In Pursuit Of Creative Conflict Management: An Overview

In Pursuit Of Creative Conflict Management: An Overview

Winston A. Richards, D.Min.

Library of Congress Control Number:		2019909698
ISBN:	Hardcover	978-1-7960-4626-7
	Softcover	978-1-7960-4625-0
	eBook	978-1-7960-4627-4

Rev. date: 07/17/2019

To order additional copies of this book, contact:
Xlibris
1-888-795-4274
www.Xlibris.com
Orders@Xlibris.com
767230

CONTENTS

PART 1

Some Theological Reflections on Conflict Management and the Ministry of Reconciliation

PART 2

*Review of Current Conflict-Management Literature and
Development of Proposed Seminar Modules*

APPENDIXES

FIGURES

TABLES

Author's Note

You are about to read a book that gives a concise, sensible, and simple look at conflict that offers a theological and practical rationale for coping with it. This book offers a cursory glimpse at the nature of man that often influences one's approach in facing conflict. It further reflects on the effects of reconciliation, resolution, restitution, and forgiveness in the arena of dealing with conflict in the workplace and the Church. It calls all leaders to reflect on their personal power base, ego, self-esteem, and defensive tools as they respond to conflicts.

This book will encourage each one to practice good communication skills of listening in combative situations and to learn preferred modal choices and how to be more relaxed rather than be fearful or frustrated in facing differences. This book will provide a toolbox with tools to handle the various aspects of conflict in the family, in the Church, in group settings, and in the boardroom. A serious reading of this book could lead the readers to attempt some of the exercises in the modules to practice in coping better with the common challenges of life. Although this study does not claim to be definitive or conclusive on the subject, it is simply an attempt to better understand the practice and purpose of conflict management. It offers to show, however meager, how conflict, if handled creatively, can be used to advance the functional goals of the Church, educational institution, industry, and boardrooms by appropriate choice of conflict models.

This book is written to provide information for both clergy and laity who serve the Church in various offices while simultaneously meeting conflicts. It should also empower readers to confidently face the challenges of differences in their interactions resulting in collaborative coworkers. This book will offer to change church leaders into creative conflict-management practitioners who understand the role of the Church in leading the saint into being a cooperative member of the assembly of the reconciled. Learning how to manage conflicts creatively will decrease the odds for a nonproductive escalation of morale. Remember, it is not the absence of conflict that is the ideal but the ability to handle and cope with conflict when it appears. Creative conflict management in the body is therefore contingent upon the health of its members.

Dr. Winston A. Richards, Retired Pastor
Chattanooga, Tennessee
2019

Acknowledgments

I wish to express my sincere appreciation and gratitude to those who have directly or indirectly contributed to the completion of this study:

To my family, for the numerous personal sacrifices they have made; to my wife, Dorothy, who gave moral support, love, advice, and encouragement; to my three daughters—Althea, Karolyn, and Sharon—for their growing appreciation and interest in this topic; and to my sister-in-law, Dr. Gloria Wright, who helped with data collection in Jamaica.

Above all, I thank God for the health and stamina to complete this task and convert my doctoral thesis into this book format.

PART 1

Some Theological Reflections on Conflict Management and the Ministry of Reconciliation

CHAPTER 1

Introduction: An Overview of the Study

An important field of expanding interest is the management of differences in the Church. Changes have taken place that challenge the very existence and fiber of organizational structure and relational growth in the church setting. There are several reasons for the increasing need for efficiency in the field of conflict management. One basic reason is the potential for dysfunctional and functional effects that conflict can have on any congregation or institution or boardroom. Adequate conflict management can prove to be a critical skill for the healthy management of differences. Consequently, potential and practicing ministers need special and continuing training in this field so that when young new ministers enter ministry, they can face differences with a toolbox equipped to handle them.

Starting active pastoral ministry can be traumatic. The transition from classroom lectures and practice preaching into the real world of ministry is not always smooth. The anticipation of putting into practice the ideas arising from one's education is dampened by the emergence of opposition. Experience leads the youthful pastor to recognize the need to balance zeal, knowledge, and enthusiasm with improved interpersonal skills.

He learns that his instant solutions do not carry over into instant conversion, trust, respect, and obedience. Challenges arise that test his unprepared psyche, and the honeymoon of ministry is over. He begins to realize that ministry is not only pleasant and prestigious but it also involves hard work. The words of Christ as reflected in the gospel song "So Send I You" begin to take on new meanings.

> So, send I you—by grace made strong to triumph
> O'er hosts of hell, o'er darkness, death, and sin,
> My name to bear, and in that name to conquer
> So, send I you, my victory to win.[1]

He now begins to recognize that even in the ministry, there are challenges and conflicts to overcome.

Statement of the Problem

It is my opinion that many Seventh-day Adventist pastors do not have a clear understanding of the functional and dysfunctional attributes of conflict in the church. This may be due to the lack of opportunity for basic exposure and training to the organized study of conflict management as a viable and effective tool in successful church administration. There is a need to sensitize ministers to the positive values of conflict management in their task of ministry, while not underestimating or encouraging the negative aspects of it to church and community life.

It is the intent of this study to design seminar materials that might bring deeper awareness of and sensitization to the various aspects of conflict management to pastors. This deepened awareness and sensitization, it is hoped, will lead ministers into an intentional ministry of dealing with conflict as they seek to fulfill their own ministry of reconciliation as well as that of the saints in their role as reconcilers. This awareness will be improved by the deeper understanding of the theological rationale behind dealing with conflict especially in the Church setting.

Justification of the Project

My pastoral experiences and observations over a span of forty years have led to my conviction that there is a need for formal training in handling

---

1   *Seventh-day Adventist Hymnal* (Washington, DC: Review & Herald, 1985), no. 578.

conflicts in ways that tend toward positive results. Involvement in building programs, single- and multiple-island pastoral districts, multichurch districts on some islands, pressures for goal achievements, and massive evangelistic agendas all lead culminatively to create various levels of fear, frustration, and anxiety for pastors in their work.

To deal with these areas successfully, another vital task is necessary—the task of utilizing proper management and interpersonal skills, which enable the appropriate handling of the situation at hand. My experiences further indicated the need to understand how one should relate to the ascribed and acquired roles inherent in pastoral ministry.

Conflicts are not unique to ministry, and they can be considered occupational hazards capable of causing a high drop-out rate. Although many ministers succeed in filling divergent and incompatible roles[2] without obvious undue frustrations and/or disorganization, it is clear that "some conflict must inevitably be experienced, for role expectations are at times irrational, exaggerated and unrealistically or impossibly idealistic."[3]

In trying to meet expectations of others, pastors may react "with excessive rigidity, compulsiveness, aggressiveness, dominance, passivity, perfection, dependence, emotional detachment, self-depreciation, anger or deference,"[4] and many times these devices are of their own manufacture. It is at this point—where coping mechanisms and activities fail—that

---

2   Thomas C. McGinnis observes that "community persons look to the pastor as a champion of great social and moral issues, a community relations expert, a religious denominational representative, or, at least, a distinguished figure in the professional activities of the community." Also "parishioners expect the pastor to be their spiritual leader, religious authority, preacher, teacher, scholar, administrator, organizer, fund raiser, home visitor, relief agent, arbitrator, confidant, comforter, matrimonial and family relations expert and skillful counselor." And his family expects him to be the "ideal father-husband who is capable of meeting many of their needs for affection, prestige, and economic security." The clergyman "may even demand that he himself be friendly, understanding, empathetic, tolerant, sincere, humble, even-tempered, emotionally stable, and generally, a model of personal and family happiness." Thomas C. McGinnis, "Clergymen in Conflict," *Pastoral Psychology* 20 (October 1969): 14.

3   Ibid., 16.

4   Ibid.

---

expectations cause intra/interpersonal stress, creating a new cycle of conflicts.

Lee and Galloway argue along similar lines. After partially blaming seminaries for inadequate training given their students in conflict management, they observe, "Today's pastor must have two additional qualifications: technical competence in the art of conflict management and personal ability to engage in conflict without undue anxiety."[5]

Based on my personal experience as a minister, it appears that pastors often tend to be defensive and resistant to opposition from their church members, and these reactions often hasten the very thing feared—failure. Many parishioners live with open conflict in their workplaces and have learned to confront issues and persons. On the other hand, pastors feel guilt when open conflict disrupts the peace they have been taught to value in their congregations. They are at a loss as to how conflict should be handled. Sometimes they feel threatened and hurt when church members request conference leaders to come and settle a problem. Thus, it is often that the pastor who tries to suppress tensions within his parish fails to appreciate the value of third-party intervention, which is so often crucial to handling conflict.

It seems to me that pastors will continue to find conflict with disruptive laity and peers until they are able, or enabled, to lower their defensiveness and resistance to differences of opinion and, instead, give full empathetic hearing to the other side. Lee and Galloway suggest, "The key to changing the church's attitude toward conflict lies with the pastors more than the laymen."[6]

Pastors need to recognize anew that although their work should be person-oriented, it is the problem-centered issues that usually dominate the decision-making process. Consequently, to satisfactorily handle conflicts, pastors dare not overlook people's feelings, perceptions, interpretations, or even off-the-cuff evaluations. Empathetic understanding must be present, especially as they deal with the emotions, self-esteem, and power of others.

Members of the clergy are often called upon to mediate in interpersonal differences because most of them have also taken courses in pastoral counseling and pastoral psychology. By utilizing various principles of the

5   Robert Lee and Russell Galloway, *The Schizophrenic Church* (Philadelphia, PA: Westminster Press, 1969), p. 187.
6   Ibid.

helping profession,[7] they can come to the task of conflict management with greater creativity as they pursue their roles as third-party negotiators. Consequently, the need for special training in creative conflict management is not only appropriate but necessary.

Blizzard[8] distinguished six practitioner roles in the work of the parish minister as those of administrator, organizer, pastor, preacher, priest, and teacher. He observes that parishioners do not want the general practitioner but a specialist. He views the chief task of the pastor in this six-fold mix as taking care of "interpersonal relationships." This would implicate the pastor as failing in his task expectations if he were to be less than a specialist in dealing with conflicts within his parish. A carefully orchestrated conflict-management seminar could serve to help bring pastors to a higher level of efficiency in dealing with the conflicts in interpersonal relationships.

The pastor in the cross fire can only remain in the cross fire if he is able to manage conflict and identify his own strengths and weaknesses in the situation. He need not run away at every major conflict. At least one study has shown that conflicts occur about three to six months and eighteen to twenty-four months in the pastorate,[9] and it is this second conflict that often determines the length of tenure. Consequently, ministerial efficiency in handling the skills of conflict management would aid in discouraging ministerial dissatisfaction, stress, burnout, and occupational change.

Misunderstandings between pastors are not unusual and may well be due partly to the lack of mutual self-disclosure. The inability to realistically face one another can eventually result in forced transfers, "created" positions,[10] stagnation, and change of vocations. One goal of this

---

7   Ibid.

8   Samuel W. Blizzard, "The Minister's Dilemma," *The Christian Century* (April 25, 1956): 508–510. Lee and Galloway contend that one of the chief causes of the church's schizophrenia has been "its failure to develop adequate tools for conflict management, and that the benefits which may flow from the conflicts will be lost unless the church increases its expertise in this area" (165).

9   Larry L. McSwain and William C. Treadwell Jr., *Conflict Ministry in the Church* (Nashville, TN: Broadman Press, 1981), p. 144.

10   "Created" positions are posts initiated in or by a conference or institutions in immediate response to organizational conflict and often have loose job descriptions.

study is to encourage appropriate assertiveness and confrontation to deepen relationships and regulate conflicts.

Research by church leadership specialists[11] indicates that church fights are often unavoidable but, if handled creatively, could extend pastoral tenure, improve the health of the pastor, increase general relational growth, strengthen the health and climate of the church, aid in the reduction of the use of legal suits, and diminish unproductive results of conflict.

An intentional use of reconciliation processes can help bring mature Christian harmony to the church. The practical aspects of conflict management and reconciliation can have greater impact and meaning on church life. It is my belief that pastoral success at conflict management could improve confidence in the decision-making processes within the church and discourage the growing tendency[12] toward court adjudication of matters between church members and between church members and the church or its institutions.

This study is justified in that, inherently, it would seek to balance the mutual interaction of tasks and objectives with relationships. In no other discipline should there be as much concern that one can win a battle and yet lose the war, win a case but lose a friendship. In the context of the caring church, no decision should be evaluated as being won where it results in the termination of a formerly trusting relationship between persons, groups, or institutions.

---

11   See Lynn Buzzard and Laurence Eck, *Tell It to the Church* (Wheaton, IL: Tyndale House, 1985); Paul Kittlaus and Speed B. Leas, *Church Fights* (Philadelphia, PA: Westminster Press, 1973); Lyle E. Schaller, *Community Organization: Conflict and Reconciliation* (Nashville, TN: Abingdon Press, 1966); Norman Shawchuck, *How to Manage Conflict in the Church* (Indianapolis, IN: Spiritual Growth Resources, 1983); R. C. Worley, *Change in the Church: A Source of Hope* (Philadelphia, PA: Westminster Press, 1971); and Marshall Shelley, *Well-Intentioned Dragons* (Carol Stream, IL: Christianity Today, 1985).

12   It must be noted here that the suit consciousness of North America has not yet permeated the Unions under study, but because many of its leaders and membership have received North American training, the potential for its development has increased. Consequently, as ministers get trained in conflict management, they may be able to delay the entry of litigation as a normative process of resolving problems in church life.

Conflict management recognizes the inevitability of conflict and seeks to do something about it. Johnson and Johnson have stated it succinctly:

> It is not the presence of conflict—but rather the destructive and ineffective management of conflict that causes psychological distress, violence, termination of relationship, social disorder and group disintegration.[13]

Limitation of the Study

This study and overview are concerned with the attitudes of ministers to the management of differences and the introduction of changes without significant regard to age, education, marital status, and conference relationship. This study is concerned only with the views of the West Indies and Caribbean Union ministers and senior ministerial students about conflict management and conflict resolution. The assumptions were based only on the questionnaires administered and the literature reviewed.

Finally, this study, as a primer for the Caribbean context, cannot claim to be exhaustive or definitive but simply to create a path by which other investigators will seek specialization.

Definition of Terms

Administrators or church administrators. The term used to identify conference or mission presidents, secretaries, and treasurers.

Caribbean Union College. The senior college operated by the Caribbean Union of Seventh-day Adventists, sometimes abbreviated CUC and is presently known as the University of the Southern Caribbean (USC).

Church. This may be understood as the Christian church or the Seventh-day Adventist Church or a local congregation of the Seventh-day Adventist Church.

Conference. The structural unit of the Seventh-day Adventist Church within a geographical area that combines and supervises several churches

---

13 David W. Johnson and Frank P. Johnson, *Joining Together* (Englewood Cliffs, NJ: Prentice-Hall, 1975), p. 230.

and whose administrators are elected by delegates of the churches in the business session.

Conflict. Refers to any perceptual and/or behavioral situation within a person or between people or groups that identifies incompatible aims, values, methods, or goals and may or may not be antagonistic in nature.

Conflict management (CM). The process that regulates or controls reactions to incompatible aims, methods, goals, and behaviors.

Conflict resolution (CR). The convergence of aims, methods, goals, and behaviors that returns relationships to a state of trust and harmony.

Creative conflict management. The intentional use of skills and processes that tend to encourage and maintain positive responses to conflict situations.

General Conference. The central, worldwide governing structure of the Seventh-day Adventist Church.

Inter-American Division (IAD). Refers to that geographical section of the General Conference of Seventh-day Adventists that includes Mexico, Central America, Columbia, Venezuela, the Guianas, and the Caribbean Islands.

Laity. The members of the Christian church or members of the Seventh-day Adventist Church that are not part of the appointed clergy.

Ministers. Ministers include ordained and/or unordained members of the clergy and/or senior ministerial students.

Mission. A conference whose president, secretary, and treasurer are appointed by the union and is not self-supporting.

SDA. The abbreviation for Seventh-day Adventists.

Union conference. The territorial level of church structure between division and the local conference.

West Indies College. The senior college operated by the (then) West Indies Union of SDA, sometimes abbreviated WIC and is presently known as the Northern Caribbean University.

Workers. Refers to administrators, ministers, and/or any other paid category of employees of the Seventh-day Adventist Church.

Overview

The following four illustrations are mere examples of pastoral conflicts in the church. A pastor comes to a district after the nine-month interim ministry of a well-loved elderly pastor and immediately meets unexplained opposition. The ingredients of strife, conflicts, and misdirected energies are in place for an unhappy entry. What should the pastor do in this situation?

A talented and influential medical doctor is taking advantage of his influence and is cautiously counseled by the pastor about his actions. He resigns as temperance and health director of the popular community-wide health awareness program of the church. Some members interpret the resignation as interference by the pastor. Avoidance and coldness exist in the sixty-member rural church. Can conciliation be experienced in this church during the tenure of the pastor? How?

Differences of opinion exist between the music committee and the choir leader over choice of renditions and the theology of the songs. Some of the choir members are interested in contemporary music while others are siding with the committee in favor of that which is more traditional. Three consecutive Sabbath/Sunday services have been conducted with a congregational song replacing the choir special. A church fight is in its genesis. What might be considered the route back to a meaningful choir ministry? Or is a choir ministry needed?

A growing 175-member rural church plans to build a new tabernacle to seat 450 members, and they have the capability to do so without any major problems. However, the conference has plans to suggest consolidation of this church with a 90-member city church that has been losing members. The conference wants both churches to move to a median area to better service both communities. The larger church has heard rumors and is insisting on going ahead with its plans, especially since it does not need conference financial help. If the rumors are accurate, how does the pastor plan to cope with this role conflict—especially since he also pastors both churches?

These kinds of situations constitute the theme of this study: How does the pastor deal with conflict in such a way that it provides relational growth?

It is an accepted fact in the related literature that conflict is inevitable—even in the church setting. Sometimes its impact in religious settings is very intensive because of the guilt due to false perceptions of conflict. Paul Tournier, among others, contends this:

> It is not possible for people to work together at a common task without there being differences of opinions, conflicts,

jealousy and bitterness. And in a religious organization they are less willing to bring these differences out into the open. They feel quite sincerely that as Christians they ought to be showing a spirit of forgiveness, charity and mutual support. The aggressiveness is repressed taking the form of anxiety.[14]

For political scientists, conflict results from competition for influences; for economists, conflict results from scarce resources; for organizational theorists, conflicts arise from faulty management procedures; and for psychologists, conflict is fostered by personal motives. As different as these may seem, they are all current approaches to the phenomenon of conflict. These views may serve to suggest that a combination of all these issues constitute the dimensions of church conflicts.

Although the term *conflict* gets its basic meaning from the behavioral sciences, various definitions allow descriptions varying from marital disagreements to international wars. Church conflicts can display aspects of structural conflict, group conflict, and cognitive conflict, and its variations complicate definitive taxonomy.

Nebgen[15] defined *conflict* as "any situation in which two or more parties perceive that their goals are incompatible." She further argues that the word *perceive* is significant to this definition as it is quite possible that the parties involved may misperceive the objective, and a conflict may occur where there is no actual goal incompatibility.[16] This argument may go both ways in that misperception can lead parties to affirm goal compatibility where none exists.

---

14   Paul Tournier, *The Meaning of Persons* (New York: Harper & Row, 1957), p. 38. Elisa DesPortes observes, "The inability of parishes to face conflict and develop constructive ways to utilize it is caused by the existence of a norm which rejects behavior tending to open up conflict and rewards behavior which tends to suppress it" *Congregations in Change* (New York: Seabury Press, 1973), p. 28.

15   Mary K. Nebgen, "Conflict Management in Schools," *Administrator's Notebook* (Chicago: University of Chicago, 1977–78), 26:7.0.

16   Ibid.

For Robbins, "Conflict is simply all kinds of opposition or antagonistic interaction."[17] Deutsch stated that "a conflict exists whenever an action by one person or group prevents, obstructs, interferes with, injures, or in some way makes less likely the desired action of another person or group."[18] Kriesberg defined *conflict* as "a relationship between two or more parties who believe **they** have incompatible goals."[19] Tedeschi, Schlenker, and Bonoma defined *conflict* as an "interactive state in which the behaviors or goals of one actor are to some degree incompatible with the behaviors or goals of some other."[20]

The tendency to require at least two parties for conflict to exist discredits the reality of intrapersonal (conflict within oneself) conflicts.[21] The emphasis on antagonism is somewhat strong, although the level of antagonism could well determine the intensity or direction of conflict. Nebgen's and Kriesberg's stress on perception takes on meaning in factoring conflict. Whether conflict is seen in terms of an action, an interaction, or a relationship, they all combine to suggest the meeting of incongruent and incompatible goals or solutions to a situation.

In this study, *conflict* will be used to refer to any perceptual and/or behavioral situation within a person or between people or between groups that identifies incompatible goals and may or may not be antagonistic in nature.

Wallace[22] suggests that the intensity of church conflicts is heightened by the historical, social, and spiritual influences on Christian behavior. To him, relating to others is a learned process. When people come into the church, they often tend to continue the use of the same patterns of relationships they have learned. Socially, people bring into the church

---

17 Stephen P. Robbins, *Managing Organizational Conflict: A Non-Traditional Approach* (Englewood Cliffs, NJ: Prentice-Hall, 1974), p. 23.

18 Morton Deutsch, *The Resolution of Conflict* (New Haven: Yale University, 1973), p. 10.

19 Louis Kriesberg, *The Sociology of Social Conflicts* (Englewood Cliffs, NJ: Prentice-Hall, 1973), 17.

20 James T. Tedeschi, Barry Schlenker, and Thomas V. Bonoma, *Conflict, Power and Games* (Chicago: Aldine, 1973), p. 232.

21 See Romans 7:15–25 and James 1:12–15 for the reality of intrapersonal conflict.

22 John Wallace, *Control in Conflict* (Nashville, TN: Broadman Press, 1982), pp. 66–68.

the influences of world events, behavior trends, the spirit of protest, and extreme individualism. The feelings that often were repressed for fear of humiliating self-disclosure often find "vent at church." Spiritually, there are influences coming into the church having their origin either in the Spirit of God or the spirit of the evil one.

Although the tendency exists to credit the evil one with the initial responsibility for the origin of conflict, and rightly so, it must not be overlooked that human beings have often given him gigantic support for the extension of conflict's debilitating effects. So widespread is this cooperative arrangement that the very word *conflict* reveals the evaluation bias in the language and inspires negative vibrations, especially among Christians. Positive interactions can result from facing the challenges of conflict.

To the concern that conflict can serve to bind together antagonists, Lee and Galloway observe, "The open expression of conflict and the subsequent reconciliation can give rise to a sense of community which can make worship a truly exalting experience."[23] They rightly associate conflict with reconciliation. Reconciliation with its accompanying by-products of peace, harmony, forgiveness, and conciliation form important dimensions of successful conflict management. Conflict management, then, can be employed in the service of reconciliation and in improving mature, supportive, and familial interpersonal relationships among Christians.

Man's acts toward reconciliation have shown a parallel, partial though it be, to the divine act of atonement. The word usage today tends to equate *atonement* (a word seemingly lost from the pulpit) to the purely soteriological act of God and *reconciliation* as the human counterpart in man-to-man relations. Without literary expansion at this point, it may be posited that atonement is the act of God with reconciliation as its primary result. Adequate conflict management can serve to encourage reconciliation, the resolution of disputes,[24] and the alignment of interests and incongruences.

---

23 Lee and Galloway, p. 174.

24 The great conflict between God and Satan has been reconciled; God knows of final victory, Satan of final defeat. However, total resolution will be at the end of world. The conflict has not escalated beyond God's control, and through the services of the Holy Spirit, God retains regulatory influence and determines the time of final resolution.

Mankind's ability to distort is balanced by his ability for reclarification of perceptions. The very germ that breeds distrust, hate, and alienation is balanced by an internal cry for reconciliation and healing, and the scale tips positively where Christian faith and hope are exercised. Just as conflict management becomes a necessity to meeting conflict, reconciliation of relationships, personal or organizational, must be perceived as a possibility—even though the precipitating conditions for alienation may be unresolved.

This possibility must be fundamental to the understanding of religious conflicts and their potential intensity. Not only have "religious attachments been among the most powerful men can feel," but sociologist James S. Coleman argues that "in so far as religion is important to men, it constitutes the potential battle lines along which men may divide when conditions are right."[25]

The presence of the Holy Spirit does not terminate the potential for conflict in religious settings, but it does offer aids for handling conflicts. Christians must recognize that religious conflict can exist between established religious groups (e.g., Adventists versus Baptists); within a religious group (e.g., choir and music committee; medical department versus ethics committee); or even between religious groups and secular society (e.g., church versus state; church versus mass media advertising of condoms against AIDS).

Coleman names "the private nature of religious experience," "the power and status functions of religious leadership," "religion as a source of alternative values," "the genesis of cleavage by association and dissociation," and "generational transmission" as significant peculiarities in religion, which make it particularly susceptible to conflict.[26]

Here again, the skills of the pastor become a crucial influence in the conflict cycle. The noted church-administration expert, Alvin Lindgren, contends that "yesterday's administrative approach is not adequate for

25 James S. Coleman, "Social Cleavage and Religious Conflict," *Journal of Social Issues* 12 (1956): 46.

26 Ibid., pp. 49–54. The private nature of religious experience and the genesis of cleavage by association or disassociation may well explain certain intrareligious conflicts. Cf. Roger Dudley's treatment of generational and moral transmission in his book *Passing on the Torch* (Hagerstown, MD: Review & Herald, 1986).

today's changed and changing world."[27] He expands this contention by stating unequivocally the following:

> Not only are there new sets of problems confronting today's church, but a whole new context is demanded to deal with them properly. Diagnosis, planning, problem-solving must be done by the people involved and not handed down from above.[28]

He offered five suggestions that, if taken seriously, could aid today's clergymen in contemporizing church administration. This would bring it in line with the progressive methods used by government, education, and industry to maximize human potential. They are enumerated as follows:

1. Today's church administration must become aware of today's social problems confronting humanity.
2. An understanding of why persons behave and react as they do is a must for the modern church administrator.
3. The administrator must be skilled in working with groups to facilitate their functioning at the best level possible for that group. (He must understand the motivating factors in the behavior of individuals that sometimes lead to group think.)
4. The alert administrator must develop skill in the whole area of planned change.
5. There must be a willingness to use several current models in other areas for getting things done, e.g., the clinical training model, coalition model, or action-oriented task forces.[29]

In summarizing his guest editorial, Lindgren "calls for a church administrator who is trained to think theologically in identifying and

---

27 Alvin Lindgren, "Contemporary Church Administration (Editorial),"
    Pastoral Psychology 20 (September 1969): 15–16.
28 Ibid.
29 Ibid. The clinical training model is learning while doing a task under supervision and reflecting on the experience with one's peers. The coalition model involves teaming up with other groups sharing a common interest even if all interests of the groups involved are not common ones. The action-oriented task forces are used to either lift up a need or to do a job.

---

stating goals and one trained in behavioral science processes to act in ways effective in communicating to and changing modern man."[30]

All the points made by Lindgren seem to suggest aspects of conflict management and reconciliation for pastors bring human beings up to their high potential of productivity. The call is relevant; it involves dovetailing theory and practice, conflict, and reconciliation.

Although it is commonly accepted that "the good of the organization takes precedence over other value consideration,"[31] my argument for reconciliation is that the good of the individual as it applies to the relationship must take precedence over other value considerations. The creativity and genius that have been concentrated on efforts to avoid conflict ought now to be used in developing better processes and expanding present positive practices for confronting conflict and for cementing relationships in and for trust.

It may be posited here that styles of conflict management and reconciliation can be cultivated systematically through special techniques in training. This being so, it may well be that many of the initial consequences of dysfunctional conflict could be prevented through carefully planned and orchestrated educational efforts. It is for this reason that andragogical principles are applied in the development of the modules. To this end, this study offers a contribution so that conflict will be intentionally dealt with and conciliation effected.

This study has been developed in two distinct sections: (1) theological and (2) the seminar development. Section one has three (1–3) chapters, and section two has three (4– 6) chapters.

Chapter 1 introduces the mechanics of the paper. It contains an overview of the general subject of conflict and reconciliation and gives the organizational plot of the study.

Chapter 2 gives a general theological context and rationale for relating to conflict.

Chapter 3 develops the reconciliation motif in creative conflict management and its potential impact on forgiveness, peacemaking, and restitution.

---

30 Ibid., 16.
31 Roy Pneuman and Margaret E. Bruehl, *Managing Conflict* (Englewood Cliffs, NJ: Prentice-Hall, 1982), p. 76.

Chapter 4 reviews some of the secular literature about conflict management.

Chapter 5 reports a questionnaire analysis and contains the module rationale and seminar development.

Chapter 6 includes summary of the project with recommendations growing out of this review and study.

CHAPTER 2

A General Theological Context
for Relating to Conflict

Introduction

No apology is advanced for seeking a biblical rationale for a subject that seems rooted in the behavioral sciences. Any real appreciation for the contributions of these sciences must be evaluated according to the level of consistency they bring in amplifying the biblical themes. Although the Bible may not give a step-by-step procedure for conflict management (apart from Matthew 18), it recognizes the reality of conflict and offers principles that are applicable in dealing with conflict management and conflict resolution.

The Bible points out that war began in heaven between the Creator and his creatures (Rev. 12:7–9). This war challenged the justice of God, the obedience of the creature, the power of choice, and the plan of God for mankind. The envy and jealousy of Satan against Jesus Christ soon gained sympathy from undiscerning angels, and E. G. White says, "There was contention among the angels. . . . There was war in heaven. . . . The Son of God and true, loyal angels prevailed; and Satan and his sympathizers

---

were expelled from heaven."[32] Thus the first casualty of the power of choice resulted in the expulsion from heaven of Satan and his angels.

Satan was banished but not destroyed. When God created mankind, Satan was allowed to test the first parents in their pledge of obedience, faith, and love to God. Although they were warned of potential treachery from Satan, the first couple disregarded the warning and fell victim to the first major conflict facing human beings. When confronted by God about their nakedness, the couple disagreed about the cause (Gen. 3:11–12). Adam blamed Eve; Eve blamed the serpent, and thus began conflict within the sphere of human relationship.

The Bible is replete with disputes, clashes, and controversies, and the picture is the same today; every congregation experiences some dissension. It ranges from differences between individuals who hold traditional versus innovative viewpoints. The intensity of the conflict can also be increased by the natural differences caused by age, race, social status, financial standing, sex, educational level, or even spiritual maturity.

A cursory review of the Bible shows that various words are used with the general connotation and implication of conflict. Some of these words include *conflict, contention, contradiction, discord, division, schism, strife*, and *variance. Conflict* is sometimes translated as *dissension* and often suggests combat, contest, struggle, concern, fight,[33] or difference of opinion.[34] Several of these words can be safely used in synonymous fashion without injury to the context, as the NIV has shown.

The Bible records examples that show the forgiveness-peace strain of reconciliation as a necessary constituent of a return to the state before alienation began. Reconciliation therefore implies activities of peacemakers, but it must not be overlooked that in a search for forgiveness and peace, there is room for repentance and restitution.

---

32 Ellen G. White, *The Story of Redemption* (Washington, DC: Review & Herald, 1947), pp. 13–19. Ellen G. White (1827–1915) was one of the key designers of the growth strategy of the SDA Church. Her prolific writings have led many to hold her in high esteem, and on occasions, she has been referred to as a prophetess, although she has never used the term herself.

33 W. E. Vine, *An Expository Dictionary of New Testament Words* (Nashville, TN: Thomas Nelson, 1952), p. 218.

34 William F. Arndt and F. Wilbur Gingrich, *A Greek-English Lexicon of the New Testament and Other Early Christian Literature* (Chicago: University of Chicago Press, 1979), p. 15.

In this chapter, I will attempt to outline what appears to be a theological rationale and context for dealing with conflict. In this pursuit, I address the subject of the nature of mankind to find whether there are characteristics in human beings that may serve to aid or inhibit creative conflict management. Further effort is given to identify some lessons from biblical incidents of conflicts. Finally, the reaction of Jesus to conflicts and the views of one famous Christian writer of the late nineteenth century is examined.

Nature of Mankind

One theory of psychology suggests that when certain conditions are held stable, certain responses are predictable. Consequently, the capacity to predict and to control behavior has developed with equal rapidity. The study of conflict management is predicated on the fact that man can do certain things to affect the conflict cycle. The way one engages in conflict management or in the search for reconciliation may be directly related to his view of the nature of humanity.

Various views exist concerning the nature and doctrine of mankind, and an overview of this subject can aid in the understanding what is really involved in restoring humans together in conciliation.[35] At least seven views of mankind are surveyed in this section, all of which have various interpretations within its own context. They include (1) man as the divine image, (2) man as holistic, (3) power of choice with its freedom and responsibility, (4) man as social being, (5) man and self-esteem, (6) man as sinner, and (7) man as saint. Man brings all these aspects to his encounter with conflict, and consequently, one's attitude to these themes influences his/her theology of hope or theology of rift. No wonder the presence of conflict is often attributed to the work of the evil one, Satan.

Mankind in the Image of God

God's satisfaction with his creation is expressed by the phrase "It was good" (Gen. 1:25), but after he went on to create man in his own image (Gen. 1:26–27), he reevaluated the creation as being "very good" (Gen.

---

35 Conciliation is the restoration to friendship, harmony, and communion; it is the settling of differences.

1:31). God was satisfied, for man, "the one for whom the beautiful earth had been fitted up, was brought upon the stage of creation."[36] Man was made in the image of God, but Adam and Eve distorted our resemblance to God. As such, man made in the image of God have the capacity to love, think, choose, and feel. Berkhof observes, "The Bible represents man as the crown of God's handiwork whose special glory consists in this—that he is created in the image of God and after His likeness."[37]

Any picture of man that undermines the impact and reality of mankind's divine origin belittles this creature of enormous potential. The psalmist caught a glimpse of mankind's priceless value to God and declared in exclamation the following:

> When I consider your heavens, the work of your fingers, the moon and the stars, which you have set in place, what is man that you are mindful of him, the son of man that you care for him? You made him a little lower than the heavenly beings, and crowned him with glory and honor. You made him ruler over the work of your hands; you put everything under his feet. (Ps. 8:3–6)

Man, even in his greatest depth of trouble and alienation, is still of supreme value and the object of God's love.

Although for centuries, attempts have been made to distinguish between the "image" and "likeness" of God (and without resolution), Rice argues for a functional rather than qualitative aspect of resemblance to God. Man's dominion was restrictive; it extended only to the rest of creation—not to other human beings. Rice further contends that

> the expression "image of God" . . . reminds us that humans are God's representatives in the world. They are not His replacement. In creating man in his image, God did not abandon the world to human whims. . . . And

---

36 Ellen G. White, *Patriarchs and Prophets* (Mountain View, CA: Pacific Press, 1945), p. 44.

37 Louis Berkhof, *Manual of Christian Doctrine* (Grand Rapids, MI: Wm. B. Eerdmans, 1933), p. 127.

because all human beings bear the image of God, we are not to exercise dominion over each other.[38]

Attempts that are made to distort this biblical picture of man as being in the image of God, capable of cosmic dominion, are candidly attacked by White: "Men are so intent upon excluding God from the sovereignty of the universe that they degrade man and defraud him of the dignity of his origin."[39] Man's creation brought him into mental, moral, and social accountability to God with an affinity to the good and to God.

Because mankind is made in the image of God, there is the potential for movement toward peace in dealing with conflicts. The image of God in humans also provides the environment for positive intentionality toward interpersonal relationships and collaborative integration of goals. Human beings with their creative potentialities for good can learn to manage conflicts so that conflicts need not become destructive of relationships or successful task fulfillment. Human beings created in the image of God have the continuing potential to be both peacemakers and peacekeepers.

Mankind as Holistic

Man is made up of parts—body, mind, and spirit—so closely interrelated as to be almost indivisible. So man is not only a soul but behaves as an entity. In fact, animals can be considered souls also, since it is the same breath that animates life. Rice nominates "freedom, symbolism and self-determination"[40] as particular aspects of mankind's uniqueness over animals. It is man's rationality that makes him accountable for his actions.

The nature of mankind as being holistic suggests that response to conflict behavior by others should be a holistic approach. An understanding of the setting in which behavior takes place can aid conflict management and reduce the tendency to underestimate the hidden aspects of the behavioral context. The holistic aspects of man make him intentional rather than instinctive (although he appears that way at times). Harkness observes, and rightly so,

---

38 Richard Rice, *The Reign of God: An Introduction to Christian Theology from a Seventh-day Adventist Perspective* (Berrien Springs, MI: Andrews University Press, 1985), pp. 110–113.

39 White, *Patriarchs and Prophets*, p. 45.

40 Rice, p. 114.

> man's spiritual nature gives him the capacity to
> transcend the lower impulses of his nature in pursuit of
> higher ideals and goals. . . . It is present in man's capacity
> to judge between conflicting values in any field, and thus
> to make decisions as to the better or the worse.[41]

Power of Choice: Freedom and Responsibility

With the power of choice comes the responsibility for consequences. Responsible freedom is the right use of the power of choice. Although White identifies man as being made in the image of God with no inclination or even propensity toward sin, she modifies the situation to recognize the possibility of departure from moral uprightness.

> God made man upright; He gave him noble traits of
> character, with no bias toward evil. He endowed him with
> high intellectual powers and presented before him the
> strongest possible inducements to be true to his allegiance.
> Obedience, perfect and perpetual, was the condition of
> eternal happiness.[42]

The test in the garden was to develop trust, which would be strengthened by the correct choice of options. These options included life or death—defeating Satan or following Satan. What a person chooses is determined by himself. Motives and experiences often form the basis for choices but are not the ultimate determinants of choices. Present options may, however, be affected by previous choices. The freedom resident in the power of choice creates our choices. A choice therefore is not an incidental occurrence or event but results from reason and motives. Motives inform and influence choices, but the individual *must* make the choice and become fully responsible for the results and consequences of choices made.

The power of choice has meaning to conflict management and may well be limited because of previous decisions. Carl Rogers notes that behavior is not caused by something that occurred in the past. "Present tensions and present needs are the only ones which the organism endeavors to reduce

---

41 Georgia Harkness, *The Ministry of Reconciliation* (Nashville, TN: Abingdon, 1971), p. 60.
42 White, *Patriarchs and Prophets*, p. 49.

or satisfy."[43] He argues that while it is true the past has served to modify the meaning that will be perceived in present experiences, "yet there is no behavior except to meet a present need, and as it may be calculated to meet future eventualities."[44]

Of man's ability to choose in responsible freedom Harkness posits the following:

> It is only because man has some freedom of choice that he can decide between good and evil and direct his actions accordingly, employ his intelligence to discover truth, become sensitive to beauty and love, appropriate meanings from the past or project them as goals into the future and increase the values of the society around him. Furthermore, it is only through freedom that he can come into a conscious relationship with God.[45]

It is this power of choice that God gave to man to help him in his relational growth with his Creator and fellowmen. Power of choice indicates human beings have full responsibility for their reaction to conflict situations. This power of choice also addresses the notion of the problem-solving sequence to conflict management and credits human beings with the ability to make informed decisions trending toward positive result and the acceptance of consequences.

It must be noted that Adam and Eve had a choice in Genesis 3, and it is because God loves us that he gave man the freedom to make choices (Gen. 2:16–17). John 16:13 promises man that he is not alone in making choices, and the Bible offers at least four principles in making choices. (1) We are free to obey God in our choices (Deut. 28:1–2). (2) We are free to disobey God in our choices (Deut. 28: 15). (3) Making right choices might bring suffering or even death, but it will bring God's eternal blessing (Acts 7:54–60). (4) Man is responsible for the choices he makes (Deut. 30:19–20) (Jimmy Ray Lee, *Free to Grow*, 38–39).

---

43 Carl R. Rogers, *Client-Centered Therapy* (Boston: Houghton Mifflin, 1951), p. 492.
44 Ibid.
45 Harkness, pp. 61–62.

Human Beings in Society

Man is not alone and should not be alone. At creation, God confirmed this fact by creating a partner for Adam. Man, in his family or in his community, is both personal yet corporate. God finds ways to continually love humanity, but he also loves the individual person. To avoid positive involvement in problem situations or persons, human beings often try to label the situation or the person. This labeling sometimes worsens the situation and reduces the cooperative spirit. It means then that humans in society can aid conflict management and relational growth by recognizing and using the forces that promote continuity and community.

Inability to maintain continuity will call for either reeducation or readjustment and sometimes even rediagnosis of the situation involved (Phil. 4:7). When rediagnosis or readjustment of the situation is not experienced, Anderson suggests man is isolated from the community and "like Cain in his banishment, he suffers the greatest loneliness and misery."[46]

Although in society, man is sometimes viewed as irrational, unsocialized, and destructive of himself and others, Rogers views man as "basically rational, socialized, forward-moving, and realistic." He contends that when man is freed from defensiveness, his reactions (unlike scapegoating or labeling) are "positive and constructive," and his self-regulatory impulses move him toward "self-actualization."[47]

Mankind's movements toward self-actualization sometimes come in conflict with attacks upon self-esteem. Consequently, it may be suggested

---

46 Bernard W. Anderson, *Understanding the Old Testament* (Englewood Cliffs, NJ: Prentice-Hall, 1964), p. 370.

47 Carl Rogers, *On Becoming a Person* (Boston, MA: Houghton Mifflin, 1961), pp. 194–195. For a fuller view of Rogers's philosophy of man, where he argues that "feelings even more than environment influence behavior," and his development of the concept of perception as reality, see his *In Therapy and In Education* (Boston, MA: Houghton Mifflin, 1961); *On Becoming a Person* (Boston, MA: Houghton Mifflin, 1961); *Carl Rogers on Encounter Groups* (New York, NY: Harper & Row, 1970); and *Becoming Partners* (New York: Harper & Row, 1972). To Rogers, it is the perception that often determines the behavior based on the meaning given to things observed or heard or seen or sensed. For Rogers, experiences have meaning only to the extent of the meaning and feelings they expire or inspire in people, and thus, he has some space in his therapeutic economy for rational emotive therapy (RET).

that the choice of a conflict-management strategy may be influenced by attempts to defend one's ego—the personhood of the individual.

Of man in his relationship in society, it might be concluded that biblical man is both corporate and individual or, rather, "he is a responsible individual who is a part of the group, whose responsibilities derive from his membership in the group."[48] This aspect of man can give an idea of the role of status quo in maintaining continuity of lifestyle or process. Conflict can occur when behavior disturbs maintenance of continuity and the pillars of self-esteem. The role of persons in society involves interaction, and the closer these interactions are, the greater the potential for conflict. Since closeness and dependence are related, when conflicts threaten this closeness or dependence, the intensity of reaction is increased. Creative conflict management becomes a necessity for peaceful coexistence.

Mankind and Self-Esteem

No direct relationship seems to exist between a preferred conflict style (one's usual method of dealing with conflict) and self-esteem; however, it appears probable that a person with a positive picture of self will more willingly explore a wider range of conflict-response options. Fifteen characteristics of self-esteem are listed in the writings of Abraham Maslow, and at least ten seem to have impact on conflict response.

Maslow[49] wrote that persons with positive feelings of self-worth or with high self-esteem perceive life situations realistically, tolerate ambiguity, accept limitations in self and others, are oriented to important life problems outside themselves, have high social concerns, are able to maintain relative independence of culture and environment, are capable of deep and profound interpersonal relations, have a sense of humor, have basic respect for all peoples, and show a sense of creativeness.

These aspects of self-esteem make it more likely that the person will accept the challenges inherent in creative conflict management. Deutsch is not alone when he argues that ego strength may develop in individuals as they experience "coping successfully with external conflict . . . and with failure."[50] Greenlaw posits that

---

48 Wulstan Mork, *The Biblical Meaning of Man* (Milwaukee: Bruce Pub., 1967), p. 13.

49 Abraham Maslow, *Motivation and Personality* (New York: Harper & Row, 1954), pp. 199–234.

50 Deutsch, p. 45.

---

poorly handled conflicts result in damage to an individual's self-worth and usually leads to continuous disharmony that prevents proper functioning. However, when conflicts are properly resolved, the individuals involved are affirmed and their self-worth built. It is thus evident that proper conflict management builds people and allows them to be better able to function in their interpersonal relationships.[51]

Failure or success at coping with conflict not only destroys or builds self-esteem but it could also be an integral determinant in one's perception of conflict. This perception can, at times, lead to an unwillingness to use strategies that are better geared to mutual benefits in favor of styles engineered to ego maintenance. Understanding of mankind's constant involvement in self-defensive activity can explain why some conflicts deteriorate into personality assassinations rather than moving on to exploring potential options to resolutions.

It is here that mankind needs the ability to balance the tension between self-esteem, self-worth, and self-centeredness, and thus kill his tendency to psychological self-destruction. White observes, "The Christian's life must be one of conflict and sacrifice. *The path of duty should be followed, not the path of inclination and choice!*"[52] (emphasis added). With this approach, conflict results are not evaluated as personal victories or personal defeats but as mutual benefits from cooperative problem-solving. It reduces the response to conflict becoming sinful.

Mankind as Sinner

51 David E. Greenlaw, "An Interpersonal Relationship Workshop Designed for Seventh-day Adventist Congregational Use" (DMin project, Andrews University, Berrien Springs, MI, 1984), p. 35. For further reading, see Mark Kinzer, *The Self-Image of a Christian* (Ann Arbor, MI: Servant Books, 1980), p. 18 passim; Robert Shuller, *Self-Esteem: The New Reformation* (Waco, TX: Word Books, 1982); Josh McDowell, *Building Your Self-Image* (Wheaton, IL: Tyndale House, 1984); and S. Bruce Narramore, "Parent Leadership Styles and Biblical Anthropology," *Bibliotheca Sacra* 135 (1978): 345–357.

52 Ellen G. White, *Testimonies to the Church*, 9 vols. (Mountain View, CA: Pacific Press, 1948), 3:538.

Man's depravity and corruption are evidenced throughout the OT (e.g., Psalm 14:1–4 and Isaiah 59:2–15) and have on occasionally resulted in alienation. The Bible does not project man as being left alone in his depravity and corruption. God's Word is presented as evidence of God's conciliatory attitude (cf. Jeremiah 3:6–4:4). Isaiah shows his people that God has left his lofty position to take his place amidst man's lowliness, depravity, and corruption: "I live in a high and holy place . . . I will not accuse forever; . . . I will guide him and create peace to those far and near; I will heal them" (Isa. 57:14–19). To J. H. Roberts, God's retribution "is but a passing moment: his word assures them of his lasting grace, his never-ending fidelity towards his covenant whereby lasting peace will be their portion, Isa 55:10, 11."[53]

The beginning of sin has been credited to Eve not in the causative sense but rather in the temporal sense. Barclay argues concerning the use of *tehillah*—that "this means that the act of Eve was the beginning of the history of sin as far as man is concerned."[54] Of man as sinner, Williams sees Paul identifying "the only hope for a licentious, notorious, immoral Corinthian church was their reconciliation to God."[55]

Paul's testimony about the desirability of the forbidden (Rom. 7:7–11) is not unique. Barclay contends that the law identified man "as inextricably and inescapably involved in sin,"[56] in need of an emancipator, which God provides.

> In Jesus Christ who is perfectly man, mankind makes a new beginning. Adam by his disobedience sinned, and thus rendered all men sinners. Jesus Christ by his perfect obedience conquered sin, and thus opened to all men the possibility of righteousness. Men were constituted righteous in the new man Jesus Christ.[57]

---

53 J. H. Roberts, "Some Biblical Foundations for a Mission of Reconciliation," *Missionalia* 7 (April 1979): 4.

54 William Barclay, *Great Themes of the New Testament*, ed. Cyril Rodd (Philadelphia, PA: Westminster Press, 1979), p. 46.

55 A. M. Williams, "Reconciliation with God," *Expository Times* 31 (1919–20): 281.

56 Barclay, *Great Themes*, p. 55.

57 Ibid., pp. 54–55.

The concept of sin must be retained in man's consciousness for a developed theory of reconciliation to have meaning. The idea of sin must not be eradicated. Harkness observes, "The need of reconciliation, whether inward or outward, is much related to sin, though this is not its only source."[58] The presence of sin in human experience makes it necessary for the conflict manager to be constantly aware of this aspect of human nature. The manager of conflict needs to be encouraged to utilize skills and processes in communication calculated to discourage sinful responses to conflict situations.

Mankind as Saint

Paul addressed several of his epistolary letters to saints and, as such, saw the results of reconciliation. As depraved and corrupted as man may be, the Christian faith has room for change. Sin, guilt, and inferiority complex can be terminated. Justification speaks to the sin problem. Man can participate in the divine intervention by choice and make redemption efficacious.

Human beings depraved by the fall can be changed and restored to the image of God's original planning. The fact of God's willingness to initiate the ministry of reconciliation through the offering of the Son on man's behalf opens anew man's high position of colaborer in the ministry of reconciliation (2 Cor. 5:19). This new position as colaborer with God brings dignity to man and combines the ethic of humility with the creation of a high Christian self-esteem. Man does not replace Christ but acts as his representatives.

Paul replaces the sinful man with the renewed man in Ephesians 4:22–32. Of this new spiritual nature, A. B. Come says, "God's reconciliation in Christ brings not only restoration but also realization of that destiny meant for man but never attained."[59] Man redeemed can attain God's potential for him—Christlikeness. With this positive view of mankind, conflict managers can take hold of their task of initiating reconciliation and peacemaking and, where possible resolution, with the new dynamics of hope and expectation. The gigantic task of successful conflict management is therefore not beyond the scope of human potentialities.

---

58 Harkness, p. 66.
59 Arnold B. Come, *Agents of Reconciliation* (Philadelphia, PA: Westminster Press, 1964), p. 35.

Summary

A theological bias toward mankind's inherent goodness must be considered equally dangerous as a theology of absolute depravity. The answer lies somewhere between both poles, with the constant potential to exchange polarity. The various views of human beings identify the complex creature in conflict situation, especially when power and self-esteem influence the reaction.

It is clear, however, that it was never God's plan for man to dominate other human beings, and it is often this domination with its various power currencies that influences an ego defense. The power of choice with its mature sense of responsibility elevates man above animals and gives him the potential for rationality. From this sense of rationality, man can navigate and evaluate the crisis of conflict and behave in ways calculated to bring mutual satisfaction. Maslow's pyramid of needs offers ideas as to why some persons act the way they do at the level of their need expectation.

However, it may be concluded that a machinery is in place to maintain a spirit of conciliation and safe living. White addresses the subject of the "moral machinery" of the heart;[60] and Galatians 5:16–18, Isaiah 1:18, and Romans 7:18 identifies the passions of nature, reason, and will as constituent parts of that machinery. Not only are "the natural appetites given by God,"[61] but appetites must be brought under sanctified reason for "everything depends on the right action of the will."[62] (Freedom of choice can influence conflict outcome.)

When the depraved, corrupted person goes to Christ, he is given a new moral taste. So one needs to bring his passions of nature under reason, and by yielding one's will to God, one can control any situation. So since "character is revealed according to the tendency of life"[63] and God sees "every motive that prompts every action,"[64] the Christian can enter every conflict situation with the motive for conciliation. His inner desire is characterized by conciliation, for he knows God judges by motives, not by results.

---

60 White, *Testimonies*, 4:85.

61 Ellen G. White, *Temperance* (Mountain View, CA: Pacific Press, 1949), p. 12.

62 White, *Testimonies*, 5:11.

63 Ellen G. White, *Steps to Christ* (Mountain View, CA: Pacific Press, 1956), p. 58.

64 Idem, *Sons and Daughters* (Washington, DC: Review & Herald, 1955), p. 71.

The saint in conflict must demonstrate no relish for dysfunctional conflict. He seeks to pursue his task of ministry of reconciliation, and he rejoices in the robe of Christ's righteousness (Isa. 61:10). As saints, Christians do take on Christ's character and righteousness, and they come better prepared to the inevitable conflicts of church life. They can now help each other to be reconciled, for they share the benefits of the covering of Christ's righteousness.

Lessons from Biblical Incidents

The Bible is filled with experiences that identify real and potential conflictual situations. The catalog of conflict-related situations mentioned in the Bible suggests that conflict is an inevitable aspect of life from which the church is not exempt.

In this section, some OT and NT passages,[65] which have a bearing on the theme of conflict and reconciliation, are reviewed with the hope of trying to identify the methods, processes, and hints that were used to resolve these situations. The passages chosen are those which may be most familiar to the reader to aid the process of moving from the concrete to the abstract.

Old Testament

The Bible reveals that conflict situations increased in frequency as the world's population increased and as corruption and wickedness grew more serious (Gen. 6:11, 13). To regulate corruption and violence, God sent the Flood, and the world had a new start. But by Genesis 13, there was quarreling between the herdsmen of Abram and Lot; in Genesis 14, there was war; and in Genesis 16, there was a family dispute in Abram's household. Then there was the conflict between David and Uriah (2 Sam. 11), which led David to plot Uriah's death to preserve his own reputation (vv. 8–14). Then on and on through the pages of the OT are repeated the experiences of conflict.[66] The examples chosen reflect a sampling of the various approaches, which appear to have been taken to resolve conflict in the OT.

---

65 Old Testament and New Testament are abbreviated to OT and NT, respectively, in this study.

66 The experiences of Moses, the judges, the priests, and the prophets show their familiarity with conflict.

Herdsmen of Abram and Lot (Gen. 13:5–12)

Conflict arose among the herdsmen of Abram and Lot concerning the inadequacy of land to keep the cattle grazing. Quarreling began, and Abram intervened by approaching Lot with a possible solution to the situation. Lot accepted the suggestion, going his way, and Abram went his way too. Noticeably, Abram and Lot were not involved; it was their herdsmen who were in conflict. However, before it got out of hand and developed into further dysfunctional proportions, Abram was willing to expose himself to the possibility of rejection by initiating resolutions. There was the potential for Lot to deny the presence of conflict, but Abram's acceptance of it created the climate for Lot to respond positively (v. 11). Genesis 14:16 indicates that reconciliation existed between Abram and Lot, and both experienced satisfaction in the resolution. This was one of the earliest examples of peacemaking in the OT.

Abraham and Sarah (Gen. 21:9–14)

After Sarah gave birth to Isaac, interpersonal relationships continued to deteriorate in the family circle. On one occasion, Ishmael mocked both Sarah and Isaac, and Sarah complained to Abram, requesting him to get rid of Ishmael and Hagar. It caused Abram distress, but to appease his wife, he arranged to send them away. He compromised the whole situation. Both Abram and Sarah acted in fashions to protect their egos and, to a lesser extent, their distorted perceptions. The tone of the discussion indicated some other concerns of Sarah, which were not ventilated in the original complaint to Abram. She showed no sign of willingness to settle for a mutual coexistence.

Pharaoh and the Children of Israel (Exod. 5:1–21, 12:51)

An OT example of labor-management conflicts is "the bricks without straw" episode recorded in the fifth chapter of Exodus. Management (Pharaoh and his taskmasters) had established a production standard. A specified quota (tale) of bricks was to be produced each day, and that requirement had existed for some time. Management changed the standard unilaterally by requiring the workers to make the same number of bricks but also to secure their own straw.

It was a retaliatory action after the union leaders (Moses and Aaron) had asked for a three-day vacation for a religious observance. The ultimate result of that incident was probably the longest strike on record.

The children of Israel quit their jobs and left Egypt, never to return. Interestingly, labor leaders confronted Pharaoh, but without success. The workers withdrew their labor after they realized Pharaoh had the wrong perception and showed poor communication and problem-solving skills concerning the situation. Pharaoh had no regard for their religious feelings, and this disregard generated into open conflict and confrontation.

Moses and Jethro (Exod. 18:12–27)

After Jethro visited with Moses, he observed potential burnout and administrative strain. This involved an intrapersonal situation on the part of Moses, and Jethro volunteered to intervene by suggesting some leadership principles. Moses accepted the unsolicited third-party intervention, and it became useful to him. It is possible that Moses did not even recognize the conflict pressure he was undergoing.

Solomon and the Mothers (1 Kings 3:16–28)

Moses was given unsolicited advice, but Solomon is contacted to adjudicate a clear case of conflict. Whose baby was it? Who was telling the truth? Both were expressing emotional attachment. Solomon listened to the different claims and devised a method to prove genuineness. He played on the emotion of love to get at the truth by introducing the idea of cutting the baby. Reality won out; the power of discernment occurred just when needed. This case showed that conflicts can be resolved, but not necessarily to the mutual satisfaction of all parties. Win-win methods are desirable, but not necessary, for every conflict situation. Conflict appears more difficult to handle when emotions are entangled with issues. Solomon identified the emotional intensity, and by introducing reason into the process, he could identify fact from fiction.

Summary of Old Testament Examples

These cursory examples indicate the presence of organizational conflict (Abram and Lot), victory by conquest or annihilation (Sarah and Ishmael and Hagar), and family disputes and ego defense mechanisms in conflict situations, which can lead to the ultimate negative resolution—death—as seen, for example, in the cases of Cain and Abel or David and Uriah.

New Testament

The NT adds to the picture of disputes. Personal conflict surrounds the birth of Jesus (Matt. 1:18–24), and Joseph plans how to handle the conflict in his social life regarding Mary's pregnancy. The composition of the disciples indicates the variety of backgrounds that converge in the body of Christ; Matthew, tax collector for the Romans, is joined in unity with Simon the Zealot.

No sooner had the early church begun that diversity broke out into strife. The complaint of the Grecians against the Hebrews (Acts 6:1–6); the public confrontation between Paul and Peter (Gal. 2:11–14); the disagreement between Paul and Barnabas over the young minister, Mark (Acts 15:36–40); the Corinthian leadership struggle (1 Cor. 1:11–12); the deteriorating disputes leading to court adjudication (1 Cor. 6:1–11); and the disagreement between Euodia and Syntyche (Phil. 4:2–3) all reflect the human experience of the early church.[67] In many of Paul's letters, he appeals for peace—although not at all cost. In writing to the Corinthians, he expressed the fear of finding "quarreling, jealousy, outbursts of anger, factions, slander, gossip, arrogance, and disorder" (2 Cor. 12:20).[68] The following sampling illustrates various aspects of the conflict experience of the NT.

---

67 Mention of the *church councils, crusades, inquisitions,* and *reformation* triggers memories of bitter and divisive conflicts. However, history recalls that not all church fights were dysfunctional. Any good church-history source can inform us of conflicts within the church. Cf. Roland H. Bainton, *Christendom,* 2 vols. (New York: Harper & Row, 1964); Williston Walker, *A History of the Christian Church* (New York: Charles Scribner's, 1970); Sydney E. Ahlstrom, *A Religious History of the American People* (New Haven, CT: Yale University Press, 1972); and Jaroslav Pelikan, *The Christian Tradition,* 2 vols. (Chicago: University of Chicago Press, 1974). Clyde L. Manschreck calls "pluralism, toleration and consensus" as forward steps in the church's handling of conflict. "Absolutism and Consensus: An Overview of Church History," *The Chicago Theological Seminary Register* 59 (May 1969): 40–47.

68 Unless indicated otherwise, the Bible quotations are from the New International Version (New York: International Bible Society, 1983). It is also abbreviated as NIV.

Joseph and Mary (Matt. 1:18–25)

The mysterious conception of Mary caught Joseph unprepared, but being of righteous nature, he thought of putting her away privately. The decision as to how to do it so that it did not bring disgrace to his beloved exercised his mind. The process included an evaluation of the options and consequences. Divine intervention helped him change his decision to divorce privately. He married her upon the advice of the angels. The result was that Christ was born in a way that fulfilled prophecy. Joseph married Mary and participated in a ministry of reconciliation and peacemaking. There are times when outside intervention is necessary to the creative handling of conflict.

Judge and a Widow (Luke 18:1–4)

This story does not appear at face value to involve conflict. However, the judge had a problem as to how to keep the widow from disturbing him. Eventually, he gave in to her demands, and she left him alone. He yielded his options in favor of her demands to inhibit further personal imbalances and discomfort.

Jerusalem Conference (Acts 15:1–31)

This passage contains the story of the Jerusalem conference with James apparently serving as mediator. The conflict involved the question, Should Gentiles be required to obey the Jewish rules when they became Christians? The process of dealing with this issue involved the use of discussion, logic, review of facts, and then, finally, agreement to accept one position rather than the other. The Jerusalem communique concluded, "We should not make it difficult for the Gentiles who are turning to God" (v. 19). The potentially dangerous church conflict was settled with mutual cordiality. An important aspect of this conference was the emphasis placed on communication of the decision to the Gentile believers. The first most serious division in the early church was reconciled, at least in theory.

Paul and Barnabas (Acts 15:36–39)

This conflict involved two key church leaders quarreling whether to take Mark with them on another trip. They discussed the matter heatedly, to the extent that they disagreed and eventually parted from their teamwork. Paul took Silas, and Barnabas took Mark. In this conflict, the private nature of the debate is of key importance. This private interaction gives a resemblance of the approach suggested in Matthew 18:15–18.

Claudius, Paul, and Felix (Acts 23:26–32)

Claudius was advised of a plot to murder Paul, and faced with this dilemma, he was unsure what to do. He decided to do whatever was possible to hinder further deterioration of the situation and referred the matter to Felix before it got worse. The result of this referral was that Paul was protected from the plot to murder him. This case indicates that some cases of conflict need referral. During his trial, Paul also appealed to Caesar.

Peter and Paul (Gal. 2:6–21)

Again, two key leaders of the early church (Peter and Paul) are involved in a conflict. Paul was concerned with Peter's double standards in his relationship with the Gentiles. Peter had changed his actions toward the Gentiles when the Jews arrived, and Paul called attention to his hypocritical actions. In this case, Paul used direct, public confrontation with Peter as a means of dealing with the conflict. The result of this confrontation was that Peter affirmed Paul's work with the Gentiles, and Paul affirmed Peter's work with the Jews; they, however, never worked together again.

Summary

All these passages indicate that conflict exists and ought to be faced, yet it does not seem as though any process or procedure was consistently followed in each case. Four principles that may be drawn from these passages and examples include the following:

1. Conflicts between persons, groups, nations, and within the person exist in the Bible.
2. Discussion, prayer, logic, review, and reclarification of faith and perceptions and a desire to reconcile can lead to conflict management and eventual resolution.
3. Direct confrontation, whether private or public, is sometimes appropriate, and it may include scolding, correcting, or even separation. Collective decision-making processes may also be initiated in the process of confrontation, and they are desirable.
4. At times, the best service that can be rendered in conflict situations is to seek outside help by referral or third-party interventions.

Jesus and Conflict Management[69]

The false philosophy accepted by many persons, and especially by Christians, that conflict is bad has generated momentum toward conflict avoidance. A review of the attitude of Jesus toward conflict must involve a review of conflicts in the gospels. It is believed that the life of Christ can give direction to recognition and creative management of conflict.

This position can be held firmly since the Bible states that Christ was tempted to sin in all points as we are, yet he was without sin (Heb. 4:15). Christ's example gives man hope of successfully using conflicts for functional purposes. It is therefore appropriate to seek out how Jesus managed his conflicts and whether he showed a model and preference.

The experience of Jesus does not show a disfamiliarity with conflict. Revelation 12:7–9 indicates there was a war in heaven with Christ as a party to it. The life of Christ on earth was to show, among other things, that conflict will be met in one's life experience. It was also to show that, through the example of his dependence on his Father, all men can experience creative results with their encounter with conflict.

Klimes[70] has identified six strategies to conflict management in the gospels, and almost all the situations involved Christ and/or the disciples or his followers. The strategies and their occurrences are (1) confrontation, forty-nine; (2) counseling, forty-two; (3) acceptance, twenty-seven; (4) prescription, fifteen; (5) avoidance, eight; and (6) compromise, five.

Confrontation

Jesus was often found in confrontations, to the extent that his submission to death revealed his commitment to resolve the conflict between good and evil. In the three temptations, Christ used confrontation.

---

69 The writer is indebted to Rudolf Klimes in the development of this section. *Conflict Management in the Gospels* (Berrien Springs, MI: Andrews University Press, 1977).

70 Ibid., p. 146. Under the strategy of confrontation, he included complaints, ridicules, demands, accusations, combat, and death. Klimes defined *conflict* as "a discord or struggle between opposing or contradictory forces or principles" (p. 2). Confrontation and counseling were the most used methods and compromise and avoidance the least–used methods of conflict management.

Jesus and Judas and Others (John 18:10–13)

Jesus's life was one of conflict, and he used different methods to manage it. One such method was confrontation. When faced with a potentially explosive situation when he was arrested in the garden of Gethsemane, he freely identified himself and requested his disciples be allowed to go free. His confrontation was frightening to the band of men and others with Judas. The result was that the conflict was contained at that point (vv. 10 and 11), and Christ was arrested without further opposition.

James and John (Mark 10:35–45)

Mark 10:35–45 tells of the request for James and John to be given the highest seats of honor in Christ's kingdom and how the other disciples were indignant toward them. In this conflict situation, Jesus took the initiative to discuss the contrast between heavenly and earthly approaches to power and honor. A counseling strategy was used in dealing with conflict, and it encouraged the disciples to follow Jesus's directions rather than normal inclinations.

In Matthew 18:15–17, Christ details what procedures one ought to follow when he is a plaintiff in a conflict situation. In a setting of love and forgiveness in one-to-one confrontation, the plaintiff goes to the wrongdoer. This is with the intent to restore relationship (Gal. 6:1), primarily, and maybe restitution, secondarily. Step 2 is to seek help from one or two spiritual ones (knowledgeable in the field of the conflict implication). If this fails, step 3, tell it to the church for their discernment, mediation, reconciliation, and if needs be, excommunication.

This method of Christ's should be primary in dealing with conflicts in the church. In fact, Paul uses the rejection of Christ's method in preference to lawsuit as an admission of spiritual defeat, an advertisement of the church's lack of forgiveness, and its inability "to judge matters pertaining to this life" (1 Cor. 6:1–7).

If this method is followed, it reduces the potential for uncontrolled anger and display of vengeance. This method develops a theology of hope (Rom. 15:13) and a willingness toward a ministry of reconciliation. It may be noted that sometimes complaints can lead to confrontation and even escalation of conflicts (Luke 5:17–26, 7:36–50).

Counseling and Acceptance

Jesus also used counseling procedures[71] to deescalate potentially explosive situations, and they were next in frequency as suggested above. Christ accepted conflict as being inevitable. He advised his followers to apologize when wrong. Sometimes he recognized conflict but did not act upon it. John's acceptance of Jesus's rise to popularity deescalated a potentially escalating conflict by his acceptance. Klimes observes that "Jesus was twice rejected at Nazareth but both times He accepted the rejection."[72] Christ taught submission to conflict in many ways. He taught the acceptance of persecution as a sign of discipleship and as an opportunity to witness.

Avoidance

Unlike most Christians, Christ did not use avoidance of conflict as a preferred style. Klimes observes that "avoidance of conflict in the gospels is directly related to delay of conflict."[73] While avoidance as a preferred style is undesirable, under the guidance of the Holy Spirit, it has its place. When he sent out the twelve disciples and the seventy, he not only instructed them to "not go among the Gentiles or enter any town of the Samaritans" (Matt. 10:5) but he also told them to leave wherever they met hostility (Matt. 10:23).[74]

Jesus understood his world in terms of conflict, and he faced constant conflict. He made it clear that his followers would face conflict in the form of persecution. Yet at the same time, the gospels are replete with examples of Jesus teaching his followers to seek peace (Matt. 5:9, 23–24; 18:15–17; Luke 17:3–4). Jesus, in showing avoidance/withdrawal as a strategy, stayed away, hid himself, slipped away, escaped their grasp, withdrew, and participated in private ministry (John 7:1, 8:59, 10:31–39, 11:53–54).[75]

---

71 Cf. Matthew 5:27–30; 6:1–4, 6–13, 6–18; 13:10–17; 19:9–12; 25:1–13; Mark 4:1–9; 10:1–23; 14:6–9; Luke 10:25–37, 38–42; 18:9–14; John 10:1–6; 12:1–6; and 13:1–20 for examples.

72 Klimes, p. 11.

73 Ibid., p. 5.

74 Examples of the avoidance strategy include Matthew 2:1–12, 2:13–15; 10:5, 14, 15; 16–25; Mark 6:30–37; Luke 9:1–3; 13:6–9; and John 6:7–15.

75 Paul and his companions also avoided conflict. Cf. Acts 9:23–25, 28–30; 14:5–7, and 13–14.

Prescription

Prescription occurred in only about 10 percent of the cases involving confrontational encounters. Prescription is the authoritative decision making in a conflict situation.

Compromise

From the milieu in which the early church evolved, and in which the Bible was written, it is not difficult to understand why compromise, as we know it, was not a popular modal style. Jesus used compromise amorally when it was more appropriate than to seek resolution then. These cases involved (1) payment of the temple tax (Matt. 17:24–27), (2) a woman's faith (Matt. 15:21–25), (3) the shrewd manager (Luke 10:1–13), and (4) the parable of the weeds and its explanation (Matt. 13:24–30, 36–43). The NT dealings with conflicts often demonstrate compromise; the Jerusalem council (Acts 15), Paul's confrontation with Peter (Gal. 2:6–21), and his handling of the *glossolalia* problem in the Corinthian church (1 Cor. 12–14) are good examples of this strategy.

Klimes, in analyzing conflicts in the Gospel as they involved Christ, observed:

1. Christ, to quite a large extent, lived a life involving conflict.
2. Christ faced conflict realistically and directly.
3. Christ used many conflict-management strategies, each appropriate to the situation at hand.
4. Christ, in his ministry, did not resolve—nor did he attempt to resolve—all conflict.
5. In managing conflict, Christ willingly underwent death rather than compromise principles.[76]

Forgiveness and Reconciliation in Matthew 18

Along with the examples of NT conflicts cited above, the Gospel of Matthew, and especially chapter 18, epitomizes a basic NT view of forgiveness and reconciliation as a normal expectancy of the Christian community. Matthew 18 and its themes of forgiveness and reconciliation emphasize that a good relationship among Christians is the basis for life

---

76 Klimes, p. 122.

in the church. The pattern of communal life is a life of reconciliation that is equally cognizant of the strengths and weaknesses of one another. Without this cognizance, these strengths and weaknesses can become antecedent conditions for conflict and potential alienation. The potential for offending behavior makes it necessary for the church to show itself a reconciling community.

Matthew's call to the church to become a reconciling community concedes potential failure (v. 17), yet it anticipates "the strengthening and supportive relationship to which the members of the church may strive."[77] This Matthean discourse of chapter 18 seems primarily concerned with the relationships of Christians *within* the community, unlike the other discourses and narratives that tend to give instructions for both internal and external conduct.

Matthew carefully calls attention to the eschatological and ethical perspectives of conduct and constantly implies that one's conduct should be influenced by kingdom expectations and values. He intentionally interprets the gospel message to give instructions about the conduct of daily life in the church. His call for the reconciliation and restoration of the erring might be seen in the thematic concerns of discipleship, conduct, and forgiveness in chapter 18. Matthew argues that alienation resulting either from extreme censorship or indifference cannot be tolerated as part of the ongoing scene.

By showing that it was the shepherd who went in search of the straying sheep (18:12), he argues that forgiveness may need to be initiated from outside the sinning one. The parables about the kingdom and the unforgiving servant serve to advise the community about mercy and forgiveness. They hold in tension the authority of Christians to discipline and to forgive. Mankind's reactions to conflict or alienation must reflect the fruits of righteousness. Continuity must exist between belief and action.

Matthew argues for Christians to perpetuate reconciliation and to intentionally discourage the disintegrative processes that can threaten and destroy fellowship. Kreider sees Matthew's accentuation of the need for forgiveness among believers as "the expression of life that will keep the community from disintegration."[78]

---

77 Eugene C. Kreider, "Matthew's Contribution to the Eschatological-Ethical Perspective in the life of the Early Church: A Redaction-Critical Study of Matthew 18," (PhD dissertation, Vanderbilt University, 1976), p. 208.
78 Kreider, "Matthew's Contribution," p. 199.

Although Luke (17:3) argues that a sinning brother ought to be warned, scolded, admonished, and rebuked, Matthew (18:15) suggests that the brother's sin should be pointed out to him with the intent that repentance might be effected and reconciliation achieved. Through the parallelism achieved by Matthew between the instruction on reproof (18:15–18) and the example of the shepherd going after the straying sheep, he identifies sin or alienation in the community as having potential negative consequences to the fellowship.

The desire for reconciliation and restoration is evidenced in the "procedural" passage, and it suggests that the wrongdoer, if he/she heeds counsel, can experience reconciliation. Kraybill sees reconciliation "as the first fruit of salvation."[79] Although the theme of forgiveness is not explicitly expressed here, the conversation between Peter and Jesus about reconciliation in verses 21 to 22 indicates a clear implication of Peter's concern for forgiveness in the process of reconciliation. Matthew draws a relationship between sin, repentance, and forgiveness and, thus, advances a statement about unlimited forgiveness (v. 22). Offering forgiveness to the other party, according to Jesus in Matthew, serves to characterize God's dealings with his people (18:35).

Matthew 18:15–17 addresses the subject of sinning while verses 21 to 22 mention the act that restores the relationship of Christians to each other—forgiveness. It is the feeling of the presence of Jesus among them (v. 19) in arbitration, mediation, adjudication, or any other intervention process, which gives rise for the desire to think Christ's thoughts in dealing with the erring. The perception of the presence of Christ (v. 20) negates the need for external adjudication and anticipates heaven's support for the decision for reconciliation or excommunication.

Although Matthew uses different terms, like *little ones*, to identify the followers of Jesus, the term that best characterizes the followers of Jesus in general in their relationship to one another is the term *brother*, as in 18:15–17.[80] Matthew's use of the two terms *pagan* and *tax collector* (18:17) compares with his use in 5:46–47. He uses the terms in both settings to describe "people who do not act according to the standards of

---

79   Ronald S. Kraybill, *Repairing the Breach* (Scottdale, PA: Herald Press, 1981), p. 12.
80   Cf. 5:22–24, 47; 7:3–5; 12:48–50; 18:21, 35; and 25:40.

the community."[81] The one who continues to sin, refusing to heed counsel, transforms himself/herself into a pagan and stands in greater need of forgiveness and reconciliation.

In chapter 18, Matthew clearly demonstrates his concern for conduct among Christians—conduct leading to reconciliation. Kreider contends that Matthew shaped the Christian tradition to declare this:

> The specific character of his concern for life in that community—being humble, not scandalizing the ones who were new in their experience of faith, going after the straying ones, showing unlimited forgiveness and mercy as well as exercising judgment about those who reject the demands of that life.[82]

The Christian's mandate for reconciliation must be influenced by his/her eschatological view of the kingdom. He/she lives in the present as though the future had arrived. Matthew argues that the Christian's conduct ought to be influenced by a sense of the presence and claims of the Lord on his/her life (18:7–10, 14, 35). Kraybill extends this point to suggest that "the church must take responsibility for inviting new believers, not merely to optional good works, but to participation in the concrete tasks of reconciliation, which are the primary manifestation of God's new creation."[83]

To Kraybill,[84] conflict ministries constitute "the heart of church life" and "the center of mission," and he combines the NT passages of Colossians 1:19–22, 2 Corinthians 5:17–20a, and Ephesians 2:14–17 with the OT Isaiah 59:9–12 to identify peacemakers as repairers of the breach.[85] It might be observed that Matthew argues for a conflict management

---

81 Kreider, "Matthew's Contribution," p. 73.
82 Ibid., p. 216.
83 Kraybill, p. 13.
84 Ibid., pp. 12–13.
85 Both Matthew and Paul demonstrate concern for the process of conflict resolution. In fact, while Matthew offers a procedural passage for handling disputes, Paul expresses the concern that the church is to provide a forum for resolving disputes *within* the fellowship of believers. Both stress the need for internal measures for settling differences.

that accentuates forgiveness and reconciliation within the backdrop of the Beatitudes.

Ellen G. White and Conflict Management

The writings of Ellen G. White suggest she had frequent experiences with conflict, and her counsels on the subject vary. She refers to conflict theologically and biblically as well as its impact upon interpersonal relationships. She offers strategies for conflict management and shows a great interest in third-party intervention to initiate conciliation. The controversy between good and evil is the pivot of her perception of the implications of conflict. Her writings identify the reality of conflict, identify what is acceptable conflict, mention personal spiritual conflict, and give encouragement for those in conflict.

Reality of Conflict

Ellen White refers to conflict as being in the past, present, and future. She writes of "the closing conflict," "the last conflict,"[86] "daily conflict with difficulty,"[87] "conflict to engage all the races of men,"[88] and "laboring in the heart of the conflict";[89] and she predicts "the great controversy between good and evil will increase in intensity to the very close of time."[90]

Desirable, Acceptable, and Necessary

To White, some conflicts were desirable, acceptable, and necessary. For example, she recognized the role of oneness in diversity. Speaking of the gifts of the Spirit (Eph. 4:8–13) in the context of unity (John 17:20–21), White notes, *"Our minds do not all run into the same channel,* and we have not all been given the same work. God has given to every man his work according to his several abilities."[91] She sees room for uniqueness. "While

---

86   Ellen G. White, *Prophets and Kings* (Mountain View, CA: Pacific Press, 1917), p. 627. In this section, emphasis is supplied.

87   Idem, *Adventist Home* (Nashville, TN: Southern Publishing, 1952), p. 133.

88   Idem, *Great Controversy* (Mountain View, CA: Pacific Press, 1935), p. 16.

89   Idem, *Sons and Daughters of God*, p. 16.

90   Idem, *Great Controversy*, p. ix.

91   Idem, "Comments on John 17:20–21," *SDA Bible Commentary*, 7 vols., ed. F. D. Nichol (Washington, DC: Review & Herald, 1953–57), 5:1148.

---

all their hopes are centered in Jesus Christ, while His Spirit pervades the soul, then there will be unity, *although every idea may not be exactly the same on all points.*[92]She appreciated the presence of conflict; she observed to workers, "There are many in the church who take it for granted that they understand what they believe, but until controversy arises, they do not know their own weakness."[93]

Personal Conflict

To White, conflict is not abstract; it is personal. "The Christian's life must be one of conflict and of sacrifice."[94] "Life in this stormy world, where open darkness triumphs over truth and virtue, will be to the Christian a continual conflict."[95] "Through conflict the spiritual life is strengthened. Trials well borne will develop steadfastness of character, and precious spiritual graces."[96]

Encouragement in Conflict

But amid a world shaped and conditioned by strife, conflict, and alienation, White offers encouragement under the caption "The Time of Trouble":

The Lord permits conflicts, to prepare the soul for peace.
The time of trouble is a fearful ordeal for God's people; but it is the time for every true believer to look up, and by faith he may see the bow of promise encircling him.[97]

Spiritual Nature

White recognized the spiritual nature of conflict. She points out that God himself masterminded the plan of redemption, calling for the voluntary death of his Son to effect restoration of the divine-human relationship. God's omniscience provided a way to initiate mankind's return to him from

92 Idem, *Counsels to Writers and Editors* (Nashville, TN: Southern Pub., 1946), p. 82.
93 Idem, *Gospel Workers* (Washington, DC: Review & Herald, 1915), p. 298.
94 Idem, *Testimonies to the Church*, 3:538.
95 Idem, *Christ Object Lessons* (Washington, DC: Review & Herald, 1941), p. 61.
96 Idem, *Great Controversy*, p. 633.
97 Ibid.

a state of estrangement and, in so doing, exposed Christ to the reality of conflict.

> *Not without a struggle* could Jesus listen in silence to the arch deceiver. But the Son of God was not to prove His divinity to Satan, or to explain the reason of His humiliation. . . . Christ was not to exercise divine power for His own benefit. He had come to bear trial as we must do, leaving us an example of faith and submission.[98]

Man's Savior was prepared for the conflict. Nothing in him responded to Satan's sophistries. *"He was fitted for the conflict by the indwelling of the Holy Spirit* [emphasis added]. And He came to make us partakers of the divine nature."[99]

Approaches

White saw the win/lose potential in every conflict and offered the consolation of assured victory:

> They can make advancement only through conflict; for there is an enemy who ever contends against them, presenting temptations to cause the soul to doubt and sin. . . . *But while there are constant battles to fight, there are also precious victories to gain; and the triumph over self and sin is of more value than the mind can estimate* [emphasis added].[100]

To one experiencing conflict, she counselled controlled endurance.

> Endure hardship as a good soldier. *Jesus is acquainted with every conflict, every trial and every pang of anguish.* He

---

98 Ibid., p. 119. Cf. E. G. White, *Evangelism* (Washington, DC: Review & Herald, 1946), p. 704; "Over every man, good and evil angels strive" (Idem, *Testimonies*, 3:30). "We should be armed for conflict and for duty" (Idem, *Testimonies*, 2:517).

99 Ibid., p. 123.

100 Idem, *Mind, Character and Personality*, 2 vols. (Nashville, TN: Southern Pub., 1977), 1:346.

---

will help you; for He was tempted in all points like as we are, yet He sinned not.[101]

There are times when *avoidance* is necessary, and White used Jesus's example. "To avoid useless conflict with the leaders at Jerusalem He (Christ) had restricted His labors to Galilee."[102] She also believed in *the ministry of reconciliation* and *third-party mediation*. After identifying a situation, she advised a husband, "Try to help your wife in the conflict," and cautioned in favor of "courtesy, gentleness and refinement of manners"[103]—all aspects of good communication. "If there has been conflict and strife among Christians, *there is need for reconciliation to take place as soon as possible*."[104]

She viewed *compromise* negatively and often differentiated between preferences and principles. She expressed the concern that Christians should stand true to principle, never bargaining with it. "God will accept *no partial obedience*; He will sanction no compromise with self."[105] For Joseph and Daniel to do less than that which was right would constitute compromise in the view of White. In fact, she confirms this view by stating to a member, "The church of God must not compromise with your coarse ways and low standard of Christianity."[106] Of intrapersonal conflict, she wrote to a female member, "You have a conflict with yourself in which you alone can act a part."[107]

Advantages

There are advantages to conflict. "Christ's mission could be fulfilled only through suffering. Before Him was a life of sorrow, hardship and

---

101 Idem, *Testimonies*, 2:313. White concedes that there are times when debate cannot be avoided, then confrontation is inevitable"—cf. *Evangelism*, p. 165. In *Christ's Object Lessons*, p. 146, she wrote, "When perplexities arise and difficulties confront you, look not for help to humanity. Trust all with God."

102 Idem, *Desire of Ages*, p. 450.

103 Idem, *Adventist Home*, p. 216. She was a believer of good interpersonal relations—cf. "Judge Not" (Review and Herald, February 7, 1899), p. 81.

104 Idem, *Christ's Object Lessons*, p. 144.

105 White, *Testimonies*, 4:148.

106 Ibid., p. 338. Later, on page 624, she writes, "Sin and holiness can make no compromise."

107 Ibid., p. 242.

conflict and an ignominious death."[108] Conflict, properly managed, builds character and removes hereditary tendencies.

> God gives the talents, the powers of the mind, we form the character. It is formed by hard stern battles with self. *Conflict after conflict must be waged against hereditary tendencies.* We shall have to criticize ourselves closely and allow not one unfavorable trait to remain uncorrected.[109]

Feelings

White recognized the impact that feelings can have on the conflict cycle and frequently addressed the subject of *feelings*. A sampling of statements regarding feelings include the following:

> The strongest man is he who, while sensitive to abuse, will yet restrain passion and forgive his enemies.[110]

> Every passion must be under the control of enlightened conscience.[111]

> We should not allow our feelings to be easily wounded. We are to live, not to guard our feelings or our reputation, but to save souls.[112]

> Nothing tends more to promote health of body and of soul than does a spirit of gratitude and praise.[113]

> Divisions, and even bitter dissensions which would disgrace any worldly community, are common in the churches, because there is so little effort to control wrong

---

108 Idem, *Desire of Ages*, p. 103.
109 Idem, *Christ's Object Lessons*, p. 331.
110 Idem, *Counsels to Parents, Teachers, and Students* (Mountain View, CA: Pacific Press, 1943), p. 222.
111 Idem, *Testimonies*, 4:243.
112 Idem, *Ministry of Healing* (Mountain View, CA: Pacific Press, 1942), p. 485.
113 Ibid., p. 251.

feelings, and to repress every word that Satan can take advantage of.[114]

Summary

It might be summarized that White recognized the reality of conflict and identified various views on the subject. A caring confrontation with reconciliation in mind appears a regular strategy. To her, conflict's functional value of maturing Christians for the final resolution of good or evil outweighs the potential injury inherent in the process of confrontation. Her concept of compromise being partial obedience to God is not consistent with the general use of the term, especially in conflict-management literature. She shows great concern for conciliation and the proper use of anger in the Christian community. We should guard well our feelings for fear of becoming Satan's agents. "We act out our aggrieved feelings and Satan uses us as his agents to wound and distress those who did not intend to injure us."[115]

114 White, *Selected Messages*, 2 vols. (Washington, DC: Review & Herald, 1958), 1:123.
115 Idem, *Testimonies*, 1:308–309.

CHAPTER 3

Reconciliation: The Christian Treatment of Conflict

Introduction

The concept of reconciliation is not a new one, for it has its initiation in the heart of God and was highlighted on the cross of Calvary in the supreme act of love. Since reconciliation involves restoration of damaged relationships, similarities exist between the reconciliation of God with man and mankind with mankind. However, reconciliation in these spheres does not always mean the same thing or even follow the same process whenever the parallel appears.[116]

The Christian church has taken positions in conflict situations that suggest its interest in reconciliation. An understanding of reconciliation is important since it constitutes a key goal of all conflict-management exercises. The terminology of reconciliation as applied through five Greek words is almost completely of Pauline manufacture and appears mainly in 1 and 2 Corinthians, Romans, Ephesians, and Colossians.

Although Pauline writings suggest a close relationship between reconciliation and atonement, if words with atonement overtones are excluded or omitted from a study of reconciliation, then only four

---

116 Matthew 5:24 and 1 Corinthians 7:11 do not appear to carry the same meaning or process as do many other reconciliation texts.

words constitute principally an understanding of the Pauline concept of reconciliation. The fifth word gives an extended view of the term. These words are the noun *katallagē* (reconciliation); the verb *katallassō* (to reconcile); a strengthened verbal form, *apokatallassō* (to reconcile); and *diallasso* (to reconcile or to affect an alteration). A fifth word *sunallassō*, as in Acts 7:26, suggests the mediating act of a third party attempting to bring about reconciliation.[117]

In this chapter, five aspects of reconciliation are addressed. I have made some selections of passages to illustrate the points, and although they are not necessarily exclusive, they do serve to support the points under consideration.

Vertical Reconciliation

Thompson expressed the belief that since reconciliation involved restoration of broken relationships, but when applied to God and man, "we are brought out of a wrong relationship into a right one with him and have the experience of fellowship with him."[118] Although it is difficult to discern whether the wrath of God is against sin or the sinner, it is true God never stopped loving his wayward and often unfaithful people (cf. Hosea

---

117 Although initiated by God, man has been known to mediate on behalf of others. Abraham on behalf of Abimelech and his house (Gen. 20:17); Moses at the request of Pharaoh (Exod. 9:27–34, 10:16–20); and again as intercessor after Miriam was struck with leprosy (Num. 12:13–15). Third-party attempts to reconcile do not always result in success. God can refuse reconciliation in spite of intercession, as for example, when he forbids an act of intercession in advance (Jer. 11:14, 14:11) or states that it will be without effect (Jer. 15:1–21). The most impressive mediating personality of the OT was the servant of Isaiah 53. God is not dependent on human beings to effect reconciliation; he has his own ways of which human help is only one option. Although reconciliation can be induced by serious illness (Ps. 6:23, 38), the infliction of punishment (2 Sam. 24:17), the warning words of a prophet (1 Sam. 15:24), or the prospect of liberation (1 Sam. 7:6), God always chooses means that still gives to man a choice in his decision to come back to his Creator.

118 John Thompson, "The Doctrine of Reconciliation," *Biblical Theology* 27 (September 1977): 43.

11:1–4). God "does not need to be appeased, but the people's alienation through infidelity must be overcome."[119]

The writings of the Bible demonstrate mankind's willful departure and alienation from God's plan. By the time of Jeremiah, God's reconciling act brought some humans to the point where inner commitment to God and his conciliation was written on their hearts (31:31–34). This entry into the cognitive and, at times, affective domains brought greater meaning to the acts of forgiveness and reconciliation.

God's consistent attempt at reconciliation with man was accomplished by God through Jesus Christ. The incarnation, life, death, resurrection, and glorification of Christ spoke to the divine initiation of reconciliation. God's mercy and justice kissed on the cross. Thompson writes, "In showing mercy, reconciling, God maintains and vindicates his righteousness."[120]

Not only does Christ's death bring reconciliation with cosmic results, but theologians of the stature of Forsyth, Barth, Denny, Taylor, and others all agree that the reconciliation of the world has already been achieved. It is only waiting for man's acceptance. Thompson quotes Taylor as positing that "unless the reconciliation is an act which is already accomplished outside of us, as it were, then it is not something that we can in fact receive."[121]

The cross symbolized the culmination of Christ's lifelong identification with sinners. The upper-room experience served as a *vorlage* of the greatness of the reconciliation accomplished at Calvary. It also became an introduction to the disciples' call to be ambassadors of the restored relationship. Man's substitute and surety of reconciliation was found in Christ and his love. Denny says this love "is one which owns the reality of sin by submitting humbly and without rebellion to the divine reaction against it."[122]

In Romans 5:1–11, Paul addressed several themes of which reconciliation is one. Paul argued that a changed situation was indicated between God and man, and that God initiated conciliation, replacing alienation with friendship. Romans 5:10 gives the enemies/hostility

---

119 Harkness, p. 22.

120 Thompson, "The Doctrine of Reconciliation," p. 44.

121 Ibid.

122 James Denny, *The Christian Doctrine of Reconciliation* (London: n.p., 1917), p. 234.

scenario to show the friendship/peace possibility. The action of one (God) induced reaction in another (men). The passage highlighted this initiation when Paul paralleled "while we were still sinners" (v. 8) with "when we were God's enemies" (v. 10), and it resulted in the reconciliation of man to God; enemies became friends.

Herein lies the very crux of divine initiation: God's willingness to accept his Son's sinlessness on behalf of man's sinfulness. The words "It is finished" (John 19:30), spoken by Christ from the cross, epitomized reconciliation. Christ's consciousness of his coming death and what it would mean in the schema of reconciliation met its fulfillment on the cross. This consciousness exploded in the triumphant *telelestai* cry and his intentional offering of his life in sacrificial death.

The conflict between perfect holiness and the sinfulness of man had been harmonized; in fact, it was overlaid by the perfect righteousness of Christ. Whether men are hostile to God or are objects of divine wrath (Rom. 5:6–10) may indicate "not only the hostile attitude of men but also the relationship in which God sees them."[123] Yet despite their enemy status (weak, sinners, and enemies), God reconciles them to himself.

To estranged men, reconciliation is not a completed act, yet they can participate daily in its salvific effects. Herein lies the supreme token of God's love for mankind in that he provided reconciliation in his Son, Christ. This supreme emblem of God's love lays the basis for humans to declare the word of reconciliation.[124] Describing the implications of the "in Christ" concept of 2 Corinthians 5:17–21, Hastings wrote "in Christ" the following:
(1) The affections are shifted from earth to heaven from self to God. (2) We enter spiritually into the fellowship of His sufferings so that we are crucified with Him, dead with Him, buried with Him, and rise with Him finding it a second nature to set our affections on things above. (3) Must be a sphere of freedom (Rom 8:2); a sphere of work (Rom 16:3, 9); (4) The life of humanity is a clean, sweet, ordered simple life.[125]

123 Vincent Taylor, *Forgiveness and Reconciliation* (London: Macmillan, 1948), p. 75.
124 R. P. Martin, "New Testament Theology: A Proposal—The Theme of Reconciliation," *Expository Times* 91 (1979–80): 367.
125 James Hastings, *Great Texts of the Bible: 2 Corinthians–Galatians* (Grand Rapids, MI: Wm. B. Eerdmans, 1913), p. 75.

Abbott says *in Christ* means "has become a Christian, has become a member of Christ."[126] The context suggests that the new creation is not the result of education, amelioration, reformation, or revolution. It is a new standing, new relationship, and new way of life. Hastings further suggested that this new creation was necessary "in order to get rid of sin, have peace of conscience and obtain spiritual knowledge."[127] This new creation brought a renewal of the past so that things grow continually newer.

In verse 18, Paul argues that God is the subject of reconciliation and that reconciliation is the end product of the process of reestablishing a broken relationship. Since God initiates reconciliation, Kaiser and Pesch are correct when they observed, "The confession of sin and guilt is necessary precondition for reconciliation of the individual (e.g., David, 2 Sam 7:6)."[128] Reconciliation is never possible in a state of distrust, condescension, or pity. In fact, reconciliation is made possible only through equals; thus, God sees not the sinner but *his Son* who covers the sinner. Christ now serves as a third- party agent mediating reconciliation.

To Cousar, reconciliation of verse 18 identified man's inabilities to "negotiate a truce," yet God "transforms and renews the divine-human relationship."[129] This gift of reconciliation provided the avenue through which all may become fellow workers in bringing men into a life of conscious fellowship with God.

The enemies are transformed into the ambassadors through whom God continues his appeal to estranged man: "be reconciled to God." That God should make former enemies ambassadors—that is, representatives of his divine kingdom—suggests God's willingness to demonstrate he does not keep account of sins. The former alienation is forgiven, and the future allegiance and cooperation are anticipated. The ministry of reconciliation offers a glimpse of God's willingness to reinstate without reservation. The

---

126 T. K. Abbott, *Ephesians and Colossians*, (Edinburgh: T & T Clark, 1956), p. 177.

127 Hastings, *The Great Texts of the Bible*, p. 175.

128 Odilo Kaiser and Rudolf Pesch, "Reconciliation," *Encyclopedia of Biblical Theology*, ed. Johannes B. Bauer (New York: Crossroads, 1981), p. 733.

129 Charles B. Cousar, "2 Corinthians 5:17–21," *Interpretation* 35 (1981): 182. Cf. Donald E. Bossart, *Creative Conflict in Religious Education and Church Administration* (Birmingham, England: Religious Education Press, 1980), pp. 130–133; Buzzard and Eck, pp. 12–14.

representative now serves not only for Christ but on behalf of Christ. He serves as a vehicle for God's advertising offer of reconciliation.

A third passage that identifies a holistic scope of the vertical reconciliation is Colossians 1:15–22. Paul transforms this text into an "ecclesiological assertion" by making Christ "the head of the body."[130] In this passage, reconciliation takes on one more dimension. It is not only the reconciling act of God with man, but it now includes all things on earth and in heaven. Paul's careful list of beneficiaries of Christ's activities disqualifies none from the potential grasp of Christ's conciliating activities.

Man's hostility is seen in its origin in the mind and its execution in evil behavior. Despite the movement toward reconciliation and friendship from hostility, Hastings quotes Taylor, contending that "the Christian man is righteous in the sight of God, not because he is perfect but because he has a righteous mind."[131]

In the phrases "in your mind" and "in your evil works," I identify— faint though it may be—the very early beginnings toward a definition of conflict being cognitive and/or affective. Since hostility and opposition begin in the mind, the perceptual theory of conflict becomes apparent. Mankind's hostility to God as seen in its execution in evil behavior can serve to identify conflict response as being behavioral.

Paul surrounds verse 20 with moral implications. Peace is made possible through the physical death of Christ with the design that both mind and behavior will adapt to the new experience of peace and grace. This new experience will lead to an established continuance in the apostolic faith (v. 23). This passage reminds the reader that the one who makes reconciliation possible is indeed the head of the body—the church—and, as such, earns the right to have supremacy over everything (v. 18). As the supreme head of the universe (cosmos), Christ has earned the right to initiate the redevelopment "of the potentialities of nature and man, personally and corporately."[132]

Reconciliation of man with God is accomplished. God outmatches man's voluntary departure and willful alienation from him with his Son's voluntary act of redemption and reconciliation. Christ destroyed man's

---

130 Martin, p. 366.
131 Hastings, p. 75.
132 Eugene C. Blanchi, *Reconciliation: The Function of the Church* (New York: Sheed & Ward, 1969), p. 109.

enmity by parading his sinless life against Satan (Col. 1). The malignancy created by man's enmity is overcome by God's mercy in the righteousness of Christ. God initiated all the elements necessary to bring estranged man back to himself. In these passages, we see God's successful attempt to win back members of his creation from a state of hostility to one of mutuality and love, where no trace of enmity, hostility, fear, or distrust exist. The reconciled ones become the reconciling ones.

Horizontal Reconciliation

Whereas reconciliation between God and man is viewed vertically, reconciliation between man and man must be seen horizontally. A sure by-product of the achieved vertical reconciliation is the man-to-man conciliation. The joy of upward conciliation must be matched by outward conciliation in the Christian community.

The conciliation between human beings in the OT appears to be not merely social justice but one of peace maintenance. This view is confirmed in the reconciliation of Jacob and Esau (Gen. 32–33). David and Saul reflected this point in the reconciliation, which followed Saul's acknowledgment of David's magnanimous acts (1 Sam. 24, especially vv. 16–22). David's plea for Absalom's life also reflected OT interest in the peace strain of reconciliation (2 Sam. 18:5, 31–33).

Many of the injunctions of Hebrew law[133] tended toward social justice, but reconciliation appears possible only where justice is perceived to be done. *Where perception of justice is absent, reconciliation and/or resolution will not be affected.* In fact, it is this perception of justice balanced by mercy that makes reconciliation between human beings a real potential and peace a present reality.

Harkness identifies the key Hebrew word on reconciliation of man-to-man in Leviticus 19:17–18 and sees its immediate context as a "mixture of earlier ethical insights, temple rituals, and the maintenance of Jewish law."[134]

Similarity and continuity exist between OT and NT views of reconciliation. In the OT, it refers basically to overcoming enmity and

---

133 Exodus 22:21–24; 21:2–11, 28–34; 16:20–21, 26–27; and 23:4–5.
134 Harkness, p. 32.

alienation, while in the NT, this overcoming is centered in Christ as the very agent of reconciliation. Jesus consistently linked the forgiveness of sin by God with the willingness to forgive others (Matt. 18:21–22). At least four passages of the NT address the subject of horizontal reconciliation: (1) unforgiving servant, Matthew 18:23–35; (2) forgiveness of woman, Luke 7:36–50); (3) woman caught in adultery, John 8:1–11; and (4) the cross sayings in Luke 23:24.

A basic theme of these passages is the need to identify injury and to do something positive about it. The one alert enough to identify the injury has the responsibility to initiate action geared toward repairing the injury. The classic example of reconciliation issuing from horizontal activity is seen in Matthew 5:23–24. One can safely posit that the basic tenor of the Sermon on the Mount was one of reconciliation. Matthew 5:23 speaks of worship, which imposes self-examination for fear there may be a brother who has something against you. Either party has the obligation to begin the process toward reconciliation.

Harkness disagrees with the popular position that suggests that Matthew 5:23–25 makes worship secondary to reconciliation. She says Matthew 5:23–25 is "a protest against a barren worship in which human relations are left out."[135] This passage emphasizes the need for believers to be reconciled together on their own initiative, whether adversary or offended.

The English text suggests that one is innocent, and it is this innocent one who is to initiate activities aimed at conciliation. However, the Greek word suggests that, in fact, mutual hostility exists, and thus, mutual concession is needed. Consequently, if either party was at worship and remembered the hostility, then it was incumbent on either one to initiate conciliation proceedings.

The ethical and interpersonal thrust of horizontal reconciliation is clearly illustrated in Matthew 5:23–24, and it takes conciliation out of the voluntary sphere of human experience and puts it under religious obligation. To the Christian community, conciliation is a moral and religious responsibility with its own urgency.

Man-to-man reconciliation appears to be built on the ability to forgive and to accept forgiveness. The NT does not always project conciliation

---

135 Harkness, p. 46. The call to reconciliation is put on the lips of Jesus here by Matthew.

without difficulty; consensus was not always present, but a spirit of unity was always encouraged and envisioned (Eph. 4:3). Paul entered the field of marriage counseling in 1 Corinthians 7:10–11 to encourage conciliation. Moses tried to conciliate two fighting Israelites but had to give up the attempt because of his lack of credibility as a third-party agent. Paul consistently counseled[136] the churches against contention and disharmony, but when disharmony occurred, he pleaded for reconciliation in a spirit of love (1 Cor. 13) and personal concern (Gal. 6:1).

The reconciliation between God and man makes conciliation between human beings an absolute necessity. This double reconciliation provides for the triangular arrangement between God, man, and man. So in Christ, all barriers were removed. A theology of peace, occasioned by this triangular arrangement, makes it inconsistent for churches to perpetuate differences within their ecclesiastical settings along racial, sexual, educational, social, or other lines. Even with a myopic view of the reconciliation motif of Ephesians, churches need to intentionally remove unnecessary barriers of natural divisions and antipathies and thus make the reconciliation message of Ephesians a reality.

In the periscope of Ephesians 2:11–19, Paul dramatized the alienated distance between parties and the strength of the restoration God displayed in accepting them into the body of Christ. Here, he introduced the peace-forgiveness-reconciliation trio in the passage and pointed to the reasonableness of maintenance of peace and unity in the community. Being without Christ makes one an *alien and stranger*, without citizenship. No wonder some of the Ephesians perceived themselves in a hopeless situation. Human reconciliation is possible regardless of the point of beginning, for Paul stated that, though they were "far away," they had been brought near.

The distance of alienation can be brought near in the closeness of reconciliation. Only as reconciled ones do Jews and Gentiles belong to the same church. By destroying the barrier, Jesus makes a new design for peace, for he seeks only the conciliation of enemies (Luke 9:51–55). Ephesians 2:11–15 clearly illustrates how long-standing and deep-rooted enmity may

---

136 For some good articles on counseling in reconciliation, see Paul F. Wilczak, "The Pastoral Care of Families: A Ministry of Reconciliation," *Encounter* 39 (Spring 1978): 175–188; and Garth D. Thompson, "On Pastors as Counselors," *Andrews University Seminary Studies* 22 (Autumn 1984): 341–348.

be effectively overcome. The gathering of saints ought to show itself a microcosm of a fully restored universe.

All true reconciliation reflects communal interest. Such interest is implied in the Pauline usage of terms like "citizenship in Israel," "fellow citizens with God's people," "member of God's household," and "a holy temple in the Lord." Since those far off and those nearby can hear the message of peace, reconciliation is a requirement both of saint and sinner.

When reconciliation is affected among human beings, there is peace of mind, a sound conscience, and a return to harmony and friendship is experienced. Reconciliation becomes the forum for conflict management. Even though the exercise of human conflict practices may stimulate reconciliation, the ultimate source of it is divine and involves heavenly and earthly cooperation. The Christian treatment of conflict is one of continuous intervention on behalf of reconciliation.

When vertical reconciliation occurs, it is emphatically not between equals returning to a state of cordiality. Every aspect of it demonstrates the supremacy of the divine over the human. However, in horizontal reconciliation, conciliation can still be affected whether the disputants are equal or not.

In vertical reconciliation, man accepts the accomplished fact, while in horizontal reconciliation, man must first be brought to a status of equal power or parity so that the reconciliation reflects total mutuality in the agreement. In Christ, humans have equal power of negotiation for both are seeking not only for a win but also for mutual satisfaction.

The discussion on the nature of mankind earlier in this study suggested, among other things, that inherent in mankind is the potential for being overcome by his tendency to do wrong acts, often due to his emotional involvements and his inability to activate his will according to sanctified reason. Micah (7:6) and Matthew (10:37) identify the potential for hostility and anger. There seems to be a role to be played by counselors in aiding man in his participation in horizontal reconciliation. This is especially so since Christians are not exempt from anxiety, frustration, guilt, disappointment, boredom, despair, inferiority complex, underestimation of the value of life, and paralysis of the will. Not only are counselors and counseling gaining in acceptance in Christian society, but some of their principles may well be necessary before approach toward conciliation may be successfully attempted and achieved.

Harkness argues convincingly that reconciliation in the person may be encouraged by (1) helping the person to find a new outlook on life; (2) locating and correcting, if possible, any physical or social causes of the inner disturbance; and (3) finding an object of love, loyalty, and devotion beyond one's self.[137] The Christian treatment of conflict is a movement that is essentially a movement toward horizontal reconciliation.

Forgiveness: A Two-Way Experience

The concept of forgiveness plays an important part in effecting reconciliation in Christian relationships. Whenever alienation occurs in a trusting relationship, there is a need for a granting and accepting of forgiveness for the relationship to be restored to its original status. An understanding of forgiveness and its implications for reconciliation can bring new meaning to conflict management.

Forgiveness and Conciliation

It may be noted here that some key passages that address the question of conciliation[138] refer to remission of sin but not to the remission of penalties or consequences, and this difference has implications for restitution and restoration after conciliation has occurred. Of conciliation, Taylor observes that "it is a stage antecedent to reconciliation; it is that which makes reconciliation possible."[139] This would suggest then that sorrow and the desire for amendment are noticeable conditions of forgiveness.

The NT gives great emphasis to horizontal forgiveness, and at least three parables illustrate this horizontal forgiveness motif: (1) the unmerciful servant, (2) the prodigal son, and (3) the Pharisee and publican. The parable of the unmerciful servant illustrates the human tendency to

---

137 Harkness, pp. 67–73. Cf. Gary R. Collins, *Christian Counseling* (Waco, TX: Word Books, 1980); Paul A. Hauck, *Brief Counseling with RET* (Philadelphia, PA: Westminster Press, 1980); William B. Oglesby Jr., *Referral in Pastoral Counseling* (Philadelphia, PA: Fortress Press, 1968); and Ernest E. Bruder, *Ministry to Deeply Troubled People* (Philadelphia, PA: Fortress Press, 1964).

138 Cf. Luke 24:47; Acts 2:38, 5:31, 10:43, 13:38, 26:18; Col. 1:14; James 5:15; and 1 John 1:9, 2:12.

139 Taylor, *Forgiveness and Reconciliation*, p. 13.

be unforgiving even though being a recipient of forgiveness.[140] Taylor's argument that the story of the prodigal son illustrates more "fully the concept of reconciliation rather than forgiveness" and verses 22 to 24 as "that of reconciliation"[141] makes a significant differentiation.

The wrong done by the son is cancelled by the father, and it no longer stands between them. The son is forgiven. Reconciliation requires forgiveness, but there can be forgiveness without reconciliation. Moved with compassion and love at the speech of the repentant son, the father ran to embrace him and, in that kiss of love, conveyed forgiveness and initiated conciliation. By the father's show of love, "the son feels that the past is forgiven and forgotten, blotted out forever."[142] Forgiveness results in restoration of the lost son to the joy of fellowship and full reconciliation in his home. The act of forgiveness is communicated and understood as such by the son. The whole process suggests reconciliation, and the father exhibited a forgiving spirit from the time of the son's departure with his daily anticipation of the son's return. Reconciliation is achieved in the unconditional bestowal of forgiveness as further evidenced in the celebration.

Although the word *forgiveness* does not appear in these parables, they illustrate forgiveness, and placed on the lips of Jesus, they suggest (1) the bestowal of mercy and (2) the cancellation of indebtedness or the removal of the barriers that stood in the way of fellowship.[143] No wonder then that Burquest sees in the communion service "a celebration feast of forgiveness"[144] where mankind experiences divine and human forgiveness.

Forgiveness then, whether guaranteed by divine initiative or proclaimed by human beings, suggests movement toward reconciliation and creative conflict management. Once confession follows fact clarification, sin no longer stands between the parties since sin is replaced by the clasped hand of harmony and restoration. This forgiveness can both restore prealienation status and depolarize disputants since both have invested part of themselves

---

140 White, "The Measure of Forgiveness," *Christ's Object Lessons*, pp. 243–251.

141 Taylor, *Forgiveness and Reconciliation*, pp. 17–18.

142 White, *Christ's Object Lessons*, p. 204.

143 Ibid., 15.

144 Donald A. Burquest, "A Celebration Feast of Forgiveness," *Christianity Today*, 26 (January–June 1982): 25.

in the healing process.[145] The spirit of forgiveness needs to be perceived in the act of forgiveness, and the forgiven needs to feel forgiven for it to result in conciliation. By including restitution as a bargaining chip in the dialogue toward reconciliation, it could trigger further deterrents in arriving at reconciliation.

In situations where people do not feel forgiven, even by God, true conciliation will be impossible. Forgiveness can be extended to a person without it resulting in conciliation. God can forgive a person even though that person does not feel forgiven. Forgiveness is a prerequisite of conciliation. Like conflict, forgiveness is both perceptual and behavioral. Perception of forgiveness ought to result in behavioral modification and attitudinal change.

For Smedes, forgiveness involves the active participation of all, for it involves "hurting, hating, healing, and reconciliation, and it offers release from the burdens of hurt and the reclamation of happiness."[146] The process of forgiveness presents a crisis, and its proper handling can determine the level of healed relationships. Forgiveness can be a short or lengthy process, but either way, Smedes suggests some people forgive "slowly, with a little understanding, in confusion, with anger left over a little at a time, freely or not at all, or with a fundamental feeling."[147]

There is danger in a delayed or lengthy forgiveness process since any minor injustice or misperception can trigger delayed forgiveness into escalated conflict. It is probably to this kind of concern that the biblical injunction called for conciliation before sunset. In 1 John 2:12, John reminds his "dear children" of the reality of forgiveness, the reality of their relationship with Jesus Christ, and their new ability to overcome the evil one (1 John 1:7, 9; 2:2). For them, walking in the light of forgiveness brings vertical and horizontal fellowship (1:7). The resolution of conflict gives to the believer a feeling analogous in concept to the feeling one has in the joy

---

145 Cf. Ron Lee Davis, *A Forgiving God in an Unforgiving World* (Eugene, OR: Harvest House, 1984); Harold H. Bloomfield, MD, *Making Peace with Yourself* (New York: Ballantine Books, 1985); David A. Seamands, *Healing for Damaged Emotions* (Wheaton, IL: Victor Books, 1984); and Jerry Cook and Stanley C. Baldwin, *Love, Acceptance, and Forgiveness* (Ventura, CA: Regal Books, 1981).

146 Lewis B. Smedes, *Forgive and Forget: Healing the Hurts We Don't Deserve* (Philadelphia, PA: Harper & Row, 1984), pp. 1–38.

147 Ibid., pp. 95–121.

of forgiveness. White observes, "In the consciousness of sin forgiven, the clouded hope of the Christian is brightened."[148]

Smedes is not alone with his interest in mutual forgiveness. David Augsburger[149] has written his book simply to delineate five basic steps to true forgiveness. He names these steps as (1) realizing wrongdoing, (2) reaffirming love, (3) releasing the past, (4) renewing repentance, and (5) rediscovering community. As though this were not enough, he turns the book around and defines what true forgiveness is not.

Restitution in Forgiveness and Conciliation

The question of restitution in forgiveness and conciliation ought not to be overlooked. Is there a role for restitution? When is the question of restitution addressed in the process of forgiveness and reconciliation? Ideally, forgiveness and reconciliation should precede any consideration of restitution. However, conciliation is often delayed until the details of restitution are arranged. By following this practice, at least two points are overlooked: the voluntary or mandatory nature of restitution and what should happen if restitution is impossible or would create undue burden on the restorer.

It seems that forgiveness and conciliation should be addressed without reference to restitution. To include restitution in the dialogue is to create additional issues, some of which often are not even relevant to the resolution of the key issue. This detour to finalize the details of restitution may even trigger further deterrents to resolving the problem.

There are times when restitution is impossible, or at its best, it would imply great injury and pain to the restorer. For this reason, restitution should not be mandatory. If a teenage child should destroy the family car, she/he may be unable to replace that car, but the inability should not impede forgiveness from occurring. The parents may need to depend more fully on God's ability to sustain in any difficulty (sustaining grace). It might be necessary then for forgiveness to be perceived by the forgiver as a gift, in which case the wrongdoer is under no obligation to make restoration.

---

148 White, *Ministry of Healing*, pp. 267–268.
149 David Augsburger, *Caring Enough to Forgive; Caring Enough Not to Forgive* (Ventura, CA: Regal Books, 1981), pp. 1–96; 1–75.

However, where restitution would not create *undue* inconvenience, the wrongdoer, of his own free choice and as a witness of love, should proceed to make restitution in a setting of agreement. In doing so, the wrongdoer, in experiencing the joy of vertical and horizontal forgiveness and as part of forgiveness and peace, would seek justice to repay the damage done (Luke 19:1–10). The wronged person, realizing that his sustenance is dependent on God, can match the wrongdoer's justice with his own act of mercy. This act of mercy could be the acceptance of the wrongdoer's offer of restitution or, indeed, the partial or full cancellation of the debt.

There is no room for compulsion of restitution but only for the willing experience of justice balanced by mercy. The offended person ought always to be aware that restitution is a voluntary act in the process of reconciliation. More than that, if restitution does not occur, his faith should inform him that God still takes care of his own and that in God's omniscience and in his best interest, God would not allow him to be reduced to starvation, poverty, or want. In fact, the absence of restitution may cause the offended person to learn and experience full dependence on God for life's needs and the restoration of the damage.

Forgiveness is not dependent on restitution. However, although restitution has optional overtones, there are distinct moral implications for restoration. The story of the prodigal son illustrates that the father's forgiveness was not conditioned by the son's restoration of his share of the estate squandered in wild living (Luke 15:11–31). A balance exists between restitution and forgiveness.

This position does not blot out obligation to just debt. As in the case of the unmerciful servant (Matt. 18:25–35), forgiveness does not automatically exclude one from fulfillment of his just obligations. Wherever it is possible that restitution is made, it becomes an act of peace,[150] of love,[151] of conscience,[152] of justice,[153] and of witness.[154] Absence of this act of restitution or restoration ought not to diminish the completeness of the forgiveness or conciliation in the wronged person's perception. *Things* do

---

150 1 Pet. 3:10–11; Rom. 12:18, 14:17; Matt. 4:9, 23–25; Prov. 28:13; and Isa 32:17.
151 John 13:35; 1 John 4:11; and Rom. 2:4, 13:8–10.
152 1 Tim. 1:5, 19; Heb. 8:10; Rom. 2:5.
153 Matt. 7:12, 22:38–40, 23:23–24; and Luke 12:57–59.
154 Luke 19:7, 19:8, and 19:1–10.

not guarantee reconciliation. Restitution in the pursuit of creative conflict management has several benefits, which can include the following:

- Restoring the injured party to his or her former position.
- It benefits society by making destructive behavior unprofitable.
- It gives the offender an opportunity to make amends for his/her wrongs/errors.
- Restitution is a sign of taking responsibility for one's actions.

Romans 12:8, 14:7, and Matthew 5:25 all suggest that the act of peacemaking involves confession, a request for forgiveness, and total restitution where possible. The effect of righteousness, of right doing, and of restitution where possible is peace, *but* peace ought not to be dependent on restitution. Restitution as an act of peacemaking is especially crucial and important when the wrongdoer has not been forgiven by the wronged person or where reconciliation seems distant or unlikely.

Where the ability to make restitution clearly exists, restitution should be made. Zacchaeus clearly had the ability to make restitution, even after giving half of his goods to the poor (Luke 19:8). The Holy Spirit always leads a repenting believer to make restitution when the ability to do so exists. The failure to make restitution where the ability clearly exists amounts to a rejection of harmony, peace, conscience, and justice. It then becomes a vivid expression of hatred and a show of ingratitude and ceases to be a practical celebration of the sense of forgiveness. Restitution that forces the offender to a point of undue burden and temporal difficulty serves in most cases to distort forgiveness and conciliation and, in effect, can renew a new cycle of conflict. Reconciliation does not require restitution to make it effectual, but restitution can indeed make reconciliation acceptable and effective. Yet it must be noted that forgiveness does not negate restitution.

Forgiveness is a decision and a choice that one makes. It involves a willingness to offer forgiveness and/or to accept the gift of forgiveness. It is a two-way street for the offended or offender. A thorough understanding of the doctrine of forgiveness shows why each church needs its own conciliatory ministry to teach its members the spiritual truth of reconciliation advocated in texts like 1 Corinthians 6:1–11, Matthew 7:1–3, and Galatians 6:1. Forgiveness and repentance ought to be communicated in three levels—intellectually, emotionally, and volitionally—if they are to lead to conciliation. The repentant disputant to an estrangement must transfer this emotional element to the action of removing an obstacle to conciliation, even if it requires restitution. Berkhof argues that "while it (repentance) is the sinner's present duty, it does not offset the claims of the law because of past transgressions.[155]

Regardless of one's views concerning forgiveness and its place in Christian experience, there are at least four reasons that justify participation in this preliminary act toward reconciliation: (1) forgiveness makes life fairer to the dignity of the wrongdoer, (2) forgiving is a better risk than revenge, (3) forgiving is stronger than hate, and (4) forgiving fits faulty people—and none of us are experts in forgiving.[156]

Reconciliation is more than settling disputes; its chief objective is to bring about healing and restoration between disputing parties. Genuine reconciliation is shown in thought (Phil. 4:8), word (2 Cor. 2:7), and deed (1 John 3:18). In this context, repentance, forgiveness, restitution, and reconciliation are linked together as means for defeating anger, bitterness, hurt, and a thirst for revenge. Reconciliation takes guts; fighting in courts only takes lawyers. That is one reason why it appears easier for Christians to change membership within their denomination than to confront the issue and be reconciled with each other!

Ellen G. White on Forgiveness

Forgiveness involves moral responsibilities. White consistently addressed the subject of forgiveness, and the following quotations give a glimpse of her thoughts on forgiveness:

"Christian love is slow to censure, quick to discern penitence, ready to forgive, to encourage, to set the wanderer in the path of holiness and to stay his feet therein."[157]

"Through Christ justice can forgive without sacrificing one jot of its exalted holiness."[158]

---

155 Louis Berkhof, *Systematic Theology*, p. 487. Restitution is used in the papyri to describe "a repair of a public way, the restoration of estates to rightful owners, a balancing of accounts" (Vine, p. 961). The concept of restoration to former condition of health is also seen in the use of *apodidomi* in Luke 19:8 and *apokathistemi* in Luke 6:10. In the papyri, it sometimes used financial restitution in making good the breaking of a stone by a workman, by his substituting another, and suggest patience and perseverance.

156 Smedes, pp. 123–151.

157 White, *Desire of Ages*, p. 462.

158 Idem, *Sons and Daughters of God*, p. 153.

"He who refuses to forgive is thereby casting away his own hope of pardon."[159]

"Strongest man will forgive while being sensitive to abuse."[160]

"Believer at variance with brother should ask to be forgiven."[161]

"David had a true conception of God's forgiveness."[162]

"God's forgiveness does not lessen duty to obey Him."[163]

"God's forgiveness does not mean you cannot require just dues from debtors."[164]

"There is God's forgiveness for the greatest sin."[165]

"There is God's forgiveness for the least sin."[166]

"There is God's forgiveness for the penitent sinner."[167]

Finally, it can be said that anyone who cherishes a forgiving spirit is en route to being not only a creative manager of conflict but also to becoming a true minister of reconciliation. "Love and forgiveness set up a chain reaction: the more forgiveness the more love; the more love the more forgiveness."[168] Then whenever the ability to restore exists, restitution will be done in joy and peace. Justice and mercy will clasp hands in human experience.

Peace and Peacemaking

The experience of forgiveness (and restitution) can create the feeling of peace and inspire participation in the ministries of reconciliation and peacemaking. Whenever reconciliation is needed, there is a role to be played by peacemakers, and consequently, the peacemakers of Matthew 5:9

159 Idem, *Christ's Object Lessons*, p. 247.
160 Idem, *Testimonies*, 4:656.
161 Idem, *Mount of Blessing*, pp. 58–59.
162 Ibid., p. 114.
163 Idem, *Christ's Object Lessons*, p. 247.
164 Ibid.
165 Idem, *SDABC*, 7:933.
166 Ibid.
167 Idem, *Mount of Blessing*, p. 8.
168 F. F. Bruce, *The Hard Sayings of Jesus*, (Downers Grove, IL: InterVarsity Press, 1983), p. 80.

could well be like the ambassadors of 2 Corinthians 5:20. Their basic and primary task and orientation is that of seeking after conciliation and peace.

Shalom and Eirene

Shalom and *eirene* constitute two coterminous words suggesting wholeness or well-being in the person or organization. The three parables of Luke 15 suggest the restoration and reconciliation overtones of peace. In fact, the repeated formula "peace from God our Father" found in Ephesians 1:2, Philippians 1:2, Colossians 1:2, and 1 Thessalonians 1:1 illustrates the practice of NT writers to combine the OT *shalom* strain of wholeness implied in *eirene*.[169] To Brueggemann, peace was living in harmony and security: "The central vision of world history in the Bible is that all creation is one, every creature in community with every other, living in harmony and security toward the joy and well-being of every other creature."[170]

In Romans, peace appears as the end product of reconciliation, although in Corinthians, the horizontal dimension is emphasized in the need to overcome disharmony and disturbance. Peace was so crucial in Paul's thinking that he says to the Christian married to a non-Christian, "God has called us to live in peace" (1 Cor. 7:15). For the body of Christ to experience unity and order, peace becomes a prerequisite. "For God is a God not of disorder but of peace" (1 Cor. 14:33).

To the Ephesians enmeshed in conflict between Jews and Gentiles, Paul tells them Christ is our peace, both vertically and horizontally. Brueggemann agrees with Paul with his reference to the peace motif in Hebrews and its connection with the Sabbath. He argues that "creation culminates in the peace and joy of the Sabbath [when] harmony has been brought to all the warring elements in our existence."[171] Every conflict amicably resolved is a foretaste of that heavenly Sabbath and its overtones of rest from restlessness and chaos.

In the NT, Christian distinctiveness was seen in its developing concept of peace (Rom. 14:17). Peace still meant well-being and security, but the physical characteristics gradually disappeared. Restoration of the image of

---

169 Robert Young, Analytical Concordance of the Bible (Grand Rapids, MI: Wm. B. Eerdmans, 1964), p. 736.

170 Walter Brueggemann, *Living Toward a Vision, Biblical Reflections on Shalom* (Philadelphia, PA: United Church Press, 1976), p. 15.

171 Brueggeman, p. 18.

God in fallen man became synonymous with peace. Peace was victory, but it was victory over the powers of darkness (Rom. 16:20).

Peace in the NT also had a negative aspect. It was the absence of contention and hostilities between nations. A study of NT texts—which may allow for the crusades,[172] for the just war,[173] for pacifism,[174] or for peacemaking[175]—will also conclude that the "Christian religion makes in some respects for the reduction and in other respects for the intensification of strife."[176]

This reduction and/or intensification of strife demonstrates the importance the peace concept brought to the first-century Christians. This dissonance may explain why many NT references to peace apply to peaceful relations among humans; others address peace as a blessing. Peace then is either a present reality and possession or a potentially accessible (cf. Luke 1:79, 2:14, 19:38).

Noticeably, the epistolary greetings present peace as inner peace. The concept of peace in the believer's life is developed as characteristic of the fruit of forgiveness and reconciliation. Only where forgiveness and reconciliation have occurred can the pastor or member invoke peace as a rationale for ending conflicts and misunderstandings. So Paul can say to the reconciled—the peaceful ones—"the kingdom of which you are now a part is 'righteousness, peace, and joy in the Holy Spirit'" (Rom. 14:17). He later names peace as a fruit of the Spirit (Gal. 5:22).

McPolin clearly develops the concept of peace in conflict. He uses the externally calm Johannine text as proof for the realistic hope of peace while engaged in conflict. The fourth Gospel contains the peace and conflict strain. With the Christian community's struggle between light and darkness, John offers the effective presence of the light of the world. McPolin identifies the farewell message of Jesus as one of "consolation and peace for disciples who experience conflict and tribulation"[177] (14:27–28; 16:1–4, 32–33). The peace of Christ's presence was not to be found outside

---

172 John 2:15; Matt. 10:34; Luke 12:51, and 22:35–38.

173 Mark 12:17; Matt. 17:24–25; Eph. 1:23; Phil. 3:20; Luke 2:11; 2:1, 12–14; 14:31–33; Matt. 26:52; and Luke 22:25–38.

174 Matt. 5; Luke 6:36; and Rom. 12:19.

175 Matt. 5:9.

176 Roland H. Bainton, *Christian Attitudes Toward War and Peace* (New York: Abingdon Press, 1960), p. 65.

177 John McPolin, "Peace in Conflict," *The Way* 22 (1982): 267.

the Christian community (14:27), yet believers were not to be discouraged over their mission (15:19).

While the NT teaches that all men may be reconciled to God, it is not less insistent that men should be reconciled one to another. This is amplified in 1 Corinthians 14:33 where Paul pleads for unity and reconciliation, for "God is not a God of confusion but of peace," not desiring faction[178] and strife.[179]

If Rogers is correct when he contends, "There is no reconciliation without cooperation,"[180] then this cooperation must be renewed daily. This cooperation symbolizes man's response to the divine call to human action and his involvement in a ministry of reconciliation. The person who enters the ministry of reconciliation in the spirit of peace is, in fact, the peacemaker of the beatitude.

Peacemaking

Patrick V. Rogers unconsciously alludes to mankind's constant battle with conflict. He sees reconciliation resulting in peace as God's answer to mankind's tension emerging between his "temptations to sin and aspirations to holiness."[181] Herein lies the conflict facing humans in their search for peace: avoidance of temptations and approach toward holiness.

Peacemaking is not negative work; it involves a spirit of hope instead of a spirit of rift. Whereas Luke offered an early theology of vertical reconciliation, Matthew found meaning in a horizontal reconciliation. Into a community encapsulated by deep divisions and discussions, Matthew encouraged conciliation. Of Matthew 18, Wansbrough notes, "The remarkable thing is that it is concerned almost entirely with peaceful relationships between brethren."[182]

True peace may be affected by absorbing the anger and hostility of the enemy. Jesus's method involved peacemaking rather than peacekeeping. Destruction of an enemy in conflict may only serve to postpone conflict

---

178 Cf. Rom. 2:8; 2 Cor. 12:20; Gal. 5:20; Phil. 1:17; 2:3; and James 3:14, 16.
179 Rom. 1:29; 13:13; 1 Cor. 1:11; 3:3; 2 Cor. 12:20; Gal. 5:20; and Phil. 1:15.
180 Patrick V. Rogers, "Peace through the Cross," *The Way* 22 (1982): 202.
181 Ibid., p. 199.
182 Henry Wansbrough, "Blessed Are the Peacemakers," *The Way* (January 1982): 14.

"as the evil of revenge lives on and takes up residence in other men who wait for their opportune turn to destroy their enemy."[183]

The peacemaker is a realist, recognizing conflict, and gets involved in resolving it (Matt. 26:47–56). He does whatever is legitimate to bring about conciliation, and Zehr says the peacemaker "has an implicit faith in the power of the helping hand, the reconciling word, and the listening ear."[184] The peacemaker also strives to aid anyone involved with Satan. White observes, "If all had a sense of the conflict which each soul must wage with satanic agencies that are seeking to ensnare, entice, and deceive, there would be much more diligent labor for those who are young in the faith."[185]

Productive peacemaking serves to undergird the whole concept of conflict management, and conciliation becomes an outgrowth of peacemaking. Whether conciliation appears potential or not, the spirit of intelligent peacemaking creates a hope of resolution and often inhibits discouragement. The true peacemaker operates in the arena and philosophy of hope. Hope for success is the goal of his/her activities. Brueggemann gives a positive view of peacemaking when he argues, "The central vision of world history in the Bible is that all creation is one, every creature in community with every other living in harmony and security toward the joy and well-being of every other creature."[186]

Some Key Passages about Peacemaking

Matthew 6:11–12 and 14–15 indicates the peace-forgiveness motif of reconciliation and symbolizes distantly the mutuality of individual responsibility for restoring relationships. Jesus's teachings on forgiveness reemphasize this same point in Luke 17:3–4: "So watch your selves. If your brother sins, rebuke him, and if he repents, forgive him. If he sins against you seven times in a day, and seven times comes back to you and says, I repent, forgive him." Paul takes up this peacemaker strain and encourages all in Christ to follow after things that make for peace (Rom. 14:19).

---

183 Daniel Zehr, "Portrait of a Peacemaker," Mennonite Central Committee Pamphlet, n.d., p. 2.
184 Ibid., p. 4. These are concepts basic to Carl Rogers's practice of psychotherapy.
185 White, *Testimonies*, 6:92.
186 Brueggemann, p. 15.

When one is willing to forgive, he/she shows his/her tendency to be interested in the person more than in what the person has done. Forgiveness means that one has abdicated his/her self-esteem and hurt or injury and released the individual of the wrong he/she has done. Forgiving involves regarding something that happened as if it had never occurred. Forgiveness brings freedom from bitterness and hardness of heart and is an attitude rather than an act. The one with a forgiving spirit is forever seeking for new means and ways to reduce bitterness, resentment, and the carrying around of grudges. When self-esteem and the defending of one's power base are not in question, cooperative approaches to problem-solving become even encouraging and more rewarding.

Any conversation on handling peacemaking and forgiveness ought to include the concept of an apology with the intent to cancel both the implied and/or perceived hurt and shame involved in the issue. The apology should be perceived and accepted as an acknowledgment and regret for the injury void of a defense or excuse. It can serve as a work of repair of relationships and a request for forgiveness. An apology can open the door to the former relationship. Forgiveness therefore ought not to be dependent on the acceptance of an apology—the acceptance of an apology by the offended can aid the feeling of forgiveness by the offender.

Human beings are encouraged to take the risk of expressing creative and innovative options to situations when problem-solving becomes encouraging and rewarding. The ego strength, balanced by the feeling of trust, develops openness among people and creates intentional movement toward peacemaking. Passive peacekeeping can give way to active peacemaking. Paul recognized the gigantic challenge of avoidance of evil and counseled, "Do not be overcome by evil but overcome evil with good" (Rom. 12:20).

In the role as conflict manager, the Christian is called to live in a state of justification before God and man. He is expected to maintain vertical and horizontal fellowship and to replace negative reactions with positive activity. The call to peacemaking is followed by identification of what causes peace or leads to peace maintenance. Peter points out that absence of peace, and the consequent presence of guilt, can impede conciliation and answered prayer (1 Pet. 3:8, 11–12).

Consequently, in the joint call by the writer to the Hebrews to make every effort "to live in peace with all men" (Heb. 12:14) and by Peter "to live in harmony with one another . . . [and to] seek peace and pursue it"

(1 Pet. 3:8, 11), one can identify an intentional admonition to mankind to seek and to maintain a peace that would establish a state of conciliation among mankind. Paul encourages Christians never to give up their search for conciliation—hard though it may seem to achieve.

The approach to peacemaking should be balanced by the desire for conciliation. Consequently, the peacemaker will move from the least restrictive to the more restrictive conciliatory strategy, constantly providing an open door for face-saving. Peacemaking, like conflict management, appreciates the defense mechanisms and uses strategies that allow for mutual benefit (of peace) from the encounter. White counseled in dealing with the erring to create a climate that promotes conciliation:

> In dealing with the erring, harsh measures should not be resorted to; milder means will affect far more. Make use of the milder means most perseveringly and even if they fail, wait patiently; never hurry the matter of cutting off a member from the church.[187]

Peacemaking must not be one-sided in its results; it must lead to mutual edification. Forgiveness, as a two-way exercise, results in mutual satisfaction, for there is no room for action leading to personal advantage. Power and influence must not be allowed to thwart movement toward peace. In Romans 14:19, Paul calls for conciliation of the weak and strong believer through methods that lead to mutual building up in the faith. In this milieu, peace is secured and maintained when preferences, convention, and feelings are not allowed to distort principle, conviction, and facts. Feelings often constitute the real issue of many conflicts, and when these feelings are not identified and dealt with positively, the results can often be destructive.

The maintenance of the close relationship that exists between forgiveness, peace, repentance, and restitution in the setting of conflict management and reconciliation can positively influence outcomes. Wherever there is alienation and disagreement, relationships often are impaired, and there is the conscious need for the recognition of that crack in the relationship and attempts to mend it. These attempts, which may be

---

187 Ellen G. White, "Be Gentle unto All Men," *The Advent Review and Sabbath Herald* (May 14, 1885), p. 305.

one-sided, must be communicated to the other party in a way that suggests willingness for conciliation through dialogue.

A mutual setting for conciliation offers the fruit of peace and allows for repentance. The presence of peace and repentance does not nullify restitution and may at times require it. The NT seems to indicate a preference for restoration of relationship (Matt. 18:15; Gal. 6:1; Phil. 4:17) more than mere restitution, although restitution could well demonstrate the fruit and result of the whole process of reconciliation.

In the Ministry of Reconciliation

Role of the Church

The Scriptures abound with metaphors and images of the church, and each metaphor or image creates a dimension of the concept of the church. I believe that the image that supports most strongly the church's role in conflict management is that of "a vehicle of reconciliation." The church becomes a vehicle of reconciliation when vertical and horizontal fellowship is demonstrated in its body life and in its treatment and encounter with conflict.

By active and vigorous participation in the ministry of reconciliation, the church—under all its metaphors, models, and images—plays a significant part in God's divine intention for mankind. Consequently, when one enters the priesthood of believers (1 Pet. 2:9), that person is thereby uniting with Jesus in God's redemptive purpose for the world. "The church individually and corporately is to be the 'carrier' of Christ to the world,"[188] especially since "the call of God comes to each man at the common tasks."[189] As carrier of Christ, the church shows itself the vehicle of reconciliation by constantly helping to remove all impediments to harmonious relationships; that is, it constantly seeks how to exchange alienation for friendship.

All churches ought to be servants in the service of reconciliation. In the act of initiating reconciliation, one renders a ministry of love. The very life of every member of the Church is a continuation of Christ's ministry on earth. "God's messengers are commissioned to take up the very work that

---

188 Rex Edwards, *A New Frontier: Every Believer a Minister* (Mountain View, CA: Pacific Press, 1979), p. 79.

189 Roland Bainton, *Here I Stand* (New York: Mentor Books, 1955), p. 156.

Christ did while on earth."[190] "All Christian ministry is basically one; it is a ministry of reconciliation."[191] The ministry of reconciliation can be viewed as a service of love rendered by Christians with the intention of healing the breaking or broken relationships occasioned by conflict.

The church's distinctive role in being a reconciling community is to confront men with the good news that God has already "broken down the dividing wall of hostility" between them, bringing their mutual hostility to an end "through the cross" (Eph. 2:12–16). It is to invite mankind to respond in faith to the fact that "he is our peace" because "through Him we both have access in one Spirit to the Father" so that we may become "fellow citizens with the saints and members of the household of God" (Eph. 2:14–22).

The role of the church is not merely to try to reconcile humans as citizens of this world but to call them into God's new order created in Christ, whereby they may be rescued from the dominion of darkness (Col. 1:13). The church of reconciled saints must be God's servant, bringing God's conciliation to the alienated (Isa. 49:1–6). The church serving in its role of reconciler has precedence in Christ. He was agent and agency. He brought man reconciliation; he was reconciliation, and he was peace. Into a world alienated from justice and mercy, the church is sent to offer justice and mercy to the estranged ones. The church finds its example in and for service in the life of Christ who sought to bring reconciliation wherever he went. His work was reconciliation.

Just as God in Christ entered the battlefield "to reconcile man to Himself,"[192] the church as a vehicle of reconciliation has a moral right, maybe moral obligation, to enter the battlefield of human animosity and to come out with tokens of peace. This becomes even more obligatory if this animosity exists within the *ecclesia* of God.

The church often tends to downplay the importance of human reconciliation for fear of failure or explosion. But wherever justice, hatred, and prejudice are alienating men from one another, the church is to be the agent of God's reconciliation. The church dares not lose sight of the truth that it is the gathered community sent forth into creative management

---

190 White, *Testimonies*, 9:130.
191 Edwards, p. 67.
192 J. H. Roberts, "Some Biblical Foundations for a Mission of Reconciliation," *Missionalia* 7 (April 1979): 7. Cf. Matt. 3:7–12 and 11:1–6.

of conflict and reconciliation. Roberts is correct when he posits that "the church as the sphere in which God exemplifies his act of reconciliation [is] the only sphere, within which the experience of being at peace with God and one another can become a reality."[193] The church is God's instrument for bringing about his promised peace among men.

Furnish further argues the following:

> The ministry of reconciliation serves the word of reconciliation by bringing it near, by making it present, by giving it shape and substance in the everyday world. Through the ministry of reconciliation God's reconciling love in Christ is to be established as the rule of Christ's love. To be reconciled to God through Christ means also to be reconciled with one another in Christ.[194]

Paul had a full grasp of the meaning of reconciliation and its implication for church life. He presses the concept that a ministry of reconciliation was not a thing of choice, and he used a special word to transfer this thought. The word is *appeal*. "God making His appeal through us" means more than it suggests. Furnish argues that *appeal* in 2 Corinthians 5:20 refers to "resocialization and reconciliation."[195] Therefore, God uses the formerly alienated ones as his vehicle for calling his enemies to resocialization and reconciliation. Herein lies the obligatory nature of conflict management— to call the alienated to resocialization and reconciliation.

The service of clarification of perceptions—so necessary in conflict management—is essential in a spirit of persevering faith and enlightened hope. The service of reconciliation is not to be engaged in to buttress inefficiency or inaccuracies or to suggest compromise as used in normal connotation. In fact, the opposite is true. Bennett observes, a stripped-down, relevant version of Christianity may be effective for the moment in dealing with a problem, but it provides little guidance for the complexities opened by that very problem. It fails to mediate the grace of forgiveness

---

193 Ibid., p. 14.

194 Victor Paul Furnish, "The Ministry of Reconciliation," *Currents in Theology and Mission* 4 (1977): 204–218.

195 Ibid., pp. 216–217. (Luke 15:28; Acts 16:39; 1 Cor. 4:13; and 2 Cor. 2:6–8.)

and of new life the whole person needs, and it knows little of the sources of reconciliation that society requires for its healing.[196]

Every attempt into the conflicts of society should be with a clearly defined theological rationale to aid reconciliation and/or resolution of relationships. The church needs consistency in its approach to the ills of society; no partial social action can be taken. Harkness contends that any church action that is not characterized by a sound theological rationale "will be interpreted as condescension, paternalism and 'tokenism'—all proven barriers to human relations reconciliation."[197]

In its service of reconciliation, Joseph notes that the church ought to be working in concert with other social agencies bringing healing and reunion.

> The church must be concerned in such areas of life as vocational guidance; premarital counseling; holding families together; the provision of wholesome recreation; the prevention of juvenile delinquency; resident care for the elderly; the rehabilitation of alcoholics; the prevention or the reconciliation of industrial strife; the alleviation of poverty, ignorance, racial injustice. . . . The church must in this radical secular society be ever conscious of humanity's basic needs.[198]

This consciousness of humanity's basic needs affirms the social gospel of conflict management.

Although Harkness observes that the church has not consistently converged spirit and action as the carrier of the faith and vehicle of reconciliation, she concedes that the church has, through the centuries, been the primary agent of reconciliation. "In this task, the Christian church has again and again been used by God for the reconciliation not

196 John Bennett, "The Missing Dimension," *Christianity and Crisis* 29 (September 1969): 242.
197 Harkness, p. 16.
198 Samuel H. Joseph, "A Study of the Foundations of Ministry and Laity with Special Reference to the East Caribbean Conference of Seventh-day Adventists," (DMin project, Andrews University, 1975), pp. 68–69.

only of man to God and of man to himself, but of man to man through its services to those in many forms of need."[199]

The reality of reconciliation becomes the mandate for its *kerygmatic* proclamation. The resurrection of Jesus validated reconciliation and forgiveness (Rom. 5:25), and as preachers of this realized reconciliation and forgiveness, men become "God's instruments, His messengers, the bearers of His peace, His ambassadors."[200] Thompson further states convincingly that reconciliation comes to full fruition when men and women "are united in fellowship and live a life of true reconciliation with each other in the body of Christ and in their dealings with others in the world."[201]

To adequately execute its mission of reconciliation, the church must engage itself in roles that approximate those of the evangelist, the teacher, the proclaimer, and the peacemaker. It must share its mediating grace with society. It must evangelize the message of conciliation and teach the tools of reconciliation. Its interests must no longer be centered in numerical growth only but also in the qualitative relational growth of human beings. The attempts to create conciliatory relationships within its membership must be extended to those who know not the Prince of Peace.

> Only by obediently practicing God's reconciliation in actual church life will the church's mission of reconciliation come to fruition. Only by being God's reconciled community can the church hope to be God's sign of reconciliation to the world.[202]

The ministry of reconciliation also implies a church with an in- and outreach mission, without a clergy-laity dichotomy. The laity must not be allowed to regard themselves as mere persons to be reconciled but, more positively, as the very agents of reconciliation. The task of initiating reconciliation does not lie solely on the ordained ministry. The true ministry of reconciliation recognizes this:

One "laos" called to be priestly and prophetic in the service of humanization. The laity as well as the clergy has a priesthood to exercise,

---

199 Harkness, p. 16.
200 Thompson, "Doctrine of Reconciliation," p. 49.
201 Ibid., p. 50.
202 Roberts, "Some Biblical Foundations," p. 15.

both at the altar and in the world. Laymen have a prophetic vocation both within the church and within their daily secular tasks.[203]

In the ministry of reconciliation lies the opportunity for a dual ministry (of laity and clergy) transcending ecclesiastical barriers and qualifications. A conflict ministry may even open the door for the ordained ministry to be involved in secular arbitration,[204] where one can extend the model of reconciliation into community life. At this level of involvement, clerical position may be even more highly appreciated in this secular world if it can demonstrate secular competence and sense of responsibility at the point where the community hurts most—at the level of dysfunctional conflict.

Creative conflict management is essentially an integral aspect of the ministry of reconciliation, and reconciliation may well be impossible if the source of alienation is not efficiently handled, regulated, or controlled. If one should suggest that conflict exists solely because of unregenerate hearts, then the task of reconciliation, of conflict management, becomes even more crucial and critical. "Every church should [then] be a training school for Christian workers. Its members should be taught . . . how to work for the unconverted."[205] The training of ministers in conflict management becomes a key step in training Christian workers for greater effectiveness in overcoming the dysfunctional effects of conflicts.

Involvement in the ministry of reconciliation is gospel work, and "God intends that His ministers shall be educators of the church in gospel work."[206] One can find here another justification for teaching creative conflict management as a tool in the ministry of reconciliation, "for it is through the average member that God would confront the world with the ministry of reconciliation."[207]

---

203 Bianchi, pp. 146–147.
204 This new area of city arbitrator or its parallel may be the twenty-first-century counterpart of Paul's tent-making ministry. It may well constitute an emerging ministry in a secular age, especially when and where the church experiences financial setbacks. It may offer extra vocational income, almost similar to the emerging pastoral consultant ministry. It could offer the church a practical presence in the community.
205 White, *Ministry of Healing*, p. 149.
206 Idem, *Desire of Ages*, p. 825.
207 Edwards, pp. 71–72.

The church that God intended to be the vehicle of reconciliation is a vibrant, redeeming community of compassion, mission, service, witness, love, worship, and conciliation. "It is not a fraternity of fans of the faith."[208] Therefore, all the members of the church (*laikoi*) become active with their special gift of edification, leading to the nurture and outreach of the body. Herein lies the role and use of spiritual gifts in the body. As the vehicle of reconciliation, God has given the church various gifts to help effect this task. We turn now to look at spiritual gifts as they aid the church in the mission of conflict management and reconciliation.

Role of Spiritual Gifts

All the ammunition the church needs for the perfect execution of its mission of reconciliation has been deposited with it ever since it has been given the mandate to bring the *goyim* to Yahweh. Every Christian, therefore, partakes of some aspects of that ammunition. A clear understanding of the role of each member in the ministry of reconciliation makes each person an active minister of his own special gift of grace to the rest of the body.

It appears to me that in three key passages (Rom. 12, 1 Cor. 12, and Eph. 4), where Paul discusses the theme of spiritual gifts, the activity of the *laos* is made possible through the correct use of the gifts. This word (*gifts*) further suggests that the successful execution of the ministry of reconciliation is made possible through the gifts God has given the church.

Of the various combinations of lists appearing in the relevant literature,[209] all serve the needs of the church from time to time. A cursory look at any major listing indicates that several of the gifts can have significant meaning and usefulness in conflict management. However, for the purposes of this study, we consider the gifts of mercy, word of wisdom, word of knowledge, distinguishing of spirits, and to a lesser extent, teaching as the gifts, which may be more closely connected with creative conflict management than the others.

---

208 Ibid., p. 20.

209 Cf. David L. Hocking, *Spiritual Gifts: Their Necessity and Use in the Local Church* (Long Beach, CA: Sounds of Grace, 1975), pp. 52–53; Kenneth Cain Kinghorn, *Gifts of the Spirit* (Nashville, TN: Abingdon Press, 1976), p. 41; Jack W. MacGorman, *The Gifts of the Spirit* (Nashville, TN: Broadman Press, 1974), pp. 34–35; and Edward F. Murphy, *Spiritual Gifts and the Great Commission* (South Pasadena, CA: Mandate Press, 1975), p. 43.

One's willingness to be influenced by facts, as made possible through the gifts of wisdom and knowledge, can make conflict management more effective. The use of these gifts to aid conflict management confirms God's intent that the gifts serve to equip the church for nurture and outreach. The presence and use of spiritual gifts can serve to stabilize the church, create functional responses to conflict, and strengthen the church's execution of its mission of reconciliation.

It might be noted that the discerning of spirits is primarily a judicial estimation made by judgment or separation. Since the unscrupulous can, at times, camouflage the genuine and distort reality, the conflict manager ought to acquaint him/herself with adequate communication skills. He/she must recognize the need to identify the spirit of disputants in a conflict, for credibility generally depends on the spirit and not just the personalities involved.

Several of the other gifts are relevant to the conflict manager, but the discerning of spirits has crucial implications for fact clarification, perception filtering, depersonalization of issues, and mediating skills. He needs to be alert to change of spirit and to capitalize on it to the mutual benefits of the parties.

The presence of dishonesty or conflict makes necessary the need for some help to cope with these difficulties. Naden adequately summarizes various aspects of the gift of discernment when he defines it as

> the Spirit's gift to perceive people's needs and minister effectively to them, to identify issues and conflicts that confront the members of the Body, and to identify the sources of motivation in people, as the Lord or Satan.[210]

It can be concluded that God, in his wisdom and knowledge, has indeed bestowed on his church all the ammunition needed for the successful execution of its ministry of reconciliation.

---

210 Roy Naden, "Pastoral Nurture and Religious Education" (notes of class lectures for CHMN740, Andrews University, Berrien Springs, MI, 1985).

Summary

The basic Christian treatment of conflict is an orientation toward conciliation and the healing of damaged relationships and emotions. The task of reconciling is mutual; both the wronged person (party) and the offended one (party) are under obligation to initiate healing toward wounded spirits. Reconciliation plays an important role in the creative management of conflict and, in fact, without full reconciliation, creative conflict management cannot be said to have been fully achieved.

Several deductions can be made from our study so far on reconciliation. They include the following:

1. Reconciliation implies complete reversal of attitude, change of heart, or the exchange of the position causing the strained relationship of the situation.

2. Reconciliation may be on the part of one party induced by the action of another, either by the contender or a third party. Reconciliation often implies mutual hostility and mutual concession in favor of conciliation.

3. Reconciliation implies complete removal of any alienation or impediment to unity and peace between parties.

4. Basically, reconciliation among mankind results in a new standing, a new relationship, and new ways of interaction. Objectively, any kind of reconciliation has an initializing input of the Holy Spirit, recognized or not (2 Cor. 5:18).

5. Reconciliation is never possible in a state of mistrust, pity, or guilt. There must be a parity of power and mutual desire for conciliation (cf. Acts 6:1–5).

6. Reconciliation requires the reconciled to be themselves agents of conciliation (treasures in earthen vessels), thus extending the *diakovia* of reconciliation.

7. Full and complete reconciliation has the inherent idea of restored peace of mind, which dispels worry and fear. This peace-reconciliation motif seems to be expected of both saint and sinner and is achievable.

8. Any conception of conflict that denies the potential of reconciliation defeats the sincere belief that conflict is manageable, and conciliation is a real possibility.

Yet amid this potential for strife, ambassadors of reconciliation need to execute their mission in ways that lead "to peace and to mutual edification" (Rom. 14:19). Christians need not initiate unnecessary strife, but while in strife, their effort ought to gravitate toward conciliation and mutual peace. The movement toward conciliation should not compromise principle or surrender truth. To this end, White noted, "No man can be true to principle without exciting opposition. A Christianity that is spiritual will be opposed by the children of disobedience."[211]

Peacemaking appears to be a learned discipline to which all Christians are called (Mark 9:50; Rom. 14:19; 2 Cor. 13:11; Heb. 12:14; 1 Pet. 3:8, 11–12). It also involves the concept of harmonious existence. Christians can experience peace in grief, loss, and conflict, for they find it personified in the person of Jesus Christ. Various means are at the disposal of anyone who participates in the task of peacemaking. Peacemaking is personal and is fundamental to the successful experience of conciliation and the creative management of conflict.

The church is responsible to the world to demonstrate its ability to initiate reconciliation within and without its boundaries. Its mission includes active participation in conflict management so that a peace analogous to the peace of God may be experienced in human encounters with peace-threatening situations. For this task, God has given his church the ammunition (gifts and talents) for the execution of its mission of reconciliation.

---

211 White, *Desire of Ages*, p. 356.

PART 2

Review of Current Conflict-Management Literature and Development of Proposed Seminar Modules

CHAPTER 4

Review of Secular Literature

History

There was a time when conflict was accepted as an aspect of the social fabric of life, and it was used specifically for its functional values. As the field of sociology developed toward being an applied science, managers began to be threatened by the presence of conflict in business. Conflict began to be evaluated negatively. Most of the literature on conflict developed about this time, which explains why this negative aspect came to be represented as the traditional view.

The literature on conflict during this period suggested that conflict was bad, that it should be avoided, and that its presence could discourage the smooth operation of any organization. The literature favored its discouragement at its best and elimination at its worst. Lewis Coser was the first to carry on Georg Simmel's[212] work on conflict and advocated the positive nature of it. "The inevitability of conflict has so transformed

---

212 Georg Simmel, *Conflict and the Web of Group Affiliations*, trans. Reinhard Bendix (Glencoe, IL: Free Press, 1955); Coser, *Functions of Social Conflict*.

thinking [today] that it is popularly accepted as a necessary and desirable experience of any relationship."[213]

The history of conflict management has developed through what Robbins calls "the three distinct stages or philosophical views: the traditional, the behavioral, and the interactionist."[214] Stage 1 (the traditional) suggested that conflict should be eliminated since all conflicts were destructive. It dominated the nineteenth century and continued to the middle 1940s. By the late 1940s and early 1950s, the behaviorialists (stage 2) recognized that organizations by their nature had built-in conflict mechanism, and consequently, they prescribed avoidance of conflict. They also stressed the resolution of conflict. The interactionist philosophy (stage 3) does not agree with the behaviorialists in that all conflicts should be avoided or resolved. The interactionist approach says, "Managers should continue to resolve those conflicts that hinder the organization but stimulate conflict intensity when the level is below that which is necessary to maintain a responsive and innovative unit."[215]

The literature in recent decades has not only recognized the functional value of conflict to any relationship, but it has moved the emphasis from conflict results and behavior to offering guidelines for successful conflict-resolution methods. Bibliographical entries in any major text dealing with conflict demonstrate the sophistication with which critical appraisal has been given to a variety of conflict situations. Although conflict management has, for decades, been given literary consideration by different disciplines, the formal study goes back to the spring of 1957 when *The Journal of Conflict Resolution* was first published.

213 Richard Cosier and Thomas L. Ruble, "Research on Conflict-Handling Behavior: An Experimental Approach," *Academy of Management Journal* 24 (December 1981): 816. For a history of the conflict management movement, see Donald E. Bossart, *Creative Conflict in Religious Education and Church Administration* (Birmingham, IL: Religious Education Press, 1980), pp. 26–32.

214 Stephen Robbins, "'Conflict Management' and 'Conflict Resolution' Are Not Synonymous Terms," *California Management Review* 21 (Winter 1970): 68.

215 Ibid., p. 69. C. A. Dailey cautions, "The deliberate precipitation of conflict also presupposes a high level of experience and expertise in conflict management since it may also head off a worse explosion. "The Management of Conflict," *Chicago Theological Seminary Register* LIX (May 1969): 7.

Recent interest in conflict management in various settings such as the church finds justification in the fact that "managers spend approximately 20 percent of their time dealing with conflict and rate conflict management as of equal (or slightly higher) importance compared with planning, communication, motivation, and decision making."[216]

Conflict and Change

Ambivalence concerning the nature of conflict still exists. Robbins's observation may have meaning for the church. He observed that, very often, leaders praise subordinates who "maintain peace, harmony, and tranquility" while "disequilibrium, confrontation, and dissatisfaction are appraised negatively."[217] The pastor needs to recognize the almost inseparability of conflict and change. This recognition will not only help pastors be familiar with the stages of change but it will also aid them in introducing changes and innovations with the least amount of dysfunctional conflict. Awareness, acceptance, and alternatives represent three conditions that favor change. The pastor who can offer these conditions also increases in credibility as a creative change agent. Figure 1 suggests conflict stimulates change, which brings about adaptation, and only through adapting can the organization survive.

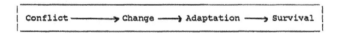

Figure 1. Conflict and Survival

Modal Preferences

A popular instrument devised by Kenneth Thomas and Ralph Kilmann has proven very useful for assessing conflict-mode style.[218] It is

---

216 K. W. Thomas and W. H. Schmidt, "A Survey of Managerial Interests with Respect to Conflict," *Academy of Management Journal* 19 (June 1976): 315–316.

217 Robbins, "'Conflict Management' and 'Conflict Resolution,'" p. 68.

218 Kenneth W. Thomas and Ralph H. Kilmann, *Thomas-Kilmann Conflict-Mode* (Tuxedo, NY: Xicon, 1974), p. 11.

---

developed along two dimensions: co-cooperativeness and assertiveness. Five behavioral patterns can be developed on this two-dimensional construct. Thomas[219] described these five patterns as follows:

Competing is assertive and uncooperative. It is a power-oriented mode seeking its own advantage.

Accommodating is unassertive and cooperative—the opposite of competing. In this mode, one neglects personal concerns to satisfy the concerns of the other.

Avoiding is unassertive and uncooperative—no concerns are pursued intentionally. Conflict is not addressed.

Collaborating is both assertive and cooperative. It involves one's attempt to work with the other person to find some solution that has mutual satisfaction.

Compromising is intermediate in both assertiveness and cooperativeness. It aims to find some mutually acceptable solution partially satisfactory to both parties. It gives up more than competing but less than accommodating and is basically the exchanging of concessions.

Although interest and emphasis are toward collaborating, the intelligent manager of conflict seeks to understand the dynamics and the characteristics of each mode. The criteria for choosing the specific mode is presented in module 4. The suggestion is that instead of mastering a preferred style, everyone should endeavor to develop a repertoire of styles that would offer more options for creative conflict management (fig. 2).

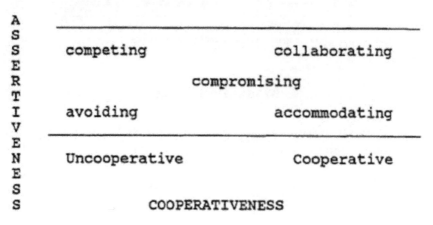

Figure 2. The Thomas-Kilmann Conflict Mode Matrix

219 Ibid., p. 12.

Power

Whether power is ascribed or earned, it plays a central role in all conflict management theories. "Power currencies of expertise, resource control, interpersonal linkages, personal qualities, and intimacy provide ways for this mutual influence to be enacted."[220] The accurate assessment of power (the ability to influence others) is difficult since it is primarily a result of social relationships. The capability to equalize power especially in conflict-management situations can create cooperation towards mutual interactions.

Some Variables Affecting the Course of Conflict

Regardless of the components of conflict situations, Deutsch has identified seven variables that affect the course of conflict:

1. The characteristics of the parties in conflict (their values, social resources, beliefs about conflict, and so forth)

2. Their prior relationship to one another (their attitudes, beliefs, and expectations about one another)

3. The nature of the issue giving rise to the conflict (its scope, its rigidity, its periodicity, its motivational significance, and its formulation)

4. The social environment within which the conflict occurs

5. The interested audiences to the conflict (their relationships and expectations to the outcomes and disputants)

---

220 Joyce L. Hocker and William W. Wilmot, *Interpersonal Conflict*, 2nd ed. (Dubuque, IA: Wm. C. Brown, 1985), p. 90. Cf. Herb Cohen, *You Can Negotiate Anything* (New York: Bantam Books, 1982), pp. 51–90.

---

6. The strategies and tactics employed by parties in the conflict

7. The consequences of the conflict to each of the participants and to other interested parties[221]

King[222] and Dailey[223] offer several propositions to be considered in developing a personal philosophy toward conflict. King argues, among other things, that the function of conflict is to maintain identity and strength, to enhance operational effectiveness, and to help deal with others. One's understanding of conflict resolution and conflict management can also influence the course of a conflict, and various definitions are given for both terms. Folberg and Taylor note that "conflict resolution and conflict management are general terms for specific processes that achieve a balance of power through non-coercive means."[224] In this paper, conflict resolution is the convergence of aims, methods, and behaviors that return relationships to a state of trust and harmony, while conflict management is the process that regulates or controls the convergence of aims, methods, and behaviors.

It is critical to conflict managers that they become acquainted with what has been called "the conflict process"[225] or the "predictable behavioral cycle."[226] Figure 3 illustrates the conflict process as four distinct stages, ranging from the antecedent conditions to increased or decreased group performance. Whether conflict is treated as a process or as a cycle, it has implications not only for the group but also for the individual.

---

221 Deutsch, pp. 4–8.

222 Dennis King, "Three Cheers for Conflict!" *Personnel* 58 (1981): 15–21.

223 Dailey, "The Management of Conflict," pp. 1–7.

224 Jay Folberg and Alison Taylor, *Mediation: A Comprehensive Guide to Resolving Conflicts without Litigation* (San Francisco, CA: Jossey-Bass, 1984), p. 26.

225 Stephen P. Robbins, *Essentials of Organizational Behavior* (Englewood Cliffs, NJ: 1984), p. 145.

226 A. Rapoport, "Conflict Resolution in the Light of Game Theory and Beyond," in P. W. Swingle, ed., *The Structure of Conflict* (New York: Academic Press, 1970), pp. 1–43. The stages are (1) tension development, (2) role dilemma, (3) injustice collecting, (4) confrontation, and (5) adjustment.

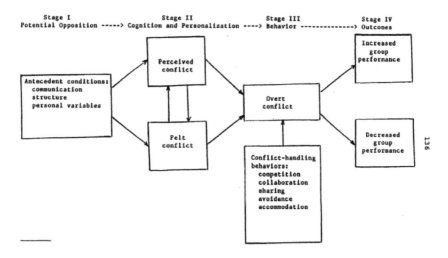

Figure 3. The Conflict Process
Source: Stephen Robbins, Essentials of Organizational Behavior (1983), p. 145

Self-esteem and feelings have vital implications for conflict management and resolution. Very often self-esteem influences the strategy used in conflict, and feelings are often hidden or suppressed only to erupt in other situations. Bossart[227] identifies anxiety, hostility, frustration, guilt, and ambiguity as five feelings that, together or independently, can influence conflict avoidance, repression, escalation, or confrontation.

Anxiety results from a threat to one's existence or relationship with others. Hostility often results after an accumulation of disappointments, hurts, and anger. Although it can be proven useful, sometimes hostility can develop into destructive intensity and thus limit the creativity brought to conflict management. Blocked goals can result in frustration and depression. Frustration is then intensified to the level of the feelings of powerlessness and hopelessness, and very often, the perception of a losing battle encourages withdrawal or avoidance.

Guilt sometimes causes irrational commitment to a cause, especially when self-interest may not appear to be in question. Guilt complicates the union of theology and practicum since anything that disturbs the equilibrium is perceived as negative or wrong, even when opposition is the correct posture to be taken. This guilt then becomes contributory to

---

227 Bossart, pp. 51–62.

ambiguity, which sometimes results in an avoidance-approach situation being reached.

Not only is Bossart correct in suggesting that feelings often dominate the church conflict scenario, but Leas extends this observation to identify five crucial pitfalls of conflicts to church life as "dropping out, blaming, attaching, generalizing, and distorted and interrupted communication."[228]

Each of these pitfalls have their effects, but generalizing or globalizing can be destructive and creative of conflict intensification. Where globalizing exists, one good offensive is fractionation, that is, the breaking down of the conflict into small issues that can be addressed. (Generalization has just the opposite reaction.) To effectively deal with generalization, the distorted and interrupted communication channels must be cleared. One example of distorted and interrupted communication that has been allowed to exist in the church is the situation in which church members sit intentionally in different areas of the church facility to ensure avoidance of communication. It must be noted here that congregational meetings are not the best settings to discuss or bisect a church problem, for these meetings tend to distort and/or to globalize the problem, leading to membership polarization of the conflict issues.

In this situation of intentional avoidance, these worshippers short-circuit vertical and horizontal reconciliation and show themselves in need of a practical interpretation of Matthew 5:23 and 25. In most cases of distorted communication, a third party is used as the channel or messenger of contact between the parties. Situations of this sort can benefit from the use of rational-emotive therapy (RET)—therapy dealing with negative emotional behavior.

Pitfalls to conflict management among members are likely to jeopardize creative conflict management and become recurrent experiences for some. In fact, Breen observes that "individuals troubled with feelings of inferiority are significantly more likely to fall back on these patterns of conflict responses."[229]

---

228 Speed B. Leas, *A Lay Person's Guide to Conflict Management* (Washington, DC: The Alban Institute, 1979), pp. 4–6.

229 David Breen, "Churches in Conflict: A Conflict Manual for Church Leaders" (DMin project, Western Theological Seminary, Holland, MI, 1983), pp. 25–26.

Some Sources and Typologies of Conflict

Several sources of conflict have been identified. Stimac[230] observes that conflict may have multiple sources and may arise in predictable circumstances or unexpected situations. Some sources of conflict are as follows:

- *Conflicting perceptions.* Individuals disagree because they perceive events differently.
- *Differing ideas.* Individuals have ideas that clash.
- *Conflicting values.* Individuals embrace different set of values that influence their perceptions and judgment.
- *Aggressive behavior.* Individuals assert their rights while knowingly or unknowingly denying other's theirs.
- *Behavior that hurts.* Individuals wittingly or unwittingly act in hurtful ways toward others.
- *Personality clashes.* Intangible personality characteristics of people create friction between them.

Table 1 gives a sampling of the various sources of conflict identified by others. It might be observed that communication, organizational structure, and human factors can influence conflict-promoting interactions tending toward dysfunction.

Various typologies[231] of conflict have been developed, and they all involve a mixture of cooperative and competitive interests. Five basic issues are involved in these interest orientations. Nonsharable resources like power, prestige, or food often constitute a "control over resources" issue. Preferences, values, beliefs, and the nature of the relationship between the parties complete this five-fold list.

Substantive versus Emotional Issues

Walton draws a distinction between these two types.[232] Substantive issues involve differences of opinion over policies, practices, and role relationships.

---

230 Michele Stimac, "Strategies for Resolving Conflict: Their Functional and Dysfunctional Sides," *Personnel* 59 (1982): 55.

231 Kurtz, "Pastor as Manager of Conflict," p. 113.

232 Richard E. Walton, *Interpersonal Peacemaking: Confrontations and Third-Party Consultations* (Reading, MA: Addison-Wesley, 1969), pp. 73–75.

Table 1. Sources of Conflict

Nebgen	McSwain-Treadwell	Robbins
Communication Problems -Poor communication -Semantic problems -Insufficient exchange of information -Noise	Attitudinal	Communication -Semantic difficulties -Misunderstandings -Noise (sender, channel, and receiver
Structural Factors -Size -Specialization -Instability of climate -Reward system	Substantive	Structure -Rules -Barriers -Organizational format
Human Factors -Personality -Job satisfaction -Role status	Emotional	Personal Behavior Factors -Idiosyncrasies -Value systems
Conflict-Promoting Interactions -Competition -Domination -Provocation	Communicative	

Emotional issues involve negative feelings between parties, such as anger, distrust, resentment, fear, and rejection. Coser[233] calls them realistic and nonrealistic conflict. Realistic conflicts are means to an end with a rational basis; in the nonrealistic type, conflict arises from aggressive tendencies as an end. Kurtz observes that "realistic conflict can be 'managed' but nonrealistic may require therapy."[234]

Functional versus Dysfunctional

Although demarcation between functional and dysfunctional is neither clear nor precise, it might be stated that "conflicts which support the goals of the organization and improve performance"[235] are functional, constructive forms. To Robbins, those that appear to hinder organizational performance are dysfunctional and destructive and need to be eradicated. For Robbins, the conflict is functional when it supports the organizational goals. Robbins perceives Filley as placing the emphasis on the individual rather than on the organization to determine functionality.[236] So the conflict that promotes the organizational goals yet leaves the individual in any continuum toward dysfunction—that conflict may be considered dysfunctional. The conflict that leaves the setting better off and in which growth occurs, preferably in both parties, is functional. The Christian orientation to conflict would allow for Filley's philosophy of making the interest of the person primary. The reconciliation that may be achieved between organizations is a reconciliation of persons, not of organizations.

Distributive versus Integrative

Win-lose conflict situations tend to make people "cautious, secretive, insecure, and belligerent." Kurtz continues his evaluation in arguing that

> hasty voting in the church on business items or other
> issues is among the more common practices that tend

---

233 Coser, pp. 48–50, 156.

234 A. Kurtz, "The Pastor as Manager of Conflict," p. 117.

235 Robbins, "'Conflict Management' and 'Conflict Resolution,'" p. 70. K. Boulding places focus on the individual more than on the organization as such and argues "the source for conflict is the intrapersonal dynamic and places the center of conflict in the self-image of the individual." *Conflict and Defense* (New York: Harper & Row, 1962), pp. 3–5.

236 Robbins, "'Conflict Management' and 'Conflict Resolution,'" p. 70.

to produce these win/lose confrontations. Integrative strategy, by contrast, aims at a win/win situation in which if I win, you win too. It seeks confrontation and consensus.[237]

Interpersonal versus Intrapersonal

Interpersonal conflict (between persons) can occur through different motivational orientations: cooperative relationship, individual orientation, or competitive orientation. Intrapersonal (with oneself) conflict is intense when anxiety, unconscious recognition of conflict, and limited ego strength are present. Smith quotes Deutsch as distinguishing between fear and anxiety on the basis that "fear comes from without while anxiety comes from within"[238] and may be accentuated by two desires simultaneously.

The win-lose intrapsychic conflict often leads to delay in action or distortion of conflict reality. Any distortion makes conflict management more difficult and resolution more time-consuming, if possible. Continuous self-deception impinges on self-esteem since repeated perceived defeats can distort self-ego. Deutsch argues that "a 'strong ego' enables the individual to cope with external difficulties and serves to regulate and integrate diverse internal processes into a coordinated cooperative system."[239]

Deutsch's Typology

A clarifying typology has been developed by Deutsch that seems to put emphasis on the *status* of the conflict rather than its *type*. The types within the Deutsch's typology are not exclusive and overlap themselves or other typologies. They are as follows:

---

237 Kurtz, "The Pastor as Manager of Conflict," p. 118. Kurtz names four dyads in connection with conflict typology: (1) functional versus dysfunctional conflict, (2) substantive versus emotional issues, (3) integrative versus distributive strategy, and (4) control versus restoration in conflict management (ibid., p. 113). For a listing of the characteristics of both the distributive and integrative approaches, see B. R. Patton and Kim Griffin, "Conflict and Its Resolution" in *Small Group Communication: A Reader*, 3rd ed., ed. R. S. Cathcart and L. A. Samovar (Dubuque, IA: Wm. C. Brown, 1979), p. 368.
238 Clagett Smith, ed., *Conflict Resolution*, p. 41. Cf. Melvin R. Nelson, "The Psychology of Spiritual Conflict," *Journal of Psychology and Theology* 4 (Winter 1976): 34–41 and his treatment on doublemindedness.
239 Smith, p. 43.

1. Vertical conflict—this is objective and is perceived accurately.
2. Contingent conflict—this is dependent on readily rearranged circumstances but is not recognized by the conflicting parties.
3. Displaced conflict—this is a manifest and underlying conflict that is not dealt with in the argumentation.
4. Attributed conflict—this is between the wrong parties and, therefore, is usually over the wrong issues.
5. Latent conflict—this is a conflict that should be occurring and is not. It is repressed or displaced. It needs consciousness-raising to be dealt with.
6. False conflict—this occurs when there is no objective base for the conflict. It implies misperceptions or misunderstandings.[240]

One thing is clear: in any conflict situation the interaction between the parties can incorporate more than one type at a time.

Some Advantages and Disadvantages of Conflict

The literature advances many advantages for conflict. McSwain and Treadwell give five advantages: clarifies identity, creates power, encourages group solidarity, encourages perseverance, and can diffuse more serious conflict.[241] A sampling of the advantages of conflict to organizational and congregational life are mentioned below.

- "Conflict sets group boundaries by strengthening group cohesiveness and separateness."[242]
- "Conflict enhances the principles of democracy and freedom."[243]
- "Conflict clarifies objectives."[244]
- "Conflict reduces tension and permits maintenance of social interactions under stress."[245]

---

240 Deutsch, pp. 12–14.
241 McSwain and Treadwell, pp. 154–155.
242 Ibid., p. 155.
243 Kurtz, "Pastor as Manager of Conflict," p. 113.
244 A. Kornhauser, R. Dubin, and A. M. Ross, *Industrial Conflict* (New York: McGraw-Hill, 1954), p. 16.
245 C. Kerr, "Industrial Conflict and Its Mediation," *American Journal of Sociology* 60 (1954): 230.

- "Conflict results in the establishment of group norms."[246]
- "Without conflict, accommodative relations would result in subordination rather than agreement."[247]
- "Performance tended to improve more when there was conflict among members than when there was fairly close agreement."[248]
- "Conflict prevents stagnation, stimulates interests and is the root of personal and social change."[249]

Human history testifies to the negative aspects of conflict in any relationship. Robbins[250] names reduced job satisfaction, increased absence and turnover rates, and less productivity as disadvantages of conflict. McSwain and Treadwell[251] see personal hurt and unnecessary rigid structures with their wasted energies as other disadvantages of conflict. Other negative effects result from poorly managed conflict. Relations often grow hostile as defensive mechanisms are exposed. There is obvious loss in momentum, motivation, relationships, self-esteem, and sometimes there is fallout.

246 D. Kahn-Freund, "Intergroup Conflicts and Their Settlement," *British Journal of Sociology* 5 (1954): 196–197.
247 R. C. Sorensen, "The Concept of Conflict in Industrial Sociology," *Forces* 29 (1951): 263.
248 J. Hall and M. S. Williams, "A Comparison of Decision-Making Performances in Established and Ad Hoc Groups," *Journal of Personality and Social Psychology* 3 (February 1966): 217.
249 Smith, p. 38; cf. Walton, p. 5.
250 Robbins, "'Conflict Management' and 'Conflict Resolution,'" p. 69.
251 McSwain and Treadwell, pp. 123–125.

Some Early Signs of Onset of Conflict

Although the onset of conflict can be experienced without anxiety, there are signs indicating that conflict is brooding. Swanson[252] names ineffective communication, identity crises, and intransigence as sources and mentions some early warning signs and prescription for conflict. Among the practical indicators of congregational unrest are as follows:

1. Sudden drop in attendance, particularly of long-established members
2. An increase in telephoning among the various members
3. Frequent resignations from positions of leadership
4. Polarization of opinion and the formation of factions.

The following are included in the prescription:

1. Renewal of contact with vanishing sheep. Pastoral calling and visitation are both counselled.
2. Slowdown of too great many simultaneous innovations.
3. Increasing of dialogue between old established families and those who have joined more recently. Increasing the dialogue between young and old.
4. Institution of long-range planning.[253]

Although Swanson's list is acceptable, Dailey's suggestion gives some simple indices of tension change that could offer significant aid to all institutions.

The following indicators are roughly arranged in order of increasing danger:

---

252 Rolla Swanson, "Planning Change and Dealing with Conflict: A Field Theory Models with Eleven Steps to Change," *Chicago Theological Seminary Register* 59 (May 1969): 26. Cf. Robert C. Worley, *Dry Bones Breathe* (Chicago: Brethren Press, 1978), p. 65. Robert T. Newbold Jr. recognizes six heralds of conflict in the Black church as (1) continued fierce expressions of competition, (2) inability or unwillingness to agree on purpose or goals, (3) unbridled jealousy, (4) expressions of unwillingness or resistance to communicate, (5) constant generation of negative feelings, and (6) different role perceptions. "Conflict in the Black Church," *Leadership* 1 (Spring 1980): 100.

253 Kittlaus and Leas, *Church Fights*, p. 76.

---

1. Voting patterns indicating the rise of opposition to the leadership
2. Direct protests of a policy or decision
3. Change in attendance at meetings (both up and down—mostly down)
4. A persisting issue of abrasive quality that we just cannot seem to settle
5. Change in revenue
6. Withdrawal of support by some of the power structure
7. Increase in polarization (formation of intense factions that habitually oppose other factions)
8. Withdrawal of key persons or groups from communication[254]

Conflict Management Strategies

Pastors can initiate creative conflict-management processes by encouraging conflicting parties to integrate their interests and goals. The pastor's credibility with disputants can lead toward integrative use of "increased excitement, creativity, motivation, and problem awareness."[255] One's understanding of the five conflict-handling modes and willingness to use them in their appropriate settings can help in the positive utilization of conflict.

Barbara Hill has identified three phases of the conflict process as
1. the "preconflict" phase: the sequence of events leading up to the outbreak of hostilities;
2. the "actual" conflict phase: the outbreak and subsequent events of the conflict itself; and
3. the "postconflict" phase: those events beginning with a covert attempt to end hostilities and concluding with a solution of the conflict.[256]

254 Dailey, "The Management of Conflict," p. 3.
255 Pneuman and Bruehl, p. 7.
256 Barbara J. Hill, "An Analysis of Conflict Resolution Techniques," *Journal of Conflict Resolution* 26 (March 1982): 109–110.

Hill believes that this initial ability to identify the phases can help pastors in managing conflict.

Traditional conflict resolution and management models used in our social, business, institutional, legal, and interpersonal relations appear in table 2. Adjudication and arbitration have proven the least satisfactory methods of conflict resolution for participants. The process allows the parties to tell their viewpoints, and the judge or arbitrator decides based on predetermined criteria.

Table 2. Conflict Resolution Processes

Process	Provider (or Decider)	Process Sequence
Adjudication and arbitration	Judge or arbitrator; higher authority	1. Listens to each side's presentation. 2. Decides options based on predetermined criteria (legislation, precedent, fairness, etc.).
Counseling	Counselor or therapist; manager	1. Gains rapport. 2. Assesses the real problems. 3. Applies intervention strategy.
Negotiation	Lawyer or agent; parties themselves	1. Orientation and positioning. 2. Argumentation. 3. Crises. 4. Agreement or final breakdown.

Problem-solving	Individual or delegated official of an organization	1. Identifies the problem.
		2. Communicates with appropriate people.
		3. Develops alternatives.
		4. Decides on alternative.
		5. Carries out action.
		6. Monitors to ensure completion.
		7. Evaluates effectiveness.
Mediation	Mediator; selected third-party facilitator	1. Introduces, structures, gains rapport.
		2. Finds out facts, isolates issues.
		3. Helps create alternatives.
		4. Guides negotiation and decision-making.
		5. Clarifies/writes an agreement or plan.
		6. Provides for legal review and processing.
		7. Available for follow-up, review, revision.

Source: Jay Folberg and Alison Taylor, Mediation (1984), p. 27.

Table 3. Basic Counseling

Counseling Model	Current situation/problem	Therapy	Goal/Outcome
Medical	Diagnosis	Treatment	Cure/stabilization
Behavior modification	Behavior to be promoted or stopped	Reinforcement/ extinction plan	Behavior change
Conflict theories	Conflict	Problem-solving	Conflict resolution
(Neo) Freudian	Id control	Psychoanalysis	Ego control
Transactional analysis	Child-parent reaction	Awareness	Adult reaction
Phenomenological	Discontinuity	Environment	Self-actualization
Perceptual	Improper perception	Learning/cues	Proper perception
Social work	Maladjustment	Services	Social order

Source: Jay Folberg and Alison Taylor, Mediation (1984), p. 29.

Counseling has been used for intrapersonal conflicts in gaining rapport, exploring problems, and applying appropriate intervention. This table 3 shows this three-step process in various therapy situations. The following sentence plots the course: The (current situation/problem), when given the appropriate (intervention/therapy/treatment), leads to the desired (goal/outcome/response). Negotiation is the most pervasive and divisive approach and is sometimes equated with bargaining. Negotiation is presently being applied to secure win-win results.

Problem-solving is a process that can be used alone or with other conflict-resolution methods. As a tool in conflict resolution, it requires negotiation, especially at the point where an alternative is chosen. This mode does not require outside facilitators for its use. Mediation uses similar stages but has the advantage of being facilitated by a neutral third party. Miller and Jackson present figure 4, which gives a diagram of the process in expressing, problem-solving, and conflict resolution.

Different names have been given to the conflict-management strategies. Pneuman and Bruehl observe that "there are only three basic choices in handling conflict: to be passive to it, to suppress it, or to manage it."[257] In other words, the several strategies devised for handling conflict all fall in the categories of passivity, suppression, or management. Most strategies indicate a preference for passivity and suppression although involvement in management approaches have been practiced.

257 Pneuman and Bruehl, p. 4.

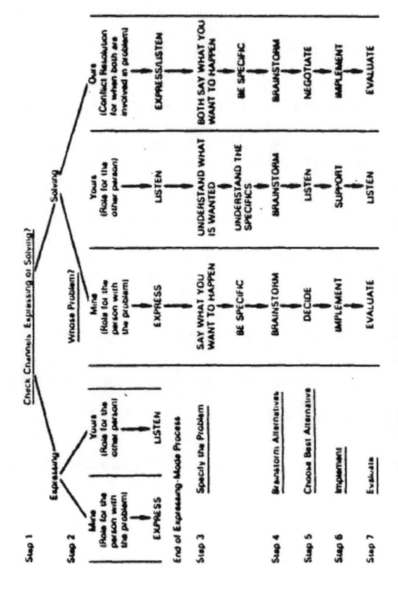

Figure 4. Expressing, Problem-Solving, and Conflict Resolution

Source: William P. Miller and Kathleen A. Jackson, Practical Psychology for Pastors (1985), p. 347.

Unlike Pneuman and Bruehl, Stimac categorizes strategies as avoidance, defense (delay), and confrontation, of which confrontation using negotiation skills seems to be most efficient. It heals wounds, reconciles parties, and provides enduring resolutions. In confrontation, the key is to make visible the issues involved by surfacing the issues, examining the assumptions, and exploring the alternatives.

Before conflict can be resolved to the satisfaction of both parties, it must be confronted. Confrontation is the most difficult of the conflict-management strategies to accomplish. It alone has the potential for clearing away crossed lines in an interpersonal relationship. Stimac[258] contends that to confront when the climate or circumstances are unfavorable or when the parties are not up to confrontation loads the scales in favor of the disaster. Figure 5 gives Stimac's characterization of the avoidance, delay, and confrontation encounter. To Stimac, conflict can often be resolved if the appropriate strategy is used. Table 4 represents Robbins's perceptions of the individual strengths and weaknesses of the major resolution techniques.[259]

---

258 Stimac, "Strategies for Resolving Conflict," p. 60.
259 Robbins, "'Conflict Management' and "Conflict Resolutions,'" p. 73.

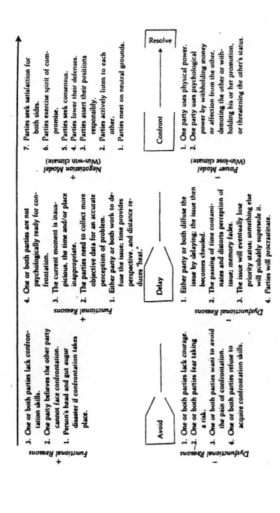

Figure 5. Avoidance, Delay, and Confrontation

Source: Michele Stimac, "Strategies for Resolving Conflict: Their Functional and Dysfunctional Sides," Personnel 59 (1982): 63.

Table 4. Resolution Techniques

Technique	Brief Definition	Strengths	Weaknesses
Problem-solving (also known as confrontations or collaboration)	Seeks resolution through face-to-face confrontation of the conflicting parties. Parties seek mutual problem definition, assessment, and solution.	Effective with conflicts stemming from semantic misunderstandings. Brings doubts and misperceptions to surface.	Can be time-consuming. Inappropriate for most noncommunicative conflicts, especially those based on different value systems.
Superordinate goals	Common goals that two or more conflicting parties each desire and cannot be reached without cooperation of those involved. Goals must be highly valued, unattainable without the help of all parties involved in the conflict, and commonly sought.	When used cumulatively and reinforced, develops "peacemaking" potential, emphasizing interdependency and cooperation.	Difficult to devise.
Expansion of resources	Make more of the scarce resource available.	Each conflicting party can be victorious.	Resources rarely exist in such quantities as to be easily expanded.
Avoidance	Includes withdrawal and suppression.	Easy to do. Natural reaction to conflict.	No effective resolution. Conflict not eliminated. Temporary.
Smoothing	Play down differences while emphasizing common interests.	All conflict situations have points of commonality within them. Cooperative efforts are reinforced.	Differences are not confronted and remain under the surface. Temporary.

109

Compromise	Each party is required to give up something of value. Includes external or third-party interventions, negotiation, and voting.	No clear loser. Consistent with democratic values	No clear winner. Power-oriented, influenced heavily by relative strength of parties. Temporary.
Authoritative command	Solution imposed from a superior holding formal positional authority.	Very effective in organizations since members recognize and accept authority of superiors.	Cause of conflict is not treated. Does not necessarily bring agreement. Temporary.

Source: Stephen P. Robbins, "'Conflict Management' and 'Conflict Resolution' Are Not Synonymous Terms," California Management Review 21 (Winter 1970): 73.

Interpersonal confrontation is a careful unmasking and exploration of defenses. It seeks the mutual review of feelings, experiences, and behavior seemingly not recognized. Confrontation should be done "in the spirit of accurate empathy, tentatively, and with care."[260] Egan has recognized potential responses from the one who is confronted as to discredit the confronter: persuade the confronter to change his views, devaluate the importance of the topic being discussed, seek support for one's own views elsewhere, change cognition to correspond to that of the confronter, and examine his behavior with the help of the counselor.[261]

Augsburger argues that not only is confrontation an art to be learned but that caring comes first and confrontation follows.

> A context of caring must come before confrontation
> A sense of support must be present before criticism.
> An experience of empathy must precede evaluation.
> A basis of trust must be laid before one risks advising.
> A floor of affirmation must undergird any assertions.
> A gift of understanding opens the way to disagreeing.
> An awareness of love sets us free to level with each other.[262]

Confrontations often lead to escalation and polarization because of inadequate skill. When confrontation occurs, it is frequently ineffective or inappropriate, and sometimes it is an attempt to unbalance the power structure. Walton argues that a third party can aid interpersonal peacemaking.

If well handled, the direct confrontation between participants can result in resolution or better control of the conflict. The third party can facilitate a productive confrontation by assessing and managing the following ingredients in the interaction setting: motivation, situational

---

260 Gerard Egan, *The Skilled Helper: A Model for Systematic Helping and Interpersonal Relating* (Monterey, CA: Brooks Cole, 1975), pp. 164–168.
261 Ibid., pp. 168–171.
262 David Augsburger, *Caring Enough to Confront* (Ventura, CA: Regal Books, 1985), p. 52.

power timing, pacing, tension level, communication signs, group norms, process skills and support relevant openness.[263]

Request for third-party intervention is not necessarily accepting defeat but could well be an intelligent evaluation of need. Under certain situations, the help of outside resources is necessary. When these situations exist, Kittlaus and Leas see "paid consultants; resources from other churches; denominational resources; and ecumenical resources"[264] as four categories worthy of consideration.

Resource Aids

Literature in the field of conflict management has been increasing rapidly. Several universities and organizations are having courses on the subject in their training programs. The church is also gradually addressing this subject as is seen in the entire spring issue of the 1980 *Leadership* magazine being devoted to it. The bibliography of this project provides an extensive list of literature on the subject, but the following entries deserve special mention for their contribution to my understanding and development of this study.

Books

Robert Bolton's *People Skills* gives vivid examples and suggestions how to use assertion, listening, and resolving of conflicts skills in the normal process of communication. It is a book that should be in every pastor's library. Donald E. Bossart's *Creative Conflict in Religious Education and Church Administration* integrates conflict with biblical and theological themes and indicates pastoral familiarity. Lynn Buzzard and Laurence

---

263 Richard Walton, p. 115. Swanson supports the idea of third-party help and concedes, "The church which bears the name of the Mediator by all means ought to be a laboratory of mediation and reconciliation," "Planning Change and Dealing with Conflict," p. 29. For further discussion on confrontation and third-party intervention, see Hill, "An Analysis of Conflict Resolution Techniques," pp. 120–138; Stimac, "Strategies for Resolving Conflict," p. 62 and passim; A. C. Filley, "Some Normative Issues in Conflict Management," *California Management Review* 21 (Winter 1978): 61–66.

264 Kittlaus and Leas, *Church Fights*, p. 76.

Eck's *Tell It to the Church* argues well for reconciling out of court by Christians. Lynn and Juanita Buzzard's *Resolving Our Differences: The Church's Ministry of Reconciliation* has a good study-guide procedure toward resolution of conflicts.

In *The Foundations of Social Conflicts*, Lewis Coser uses sixteen propositions to explore both the positive and negative impact that conflict has on society. Morton Deutsch makes a substantial contribution to conflict theory in his *The Resolution of Conflict* as he delineates the constructive and destructive processes involved in conflict management. He shows interest in cooperation rather than competition and strongly advocates the use of third parties. Alan C. Filley's *Interpersonal Conflict Resolution* suggests specific skills for developing a style of integrative decision-making. It also includes a helpful chapter on "Attitudes and Problem-Solving." Leslie B. Flynn gives a good review of church conflicts in *Great Church Fights*.

Speed Leas and Paul Kittlaus's *Church Fights* is another very key text with two outstanding experts addressing the causes of church conflict and discussing how to manage and use them for growth. This book will last long as an authoritative work on church conflicts and should be in every church's library. Speed Leas's *A Lay Person's Guide to Conflict Management* is a manual designed for the lay member and describes how to prevent, understand, and manage conflict in the church.

Clergy Malpractice, by H. Newton Malony, Thomas L. Needham, and Samuel Southard, is a particularly good book that can help give pastors direction in their task of pastoral leadership. The book brings together biblical, psychological, legal, and practical insights about malpractice and ministry in today's world and offers guidelines for dealing with the problem and directions for future pastoral work. Norman Shawchuck's *How to Manage Conflict in the Church* is an educational curriculum to aid in conflict management. It shows a strong interest in intervention processes using management concepts. The tape on the curriculum is equally as useful as the one accompanying Buzzard's *Resolving Our Differences* package.[265]

---

265 Shawchuck's *How to Manage Conflict* volumes and tapes are available from Spiritual Growth Resources, Indianapolis, Indiana (1984). Buzzard's *Resolving Our Differences* package is available from David C. Cook, Elgin, IL (1982).

Other Resources: Agencies

The Alban Institute. The Alban Institute, founded 1974, believes the congregation is essential to the task of equipping the people of God for both in-reach and outreach ministry. It provides on-site training, educational programs, consulting, research, and publishing for hundreds of churches. It provides resources to ministers, congregations, judicatories, and seminary faculty and administrators. Individual or group memberships in the Alban Institute are available. Members receive newsletters and information about the institute's publications and workshops. Their address is:

> The Alban Institute Inc.
> Mount St. Alban
> Washington, DC 20016

The Christian Legal Society (CLS). The Christian Legal Society, founded in 1961, aims at mobilizing at the local-level resources needed to advance religious liberty, biblical justice, and reconciliation. Each of its local centers offers one or more of three services to their communities: (1) conciliation services to resolve disputes out of court, (2) legal aid for the underprivileged, and (3) assistance to individuals and groups on religious liberty issues. It has interests in the preservation of the First Amendment guaranteeing the free exercise of religion. It publishes *The Reconciler.*

The Christian Conciliation Service—an arm of the Christian Legal Society—is an attempt to relate the biblical admonitions regarding reconciliation, peace, and the role of the Christian community in the resolution of disputes to the modern situation. To facilitate in the reconciliation of persons as well as the resolution of the dispute, the CCS

- encourages the use of mediation and/or arbitration guided by Christians who possess the requisite skills, commitments, and training to assist as peacemakers;
- provides literature to assist in understanding the concepts and provisions of Christian conciliation; and
- facilitates local affiliation and healing as an alternative to legal conflict within the communities.[266]

---

266 "Christian Legal Society," informational pamphlet (Oak Park, IL: n.d.).

The Mennonite Conciliation Service (MCS). The Mennonite Conciliation Service is established by the Mennonite Central Committee, a relief and social-services agency supported jointly by the Mennonite and Brethren in Christ denominations. It aims at providing training, coordination, and consultation to individuals and congregations committed to ministering amid local conflicts. It has special interest in authentic reconciliation.

The Seventh-day Adventist Church. The Seventh-day Adventist Church has also demonstrated interest in out-of-court resolution of differences and has recently established a new area of concentration dealing with conciliation under the leadership of Dr. Sara Terian on the campus of Andrews University, Berrien Springs, Michigan. Another recent development is the private organization Adventist Conciliation Service, under the leadership of Claude and Carolyn Morgan, working in conjunction with the Sacramento Christian Conciliation Service. Their address is:

> 6102 Morgan Place
> Loomis, CA 95650

The high level of litigation consciousness of society has led several Christians to consider the principles of fellowship, reconciliation, and peace among Christians with an intent to withdraw from court adjudication.[267]

Summary

Commitment to conflict management is a commitment to the integrationist philosophy of handling conflict. For this reason, conflict management and conflict resolution are not equated. Whereas resolution is one strategy among others used in conflict management, the task of the manager is "to manage conflict to maintain an optimum balance and tension between efficiency and creativity within the system."[268] Conflict

---

267 McSwain and Treadwell have identified several resources for conflict ministry, a sampling of which appears in pp. 183–190 in their book *Conflict Ministry in the Church.*

268 Pneuman and Bruehl, p. 6.

---

is both perceptual and behavioral, and variations in definitions of conflict involve the concepts of blockage, opposition, and scarcity.

Conflict has been viewed both negatively as abnormal, destructive, and cyclic and positively as a normal human experience capable of creative growth. Conflict language is always present in society and is evident even in child's play. Strategies of conflict management may be either competitive or cooperative and may take the form of avoidance, delay, or confrontation. Whether involved in avoidance-avoidance, approach-avoidance, approach-approach situations or engaged in potential win-win, win-lose, or lose-lose conflicts, one ought to have a working knowledge of the characteristics of these dyads and use the combination that best facilitates reconciliation and resolution.

Equality of power and increased self-esteem are good qualities that encourage positive attitudes to conflict and make for anticipatory conflict management. Conflict is not incompatible with stability and structure. It often leads to the creation of stability and greater dialogue between parties. As Swanson puts it, "The key issue is to identify conflict, deal with it openly and honestly, and keep it from being destructive of the well-being of the Christian community."[269]

The literature indicates that improved communication skills, ability to recognize conflict and its components, training in conflict management, knowledge of modal choices, practice in negotiating skills, and understanding and using the advantages of third-party intervention are all contributory to good creative management of conflict. Bolton argues strongly for training in conflict management when he observes that training for conflict management is necessary both for the prevention of needless conflict and for the resolution of the conflicts that are inevitable in any relationship. Conflict management skills should be taught as part of a training program that includes listening, assertion, and collaborative problem-solving skills. . . . Agreed-upon ways of preventing and resolving conflict, adequate channels of communications, mechanisms for handling grievances—these and other methods when combined with effective training are parts of a comprehensive program of conflict management.[270]

269 Swanson, "Planning Change and Dealing with Conflict," p. 23.
270 Bolton, p. 215.

Speed Leas has summarized the entire thinking on the potential for creative conflict management.

The goal of conflict management process is to move the congregation out of the chaos and confusion of enmity into reconciliation. The hope is that we will be able to help people choose to cope with the difficult situation, helping them to feel in charge of themselves and the organization . . . while not denying the right of others also to share in the control of that organization. Ultimately the goal is to move from enmity to amity, to move from malevolence to benevolence.[271]

An intelligent, assertive approach to conflict can serve to aid development of personality, perspective, and power and provide participants with new visions of the creative potentialities with which God has endowed mankind. Conflict then can be made a creative force in mankind that serves as a catalyst for fulfilling the task of facilitating horizontal and vertical reconciliation in a society gone amiss by sin.

---

271 Speed Leas, *A Lay Person's Guide*, p. 9.

CHAPTER 5

Data Analysis and Seminar Development

This chapter presents a summary of the research procedures, the questionnaire development and analysis, the seminar rationale, and the development of this project.

Method

Three basic procedures were followed in the development of this study.

1. Theological study was made in the related areas of conflict, forgiveness, nature of mankind, peace, restitution, and reconciliation in search of a biblical direction and understanding for conflict management. Care was taken to identify conflict and reconciliation examples in the Bible and how personal and third-party interventions could aid creative conflict management, conflict resolution, and reconciliation.

2. A review of the literature was undertaken to identify some of the thinking on conflict management and reconciliation processes and how this thinking may be applied successfully to the practice of ministry and other leadership roles.

3. Preparation of presentations, exercises, and other instructional techniques for the modules of a seminar was done, taking into

consideration information from a questionnaire administered to a group of ministers and others in leadership roles in the Unions under study.

Population for the Study

The population for this study included all ordained and unordained ministers of the two Caribbean and West Indies Unions of Seventh-day Adventists. From these, a sample consisting of 134 ordained and 102 unordained clergy was randomly drawn. All senior ministerial students of Caribbean Union College, presently named University of the Southern Caribbean (14) and West Indies College, presently named Northern Caribbean University (12) were also included in this sample.

Instrument Development

The questionnaire was developed after the literature was reviewed, and key conflict assumptions were identified and incorporated into the instrument. The general objective of the questionnaire was to ascertain attitudes of the population toward conflict and conflict-resolution strategies. The questionnaire was structured to help give direction to the formation of the seminar modules.

The survey instrument was revised by peers from the Caribbean and finally refined with the guidance of Dr. Roger Dudley, Director, Andrews University Institute of Church Ministry. The written questionnaire method[272] was used because it was anticipated that it would reach the population in a short time, afford opportunity for genuine and confidential expression, and further provide easily summarized and reportable data.

---

272 Six general methods of need determination have been identified as interview; written questionnaires; management records, reports, and tests; group problem analysis; job analysis and performance review; and records and reports studies. Malcolm S. Knowles, *The Modern Practice of Adult Education* (New York: Associated Press, 1970), p. 100.

Distribution and Collection

The questionnaire instruments were sent with directions to key acquaintances in the conferences for the delivery of the stamped, self-addressed, return envelopes to the participants. Each survey was given a number corresponding to the minister's name, and as it was returned, it was checked off. Table 5 shows the survey results.

Table 5. Survey Results

Unions	Ordained			Unordained		
	Amt. Sent	Amt. Recvd.	%	Amt. Sent	Amt. Recvd.	%
Caribbean	75	58	77	58	46	79
West Indies	59	46	80	44	28	64
Total	134	104	78	102	74	72.5

It must be noted also that in several conferences, the administrators and departmental directors participate directly in pastoral leadership to cope with the expanding growth in membership and churches. It is not surprising then that the internship period is often lessened so that many licensed ministers are in direct district leadership roles within six to twelve months of graduation. This also explains the reason for every district to be continually involved in building or renovating churches. This is a necessary by-product of the gigantic thrust made in evangelism. Each new church brings with it the additional challenges of facing new conflicts.

Questionnaire Review

The data analysis followed the procedure developed for the study, and the appropriate computer requests were made and served to identify (tables 6–8):

1. The top 10 issues that were perceived by pastors as the highest sources of conflict
2. The top 5 relationships that were perceived by pastors to cause the most discomfort and conflict when they were engaged in arguments or quarrels
3. The priority listing given to conflict strategies
4. The self-assessment of certain skills

5. The knowledge (cognitive and affective) of certain conflict assumptions and theories of the sample
6. The top 10 themes that would create the highest level of interest for a conflict-management seminar.

The survey results are addressed in the order in which they appear after some of the demographic information is presented.

Marital Status

Of the 204 responding pastors and students, 151 (74 percent) were married and 47 (23 percent) were single. One was separated; one was widowed; and four did not specify marital status. Of the 151 married respondents, 100 (66 percent) were ordained.

Age

Sixty-six respondents (32 percent) were between twenty and thirty years of age, and sixty-three (31 percent) were between thirty-one and forty years of age. Thirty pastors each were between forty-one and fifty years, and fifty-one and sixty years. Sixty-three percent of the respondents were between twenty and forty years of age. Only eleven pastors (5 percent) were over sixty-one years of age. All the students were under thirty years of age, and sixty-seven of the unordained were between twenty and forty years of age.

Perception of Exposure to Conflict Issues

In seeking to find their perceptions on conflict issues relevant to their districts, the question was asked, "To what extent for you is each of the following issues a source of conflict with others." A five-point scale ranging from "never" to "very often" was adopted. In the analysis, the results for "never" and "seldom" were combined; so likewise was "often" and "very often," leaving "sometimes" as midpoint. Table 6 shows the top 10 conflict issues as perceived by the categories of ministers.

There does not seem to be a significant difference in rating of these subjects among the categories. Social concerns (politics, teenage pregnancy), church standards, church music, and time management appear in the first five priorities of all categories. Pastors' leadership style does not appear as an issue for all respondents or for unordained pastors but appears in the ordained list. It may be noted that pastors' leadership style can serve to aid resolution or stimulation of conflict or even the escalation of it.

Table 7 illustrates the intensity of the discomfort felt by pastors when engaged in quarrels or disagreements within certain personal relationship. The response conforms well to the theory that conflict is strongest where relations are closest. Consequently, it is not surprising that quarrels with spouses have more discomfort than those with close friends.

Table 6. Top 10 Conflict Issues

	All Respondents	O/VO*	Ordained	O/VO*	Unordained	O/VO*
1.	Social concerns	33%	Church standards	27%	Church standards	39%
2.	Church standards	32%	Social concerns	24%	Social concerns	32%
3.	Church music	22%	Time management	20%	Time management	28%
4.	Time management	22%	Church music	18%	Member's leisure time activities	23%
5.	Church disciplinary matters	17%	Church disciplinary matters	14%	Church music	19%
6.	Theological/ biblical differences	15%	Union/conf. decision-making processes	13%	Church promotions	16%
7.	Union/conf. decision-making process	14%	Building programs	13%	Ministerial benefits	15%
8.	Church board decisions	14%	Theological/ biblical differences	12%	Church disciplinary matters	14%
9.	Building programs	13%	Leadership styles	11%	Job satisfaction	14%
10.	Member's leisure time activities	13%	Ministerial benefits	11%	Other	14%

* O/VO denotes Often/Very Often

Table 7. Top 5 Conflict Relations

All Respondents	Very Much	Ordained	Very Much	Unordained	Very Much
Spouse	23%	Spouse	27%	Spouse	22%
Boss	14%	Boss	15%	Boss	14%
Children	12%	Friends	13%	Peers	9%
Parents	11%	Children	12%	Children	9%
Peers	11%	Peers	12%	Parents	7%
Friends	10%	Parents	9%	Subordinates	6%

Modal Preferences

The survey results indicate an interesting sequence of modal preferences for ordained pastors. There is an equal tendency to confront as there is to compromise, followed by accommodating, avoiding, and finally, winning at all cost. Among the unordained, the central modal tendency is toward accommodating. Both avoidance and winning at all cost received very low responses as preferred modal choices. Among all respondents, accommodation is the central modal choice in conflict situations. The combined analysis for the students is similar to the unordained, only that the student's initial response to conflict is avoidance. Table 8 shows the preferred modal choices of the categories.

Perception of Competencies

Tables 9 and 10 indicate interesting data. For analysis, "not good enough" was combined with "fair," providing for three categories of self-evaluation: "fair," "competent," and "excellent." One hundred and twenty-three pastors (60 percent) perceived themselves competent at negotiating, 56 percent at problem-solving, and 49 percent at mediating. Thirty-eight percent (77) perceived themselves excellent at listening, and only about 16 percent (33) rated themselves excellent at mediating. Introducing changes and innovations, being assertive, or being diplomatic received only fair evaluations.

Table 8. Preferred Modal Choices

All Respondents		Ordained		Unordained	
Accommodate	28%	Confront	28%	Accommodate	35%
Confront	27%	Compromise	28%	Confront	26%
Compromise	22%	Accommodate	24%	Compromise	18%
Avoid	16%	Avoid	15%	Avoid	12%
Win	5%	Win	4%	Win	5%

Table 9. Actual Distribution of Perception of Competencies—All Respondents

Competencies	Fair	Competent	Excellent
Negotiating	31%	60%	6%
Problem-solving	31%	56%	11%
Mediating as a third party	33%	49%	16%
Listening (as in counseling)	16%	46%	38%
Introducing changes	37%	48%	14%
Being assertive	47%	41%	9%
Being diplomatic	40%	47%	11%

Table 10. Perception of Competencies According to Categories

All Respondents	C/E*	Ordained	C/E*	Unordained	C/E*
Listening	38%	Listening	35%	Listening	42%
Mediating	16%	Mediating	14%	Introducing changes	18%
Introducing changes	14%	Problem-solving	12%	Mediating	15%
Problem-solving	11%	Introducing changes	12%	Being diplomatic	12%
Being diplomatic	11%	Being diplomatic	10%	Being assertive	11%
Being assertive	9%	Being assertive	4%	Negotiating	8%
Negotiating	6%	Negotiating	3%	Problem-solving	5%

* C/E denotes Competent/Excellent

The high rating given to listening compares well with the central modal choice of accommodation. In fact, the pastor's perception of high competence in the listening skills could be very useful in implementing the various modal strategies in conflict situations. Table 11 shows a low perception of assertive and negotiating skills and only marginal competency at problem-solving. Increasing competence in these skills could aid change introduction and thus reduce dysfunctional conflict.

Attitudes to Some Conflict Theories

Section E of the instrument had twenty-seven items addressing various theories and assumptions about conflict. Certain questions addressed some of my specific concerns and may, at times, appear arbitrary; but with items of this sort, the decision is sometimes a judgment call. The reader may feel free to make his/her own arbitrary categorization of the items under consideration.

There were nineteen possible positive responses (2–8, 11–13, 15, 17, 19, 20, 23–27) and eight possible negative responses (1, 9, 10, 14, 16, 18, 21, 22) based on my judgment and the literature review findings. Eleven items (1, 2, 4, 6, 11, 14, 18–21, 25) addressed the theory of conflict (cognition). Nine items (5, 9, 10, 13, 16, 17, 22–24) addressed the affective responses, and seven (3, 7, 8, 12, 15, 26, 27) referred to potential reaction (doing) to conflict situations. The items also checked for conflict-management content, perception, and communication processes within conflict situations.

Table 12 shows the attitudes of the pastors to conflict. Most respondents (83 percent) disagreed that suppression of conflict led to peace and harmony in the long run (item 1). Eighty-nine percent (181) felt real growth can occur through properly confronting differences (item 3). Seventy-three percent (148) agreed that conflicts can be handled in a way that all parties can win and the church be stronger for it (item 12). Sixty-one percent (124) agreed that adequate opportunity for consideration of different approaches to problems was not generally provided (item 27). An inference here would be that there could be a lot of latent conflict and win-lose results in the congregations. There is need for more attention to the problem-solving process and to introducing changes.

Table 13 reports the pastor's awareness of some valuable aspects of conflict to church life. Twenty-five percent of all respondents agreed that conflict and reconciliation are incompatible. Eighty-eight percent of all respondents disagreed that reconciliation and forgiveness do not aid conflict management. Among all respondents, there was a split decision concerning the disturbing amount of conflict present in the church (item 25).

Table 13. Awareness to Some Valuable Aspects of Conflict to Church Life

	Items	All Respondents		Ordained		Unordained	
		A/SA*	D/SD†	A/SA	D/SD	A/SA	D/SD
1.	Suppression of conflict leads to peace and harmony in the long term.	13%	83%	14%	83%	11%	88%
2.	Conflict is neither negative nor positive.	41%	52%	43%	49%	31%	62%
3.	Real growth occurs through properly confronting differences.	89%	9%	92%	7%	85%	11%
10.	Reconciliation and forgiveness do not aid conflict management.	11%	88%	16%	82%	3%	96%
12.	Conflict can be handled in a way that all parties can win and the church be stronger for it.	73%	18%	77%	18%	70%	18%
22.	Hope and expectation are not necessary to handle conflict well.	19%	71%	19%	71%	14%	73%
27.	In important discussions in our church, adequate opportunity for consideration of difficult approaches is generally not provided.	61%	32%	58%	37%	63%	27%

Note: Responses of ministerial students are reflected in the "All Respondents" category.

 *A/SA combines Agree and Strongly Agree.

 † D/SD combines Disagree and Strongly Disagree.

Table 12. Awareness of Some Valuable Aspects of Conflict to Church Life

	Items	All Respondents		Ordained		Unordained	
		A/SA*	D/SD†	S/SA	D/SD	A/SA	D/SD
3.	Real growth occurs through properly confronting differences.	89%	9%	92%	7%	85%	11%
9.	Conflict and reconciliation are incompatible.	25%	69%	28%	68%	23%	69%
10.	Reconciliation and forgiveness do not aid conflict management.	11%	88%	16%	82%	3%	96%
25.	There is a disturbing amount of conflict in my church/district/ conference.	46%	48%	60%	29%	55%	39%
26.	There is frequently a small group of members who opposes what the majority wants to do.	81%	15%	84%	15%	78%	15%

Note: Responses of ministerial students are reflected in the "All Respondents" category.

* A/SA combines Agree and Strongly Agree.

† D/SD combines Disagree and Strongly Disagree.

The majority agreed a small group of members opposed what the majority wanted to do (item 26). If this opposition was not overdone, it could aid good problem-solving processes, especially when the leader is not unduly threatened by this opposing group. The presence of opposition could ensure organizational growth and creativity.

Table 14 gives the pastors' perception of the organizational structure and conflict management. For item 8, all categories showed indecision as to whether the win-lose method was the chief way most churches used in settling disputes, although 135 (66 percent) disagreed that the simple majority vote was enough to decide important matters in the church (item 14). Seventy-eight percent of all respondents agreed that the most effective organizations developed processes for managing conflict (item 20). The unordained category showed 64 percent agreeing that the organizational structure does not give adequate opportunity for full discussion on important subjects (item 27). Fifty-three percent of the unordained believed that the win-lose method was the chief method used in settling disputes (item 8).

Tables 14 to 16 illustrate the pastors' perceptions to conflict strategies, their responses to other pastor-related issues, and attitudes to skills that could influence conflict management. Most respondents (92 percent) agreed that when trust in integrity was lost, it was hard to regain (item 5). They were unsure of pastors' competencies in conflict management (item 6). Seventy-five percent (153) disagreed that conflict-management styles cannot be replaced by new styles (item 16). Ninety-five percent (194) of the pastors recognized the healthy pride members had in belonging to the church (item 24).

Table 14. Organizational Structure and Conflict Management

		All Respondents		Ordained		Unordained	
	Items	A/SA*	D/SD†	A/SA	D/SD	A/SA	D/SD
8.	The win-lose method is the chief way most churches use in settling disputes.	50%	41%	47%	47%	53%	41%
12.	Conflicts can be handled in a way that all parties can win and the church be stronger for it.	73%	18%	77%	18%	70%	18%
14.	A simple majority vote is often enough to decide important matters in the church.	33%	66%	33%	67%	30%	69%
20.	The most effective organizations are the ones that develop processes for managing conflicts.	78%	8%	84%	4%	76%	11%
26.	There is frequently a small group of members who opposes what the majority wants to do.	81%	15%	84%	15%	78%	15%
27.	In important discussions in our church, adequate opportunity for consideration of different approaches is generally not provided.	61%	32%	59%	37%	64%	27%

Note: Responses of ministerial students are reflected in the "All Respondents" category.

   * A/SA combines Agree and Strongly Agree.

   † D/SD combines Disagree and Strongly Disagree.

Table 15. Conflict Strategies

	Items	All Respondents A/SA*	D/SD†	Ordained S/SA	D/SD	Unordained S/SA	D/SD
5.	When trust in our integrity is lost, it is hard to regain.	92%	5%	94%	3%	91%	7%
6.	Pastors often lack the skills to resolve differences with creative and productive results.	49%	45%	48%	44%	50%	43%
14.	A simple majority vote is often enough to decide important matters in the church.	33%	66%	33%	67%	30%	69%
16.	Conflict-management styles cannot be replaced by new styles.	11%	75%	12%	74%	8%	80%
20.	The most effective organizations are the ones that develop processes for managing conflict.	78%	8%	84%	4%	76%	11%
24.	Overall, members share a healthy pride in belonging to our church.	95%	4%	97%	3%	93%	5%
26.	There is frequently a small group of members who opposes what the majority wants to do.	81%	15%	84%	15%	78%	15%

Note: Responses of ministerial students are reflected in the "All Respondents" category.

    * A/SA combines Agree and Strongly Agree.

    † D/SD combines Disagree and Strongly Disagree.

Table 16. Conflict-Management Skills

	Items	All Respondents A/SA*	D/SD†	Ordained S/SA	D/SD	Unordained S/SA	D/SD
5.	When trust in our integrity is lost, it is hard to regain.	92%	5%	94%	3%	91%	7%
6.	Pastors often lack the skill to resolve differences with creative and productive results.	49%	45%	48%	44%	50%	43%
7.	Church members often express their hostilities in ways that hinder and disrupt the work of the church.	68%	26%	63%	32%	76%	18%
16.	Conflict-management styles cannot be replaced by new styles.	11%	75%	12%	74%	8%	80%
17.	Self-esteem often determines the method one adopts in a conflict.	83%	8%	88%	7%	80%	11%
23.	I do not feel myself confident in dealing with conflicts in the church.	8%	89%	6%	93%	11%	85%
24.	Overall, members share a healthy pride in belonging to our church.	95%	4%	97%	3%	93%	5%

Note: Responses of ministerial students are reflected in the "All Respondents" category.

 * A/SA combines Agree and Strongly Agree.

 † D/SD combines Disagree and Strongly Disagree.

Table 17. Methodology

	Items	All Respondents		Ordained		Non-Ordained	
		A/SA*	D/SD†	S/SA	D/SD	S/SA	D/SD
1.	Suppression of conflict leads to peace and harmony in the long term.	13%	83%	13%	83%	11%	88%
3.	Real growth occurs through properly confronting differences.	89%	9%	92%	7%	85%	11%
7.	Church members often express their hostilities in ways that hinder and disrupt the work of the church.	68%	26%	63%	32%	76%	18%
11.	Conflict over facts is generally easier to manage than conflict over values.	80%	15%	77%	18%	84%	12%
18.	Most church conflicts involve reason rather than emotions.	25%	68%	30%	66%	16%	80%
22.	Hope and expectation are not necessary to handle conflict well.	19%	71%	19%	71%	15%	73%

Note: Responses of ministerial students are reflected the in "All Respondents" category.

    * A/SA combines Agree and Strongly Agree.

    † D/SD combines Disagree and Strongly Disagree.

To item 23, "I do not feel myself confident in dealing with conflicts in the church," 16 respondents (8 percent) responded "agree." An implication of these pastor-related responses shows why third-party intervention by pastors could, at times, be difficult. However, their responses to item 16 gave hope for success in teaching new conflict-management styles. Protected trust can develop cooperation rather than competition in problem-solving.

Sixty-eight percent of all respondents agreed that church members often expressed their hostilities in ways that hindered and disrupted the work of the church (item 7). They also agreed (80 percent) that conflict over facts was generally easier to manage than conflict over values (item 11), although they conceded that most church conflicts involved emotions rather than reason (item 18). Seventy-one percent of all respondents disagreed that hope and expectation are not necessary to handle conflicts well (item 22). The pastors believed that emotions caused most of their conflicts, and an implication here is for the development of listening skills to help depersonalize conflict and filter facts from emotions.

As it concerns conflict-management skills, all categories were divided on whether pastors lacked the skills to resolve differences with creative and productive results (item 6). As mentioned before, there was division on the win-lose method as a chief means of settling disputes. Results on item 14 show the simple majority as not being enough to settle important matters. Eighty-three percent of all respondents (170) agreed that self-esteem often determined the method used or adopted in a conflict (item 17).

The basic implication of these responses suggests a dissonance concerning effective modal choices and efficiency. The wrong choice of a strategy could lead to latent conflict. These responses not only have implications for introducing change and innovations, dealing with the status quo, and effective church management, but these responses also demonstrate the need for a seminar in conflict management to help clarify some perceptions on the subject.

Open-Ended Questions

Four open-ended statements appeared in the survey instrument, and the results indicate four basic sources of conflict: communication, listening, confrontational skills, and human and organizational factors. The pastors were asked to write the first thoughts that entered their minds as they read the following statements:

1. The greatest source of conflict for me in my family right now is _____
2. The greatest source of conflict for me in my work right now is _____
3. There would be less conflict in my life if _____
4. I am most likely to get into verbal disagreements when _____

Question 1 showed all categories responding about the same way. The ordained pastors identified finances, poor communication, time management, and children's education for college among their key conflict concerns. The unordained pastors mentioned time management, family expectations versus personal ambitions, insecurity, finances, and relationships with relatives as causing much conflict within the family.

Question 2 had several responses. The ordained pastors identified a lack of reconciling spirit among clergy and laity as disruptive to them while several had conflicts with certain administrative decisions. One pastor mentioned as of great personal concern, "the traditional status quo responses to changing contemporary problems." Another mentioned "the administrators who just cannot think progressively." One pastor was burdened by "the church school and church relationship." One other pastor referred to the "administration's lack of understanding of the importance of youth ministry and nurture."

The unordained were equally concerned about administration. Some mentioned "outdated policies," "not enough incentives or appraisal and recognition for work well done," and "the competitive principle which underlies most decisions made by the administration in relation to the pastors." Others showed concern about the lack of communication between senior pastors and themselves. One pastor mentioned the "uncertainty of the future and my academic growth."

Both groups were concerned about the number and sizes of congregations. Others felt their work was jeopardized by "disunity of workers." While one pastor had conflict "implementing and sustaining new programs," another found it difficult "to adjust to programs *now* that were formerly set up differently by me." Several had conflicts with conference expectations and their transportation. Internal economic conditions made importation of car parts difficult and expensive. In one island, gasoline neared eight dollars a gallon, and at times, travel allowances did not appear commensurate with the demands of a vigorous visitation program.

In question 3, several expressed the belief that improved communication would reduce the conflicts in their lives. One pastor felt that if he "read and meditated more, things would improve." There was much concern about unsaved relatives, mediocrity, and job satisfaction. Some felt that "being less analytical," "less sensitive," "reduced any tendency to doubt my call," and being "better trained to deal with conflict" would create less conflict in their lives.

Question 4 provided a good list of miscellaneous events that can trigger conflict. Physical experiences like tiredness, frustration, and overwork predisposed several to short-circuit listening and communication skills. One pastor mentioned that he was most likely to get into verbal disagreements when "decisions are made based on past practice over against the need to devise creative responses to prevailing needs." Several unordained got into verbal disagreements when policy applications seemed questionable. Many got into verbal disagreements to protest what they perceived as wrong decisions and to defend their self-esteem.

The ministerial students were no different. They were concerned about employment after graduation, lack of communication, poor quality of superior-subordinate relationships, and their desire to achieve competence and efficiency. One student summarized the general tenure of their thinking: "There would be less conflict in my life if I were certain of my fate after graduation."

Conflict-Management Seminar

The survey results indicate the population being interested in topics associated with conflict-management theories and concepts. Of the fifteen suggested subjects, the ministers indicated a high interest in ten of them. A prioritization shows the top ten as follows:

- Effective communication techniques (65%)
- Decision-making strategies (55%)
- Basic principles of conflict management (51%)
- Diagnosis and averting conflict (51%)
- The theology of conflict (43%)
- Forgiveness and reconciliation (41%)
- How to identify conflict-management strategies (41%)
- Introducing changes and innovations creatively (40%)
- The pastor as a party in conflict (39%)
- How to help others handle conflict (37%)

A consideration of the above interests and the suggestions of the literature recommending conflict-management training have led me to develop a six-module seminar of twenty-one to twenty-four hours total duration. These modules are developed in the second part of this chapter.

Module Development

This section reviews some essentials of the learning-teaching theory that serves as the foundation and rationale for the module development.[273] The extent to which this theory has influenced this project development is described and evidenced throughout the modules. This section is organized along the following lines:

1. The adult learner and andragogy
2. Some theory in teaching and learning
3. Techniques
4. Objectives
5. Summary of each seminar

The Adult Learner and Andragogy

Knowles defines *andragogy* as "the art and science of helping adults learn,"[274] although he frequently refers to the "unique characteristics of adults as learners," and to *andragogy* as a "comprehensive theory of adult learning."[275] Various writers have made pronouncements concerning the adult engaged in formal learning, and these have meaning for this study.

Some measure of conceptual confusion exists concerning a definition of andragogy; there seems to be a relation between effective techniques of facilitation and andragogical injunctions. Davenport and Davenport have pointed out that andragogy has been variously classified as "the theory of adult education," "a theory of adult learning," "a theory of the technology

---

273 The organization and development for this module design have been highly influenced by two courses taken at Michigan State University and Western Michigan University; namely, (1) Joan Webster, EAD 851A, "Organization and Theory of Education" (Summer 1986); and (2) P. Birdswell, ED 505, "Adult Learner" (Fall 1986).

274 M. S. Knowles, *The Modern Practice of Adult Education*, p. 39.

275 Idem, *The Adult Learner: A Neglected Species*, 2nd ed. (Houston: Gulf Pub., 1978), p. 28.

---

of adult learning," "method of adult education," "a technique of adult education," and "a set of assumptions."[276]

It is significant then that since the participants to the proposed seminar will be adults, the seminar format comes under the adult or continuing education umbrella. Whether the seminar is adult or continuing education, the concepts of andragogy as they impact adult learning have some bearing on the module development. For this research, *andragogy* is used to mean "the art and science of learning adopted chiefly to aid adult learning but not necessarily restricted to adults." It strongly discourages dependency and encourages independence and the application of life-long experience.

Andragogical theory is based on at least four main assumptions that are significantly different from those of pedagogy and can serve to influence any seminar development.

1. Changes in self-concept. This assumption is that as a person grows and matures, his self-concept moves from one of total dependency to one of interesting self-directedness.

2. The role of experience. As an individual matures, he accumulates an expanding reservoir of experience that causes him to become an increasingly rich resource for learning and, at the same time, provides him with a broadening base to relate to new learnings.

3. Readiness to learn. As an individual matures, his readiness to learn is decreasingly the product of his biological development and academic pressure and is increasingly the product of the development tasks required for the performance of his evolving social roles.

4. Orientation to learning. The adult has a time perspective, which is one of immediacy of application.[277]

In these assumptions, one sees the implication for potential self-directedness. In this situation, the seminar leader serves primarily as facilitator of learning, thus integrating learner desires and educator priorities to encourage appropriate two-way interaction and influence.

Many of the exercises, indirectly or directly, reflect the second assumption of andragogy—the reservoir of experiences concept. The

---

276 J. Davenport and J. A. Davenport, "A Chronology and Analysis of the Andragogy Debate," *Adult Education Quarterly* 35 (1984):152–159.
277 Knowles, *A Neglected Species*, pp. 45–46.

modules give opportunity for critical reflection on experiences. It is hoped that this collaborative interpretation and exchange of such experiences may serve to aid appropriate attitudinal change to conflict, conflict management, and differences between human beings. This assumption utilizes the concept that the new learning is not only additive to what is already known but serves to transform existing knowledge to bring about new perspectives (where necessary).

To amplify these four assumptions of andragogy, the participants will be encouraged into a critical analysis of each module during a feedback period involving a participants-initiated question-and-answer period. Through this experience, the participants will continue to develop their own theology and philosophy of conflict—which may well be the acceptance of an already-defined philosophy. This philosophy may experience delayed fulfillment since some pastors may prefer "to focus on the development of self-awareness and self-insight, rather than the development of performance-based competencies."[278]

Some Theories in Teaching and Learning

The importance of the four basic assumptions of andragogy have implications for the learning process; consequently, any workshop must be based on the knowledge of how adult people learn. Learning theorists have grouped themselves into three camps: (1) behaviorists, represented by B. F. Skinner; (2) cognitive field theorists, represented by Jerome J. Bruner and David Ausubel; and (3) humanists, represented by such persons as Carl Rogers, Abraham Maslow, and Fritz Perls. The philosophies of these theories combine to suggest that learning is doing; changing, planned, or incidental; living; and life-long. Learning is a problem-solving, reorganizing experience; and it is often unlearning. "Learning is sometimes painful but can be graciously joyous; it is hard work and growth."[279]

Presentation of seminar material can be intentional, especially when it appeals to specific ends. Gagne identifies five domains of the learning process, each with its own praxis and each capable of bringing about change:

---

278 Stephen Brookfield, *Understanding and Facilitating Adult Education* (San Francisco, CA: Jossey-Bass, 1986), p. 121.

279 Jerold W. Apps, *Study Skills for Adults Returning to School* (New York: McGraw-Hill, 1982), p. 2; cf. Martha M. Leypoldt, *Learning Is Change: Adult Education in the Church* (Valley Forge, PA: Judson Press, 1981).

1. Motor skills, which are developed through practice.
2. Verbal information, the major requirement for learning being its presentation within an organized, meaningful context.
3. Intellectual skills, the learning of which appears to require prior learning of prerequisite skills.
4. Cognitive strategies, the learning that requires repeated occasions in which challenges to thinking are presented.
5. Attitudes, which are learned most effectively using human models and "vicarious reinforcement."[280]

Although participants are not especially interested in learning theories or processes, the development of any workshop must take into consideration the five domains of learning in its planning stages. This may mean that the seminar format may need to integrate humanistic, behavioristic, and cognitive approaches to its delivery system. It will need to be humanistic since it seeks to advance personhood, behavioristic in creating behavior change, and cognitive in providing material for the thinking processes.

A review of teaching-learning theories concerning andragogy as presented by Gibb, Miller, Kidd, Knox, Brundage and MacKeracher, Smith, and Darkenwald and Merriam can be summarized as follows: Adults learn throughout their lives, with the negotiations of the transitional stages in the life span being the immediate causes and motives for much of this learning. Adults exhibit diverse learning styles and learn in different ways, at different time, for different purposes. They like their learning activities to be problem centered and to be meaningful to their life situations; they want the learning outcomes to have some immediacy of application. Past experiences affect current learning and can serve as hindrance or enhancement. Effective learning is also linked to the adult's

---

280 R. M. Gagné, *The Conditions of Learning* (New York: Holt, Rinehart & Winston, 1965), pp. 3–4.

subscription to a self-concept of himself or herself as a learner. Adults exhibit a tendency toward self-directedness in their learning.[281]

Based on these findings, successful reeducation and rediagnosis of the state of conflict management within the church can be achieved with distinction by pastors. In fact, Brookfield observes that Brundage and MacKeracher judge "adults [pastors] to be strongly motivated to learn in areas relevant to their current development tasks, social roles, life crises, and transition periods."[282] This means that the facilitator of learning ought to realize that since past experiences can help or impede learning, she/he should seek to construct designs that allow for positive realignment of past experiences with new stimuli.

This approach guarantees that, for a pastor coming from a milieu of marked conflict, this supportive climate can make that period of conflict a time of learning, of growth, of a teachable moment, and of creative rethinking. In this setting of mutual trust, the pastors use experience as a resource in learning so that the learning content and process serve to bear a perceived and meaningful relationship to experience.

As the researcher prepared the design for the modules, the six optimum conditions for learning dominated preparation. Smith notes that adults learn best when these six conditions are met:

1. They feel the need to learn and have input into what, why, and how they will learn.

281 Brookfield, p. 31. For further clarification of learning theories associated with andragogy, see J. R. Gibb, "Learning Theory in Adult Education," in M. S. Knowles (ed.), *Handbook of Adult Education in the United States* (Washington, DC: Adult Education Assn. of the USA, 1960); H. L. Miller, *Teaching and Learning in Adult Education* (New York: Macmillan, 1964); J. R. Kidd, *How Adults Learn* (New York: Cambridge Books, 1973); A. B. Knox, *Adult Development and Learning: A Handbook on Individual Growth and Competence in Adult Years* (San Francisco: Jossey-Bass, 1977); D. H. Brundage and D. MacKeracher, *Adult Learning Principles and Their Application to Program Planning* (Toronto: Ministry of Education, Ontario, 1980); R. M. Smith, *Learning How to Learn: Applied Learning Theory for Adults* (New York: Cambridge Books, 1982a); and G. G. Darkenwald and S. B. Merriam, *Adult Education: Foundations of Practice* (New York: Harper & Harper & Row, 1982).
282 Brookfield, p. 29.

2. Learning's content and processes bear a perceived and meaningful relationship to experience, and experience is effectively utilized as a resource for learning.

3. What is to be learned relates optimally to the individual's developmental changes and life tasks.

4. The amount of autonomy exercised by the learner is congruent with that required by the mode or method utilized, e.g., self-directed, collaborative, or institutional.

5. They learn in a climate that minimizes anxiety and encourages freedom to experiment.

6. Their learning styles are considered.[283]

One basic theme is clear in these conditions for learning: learning can be planned or incidental. Consequently, the researcher tried to choose his instructional aids with much thought. Whether the desired outcome was understanding, skills, attitudes, values, or interests, the most appropriate procedure or strategy was carefully chosen to ensure the desired outcome.

The theological, social, andragogical, and methodological approaches to the study served to undergird the development of the six-module seminar. This six-module seminar gives ministers exposure to skills that aid interpersonal relationships: listening, assertiveness, conflict resolution, collaborative problem-solving, and skill selection. The findings of the literature suggest that the successful church administrator will also demonstrate proficiency in interpersonal relationships and creative conflict-management skills. The position of this study is that when ministers become sensitized to the origin, process, and potential of conflicts, they can significantly influence the positive route that conflicts take by utilizing certain skills associated with conflict management and creative problem-solving.

Techniques

The choice of techniques for adult learning was also taken into consideration. There is need for informality and variety and time for socialization since, very often, the pastors are not well acquainted with one another. Attempts were made to manage learning experiences by including presentation techniques (lectures, interviews, panels, etc.),

---

283 Smith, p. 47.

audience techniques (question and answer, buzz groups, etc.), discussion techniques (guided discussion), nonverbal exercises, and skill practice exercises. These techniques imply that the learners accept a share of the responsibility for planning and operating a learning experience with its consequent commitment to it.

Since adults often perceive the grading system as an ultimate sign of disrespect and dependency, the seminar leader—as facilitator of learning, manager of the conditions of learning, and the manager of instruction—should make attempts to develop the andragogical concept of rediagnosis of learning in place of evaluation (and its connotation of testing). The motivational ingredient of the teachable moment is used to encourage behavioral and perceptual changes to conflict management.

It may be observed here that techniques form a key aspect of any design development. The task of selecting the right technique for the right task is not an easy one. However, two key guidelines may ease the challenge: (1) match the technique to the objectives and, (2) given an option between two techniques, choose the one involving the participants in the most active participation.[284] The correct use of techniques is an aid to the effective management of learning experiences. Figure 6 gives guidelines for selecting techniques.

By integrating learning outcomes and techniques, I was better able to develop objectives to meet the design plan. Printed material and handouts are provided so that the participants might (1) be encouraged to take notes, (2) fill in the blanks where appropriate, and (3) be encouraged to maintain a resource file for future reference. In each module an overhead projector is used and/ or integrated with other technological aids, e.g., PowerPoint presentations, to illustrate the study and, in some cases, to provide summations.

---

284 Knowles, *Modern Practice*, p. 294.

Techniques   Learning Outcomes

	VERBAL INFORMATION	INTELLECTUAL SKILLS	COGNITIVE STRATEGIES	ATTITUDINAL CHANGE	MOTOR SKILLS
LECTURE OR TALK	■				
PANEL	■				
DEBATE	■				
DEMONSTRATION		■			■
PRACTICE & DRILL					■
FIELD TRIP					
CASE STUDY			■		
BUZZ GROUPS		■			
BRAINSTORMING		■			
GROUP DISCUSSION		■		■	
SIMULATION & DRILL			■	■	
ROLE-PLAYING		■		■	

Figure 6. Guidelines for Selecting Techniques

Source: Malcolm S. Knowles, The Modern Practice of Adult Education (New York: Association Press, 1970), p. 294.

Opportunity is given for periodic reevaluation to encourage continued modification and immediate applicability. Finally, attempts are made to apply these techniques in three settings: group work, individual work, and activity learning situations.

Objectives

Since the format of the seminar is basically educational, objectives are developed to aid learning and to design learning experiences. These objectives will also serve to sequence units of instruction. It is significant then that the instructional objectives for each module were worded mainly behaviorally and took much planning. I sought to identify long-term goals associated with the seminar and some intermediate objectives to aid choice of module content and its development. This eventually created the objectives for the sections of each module.

According to Manager,

An objective is a description of a performance you want learners to be able to exhibit before you consider them competent. An objective describes an intended result of instruction, rather than the process of instruction itself.[285]

Using Draves's definition of goals as "long-term wishes,"[286] it was recognized that some goals would not be achieved within the parameter of the seminar but that certain aspects would be in position by the close of the seminar to make the goals ultimately attainable in the future.

In as much as each proposed seminar experience would have some collaboration in its planning with the sponsors, part of the first session of every seminar is devoted to identifying some objectives and anticipations of the *actual* participants. This on-site collaboration could bring meaningfulness to the curricula content of the seminar, clarify perceptions, and encourage the climate of mutual respect so necessary for adults—especially of the professional clientele.[287]

The conflict-management seminar seeks to develop the following:

1. Knowledge of the modern findings of research regarding conflict management and resolution
2. An understanding of how this knowledge may be used or transferred in certain practical situations to church settings
3. Skill in planning group activities and innovating changes
4. Attitudes of concern, understanding, and sensitivity to people demonstrating dysfunctional behavior response to conflict situations
5. Knowledge and practice in some communication skills
6. Awareness of some principles of reconciliation, restitution, forgiveness, confrontation, and third-party intervention

285 Robert F. Mager, *Preparing Instructional Objectives*, revised 2nd ed., (Belmont, CA: David S. Lake, 1984), p. 3.

286 William A. Draves, *How to Teach Adults* (Manhattan, KA: Learning Resources Network, 1984), p. 25.

287 Knowles and Associates have identified seven components of andragogical practice they feel are replicable in a variety of programs in almost every kind of institution throughout the world. J. S. Knowles and Associates, *Andragogy in Action: Applying Modern Principles of Adult Learning* (San Francisco, CA: Jossey-Bass, 1984), pp. 14–18.

7. Knowledge about pamphlets, books, films, associations, and other resources available for aiding conflict management and reconciliation

8. Improvement in personal competencies, movement toward self-actualization, and encouragement into future private investigation of the conflict.

Summary of Each Module

The following is a summary of the facilitator's goals and pastors' terminal objectives of the six modules of the Conflict-Management Seminar.[288]

Module 1: Understanding Conflict

Focus: A general introduction to conflict.

Facilitator's Goals: The goals of this learning module include (1) to develop in each pastor an awareness of some behavioral-science theory relevant to conflict management and group life, (2) to help pastors relate or transfer information and new skills to their job situations, and (3) to help pastors become more acquainted with some common concepts and assumptions associated with conflict and conflict management theories.

Pastors' Terminal Objectives: Upon the completion of this learning module, the pastors will be able to (1) define *conflict* in their own words, (2) explain the three philosophies of conflict management, (3) correctly identify the conflict cycle in order of its presentation in real-life situation, (4) identify some early warning signs of conflict and some prevention methods, (5) analyze and recognize the various stages one may experience while in a conflict situation, (6) identify at least five positive and five negative results of conflict, and (7) reflect orally on one experience of a conflict situation.

Module 2: Forgiveness, Reconciliation, and Restitution

Focus: An understanding of forgiveness, reconciliation, and restitution can aid creative conflict management and preserve good interpersonal relationships.

---

288 See appendix 2 for the material used during the Conflict-Management Seminar.

Facilitator's Goals: The goals of this learning module include (1) to demonstrate from Scripture that the Christian is to engage in the work of reconciliation; (2) to help pastors reflect on the forgiveness-restitution concept in reconciliation; (3) to share some views about steps and obstacles to forgiveness; (4) to give pastors opportunity for personal reflection and the examination of their attitude to church discipline and the three steps of Matthew 18:15–18, with the admonition of 1 Corinthians 6; and (5) to show that this triad can serve to prepare members for ministries of reconciliation and intervention.

Pastors' Terminal Objectives: Upon the completion of this learning module, the pastors will be able to (1) indicate from Scripture (Matt. 5:43–48) the roles that determine how a Christian views an antagonist, (2) explain how reconciliation relates to conflict management, (3) explain some practical steps of forgiveness, (4) recognize some obstacles to forgiveness and reconciliation, (5) identify some qualities of the peacemaker, (6) identify five clusters of skills associated with interpersonal relationships, and (7) recognize and explain from 2 Corinthians 5:17–21 the principle of reconciliation.

Module 3: Communicating in Conflict Situations

Focus: Improved communication skills can aid conflict management and reduce perceptual and behavioral incongruences.

Facilitator's Goals: The goals of this learning module include (1) to review some general concepts of communication, (2) to help pastors understand three key concepts in rational-emotive therapy and how feelings can influence conflict management, (3) to explain transactional analysis and barriers to good communication, (4) to help pastors recognize the advantages of confrontation in conflict management, and (5) to explain I-messages and you-messages.

Pastors' Terminal Objectives: Upon completion of this learning module, the pastors will be able to (1) demonstrate skills in the affirmative-assertive techniques as means to deepening relationships and regulating conflict's progress, (2) identify barriers to communication and the five levels of communication, (3) demonstrate some listening skills, (4) recognize the use of verbal and nonverbal communication, (5) explain three key concepts of rational-emotive therapy and recognize some effects of emotions on conflict management, and (6) distinguish between I-messages and you-messages.

Module 4: How to Identify Conflict Styles

Focus: Various conflict reactions lead to either cooperative or competitive behavior, which can be changed according to desired outcome.

Facilitator's Goals: The goals of this learning module include (1) to demonstrate from conflict theory the outcomes and approaches to conflict, (2) to help pastors identify their own preferred conflict-management style, and (3) to encourage the development of a repertoire of conflict styles.

Pastors' Terminal Objectives: Upon the completion of this learning module, the pastors will be able to (1) identify and evaluate one's preferred conflict-management style in terms of its effectiveness in resolving conflict and maintaining interpersonal relationships, (2) explain three approaches and three outcomes to conflict, (3) use the win-win problem-solving option whenever possible, and (4) identify instruments available for analyzing conflict styles and situations.

Module 5: How to Make Good Decisions and Introduce Change

Focus: Change and decision-making processes influence conflict process and management.

Facilitator's Goals: The goals of this learning module include (1) to identify certain concepts associated with power and authority as they may influence the conflict process, (2) to help pastors become more acquainted with principles and types of decision-making and their potential consequences and usefulness, (3) to help pastors become more acquainted with proven principles of introducing and selling change, (4) to help pastors recognize trouble and to deal with it efficiently, and (5) to help pastors recognize some obstacles and characteristics of effective decision-making.

Pastors' Terminal Objectives: Upon the completion of this learning module, the pastors will be able to (1) identify some aspects of good decision-making, (2) identify various sources of decision-making, (3) choose right criteria for selecting appropriate decision-making methods, (4) recognize some pitfalls causing failure in the collaborative problem-solving method, and (5) identify five to seven steps to effective problem-solving.

Module 6: How to Help Others Handle Conflicts

Focus: Third-party intervention is needed often to efficiently handle conflicts, equalize perceptions, and initiate rational responses to conflict.

Facilitator's Goals: The goals of this learning module include (1) to provide information useful to pastors that can aid successful third-party intervention and negotiation, (2) to increase confidence in using resource persons or aids in conflict management, (3) to demonstrate some advantages of referral in conflict management, (4) to encourage pastors to see other individuals as potential resources for learning, and (5) to update pastors with the contents and intent of the conciliation procedures of the General Conference of Seventh-day Adventists.

Pastors' Terminal Objectives: Upon the completion of this learning module, pastors will be able to (1) recognize when third-party help is needed, (2) identify some intervention strategies for managing conflicts, (3) identify some qualities of good interveners and demonstrate by recall some advantages of third-party intervention, and (4) intentionally enter conflict with less apprehension and fear.

Chapter 6

Conclusion

Summary

Whenever the caring-church concept is encouraged in cooperation with participative decision-making, the potential for conflict is increased and the need for skills in conflict management becomes more critical. Consequently, various methods for preventing, controlling, and institutionalizing regulation strategies are important for church harmony to be achieved and creatively maintained.

Distorted communication, hostile attitudes, and oversensitivity to differences can lead to intensification and perpetuation of conflict. Pastors can aid the conflict-management process in establishing group climate by encouraging high levels of trust, support, openness, and cooperative planning and action. Although four key sources of conflict are identified, combinations of them often account for conflict. Skills in creative management of conflict are useful to anyone involved in working with human resources. Win-lose competition need not become merely a shared expectation but can create motivation for transforming dysfunctional competition into active cooperation.

Rico offers an accurate summation of the dual potential of conflict. He observes, "The absence of conflict may indicate autocracy, uniformity, stagnation and mental fixity; the presence of conflict may be indicative of democracy, diversity, growth and self-actualization."[289] It seems obvious to me that the pastor of the future will need to properly align the actual and desired levels of conflict to generate progressive growth within the church setting.

The key to successful conflict management will lie not only in knowledge of stimulation and resolution strategies but also in the pastor's ability to use his sense of discernment, experience, and judgment to achieve reconciliation and/or from his intervention approaches. The interactionist philosophy to conflict management provides the best environment for the creative management of conflict and can set the tone for the pastor's reaction to the inevitable experience of conflict in the church.

The position of this study is that conflict has not been consistently used in the church for functional reasons and has served to dysfunctional results. The risk implied in conflict confrontation is worth the potential good that can accrue from its creative use. An organization or relationship can indeed be strengthened by the intelligent use of collaborative strategies.

Pastors, leaders of institutions or organizations, or profit or nonprofit entities can be taught to manage conflict rather than to allow conflict to determine their reaction. Pat answers to conflict management tend to discourage creative management of conflict. Solutions must be drawn from one's repertoire of options; the medicine should fit the ailment. Successful conflict management is not trial and error; it includes daily efficiency in decision-making.

This study has provided material that, it is hoped, can serve to aid the pastor, the lay member, or the boardroom leader to face daily experience with conflict with greater anticipation and creativity. It is to this end that I anticipate, among others, the following expectations.

Expectations from the Study

The main goal of this study is that I would experience great growth toward becoming an improved creative manager of conflict. It is also anticipated that I may become available to conferences, churches, and/

---

289 Leonard Rico, "Organizational Conflict: A Framework for Reappraisal," *Industrial Management Review* 6 (Fall 1964): 67.

or groups to share insights on conflict management and to help develop conciliatory attitudes toward conflict and relational growth.

It is further anticipated that this project will aid me in developing other specific workshops to be used in educational and medical institutions, with lay people and in family-life workshops. Some of these seminars would be used as special events in evangelistic meetings, e.g., "How to deal with conflicts with teenagers."

It is the anticipated expectation that whenever and wherever this seminar is given, the following will occur:

1. The seminar experience will provide pastors with concepts, exposure, and processes for leading multiple staff and congregations through conflicts in such a way that the conflict is useful and not detrimental to the further development of the mission of the church—the full and complete reconciliation of man with God and man with man.

2. There will be an improved quality of interpersonal relations between pastors and pastors, pastors and members, and members and members. Hopefully, this will discourage the existing legal-suit consciousness among members.

3. The seminar will serve as a means of improving group processes especially at committee/board level so that the fear of conflict does not inhibit constructive discussion and problem-solving processes.

4. Pastors experiencing this workshop will be aided in becoming better negotiators in their role as conciliators by using the transfer of skills acquired under pastoral counseling or from the behavioral or management fields of instruction.

5. There will be an improvement of local church and conference budgets by reducing the tendency to use withdrawal of finances or other power currencies as a means of managing conflict or displeasure.

6. Finally, it is hoped that the influence of this seminar will raise the level of interest and training in conflict management so that leaders will lend their support and influence to making training in conflict management a regular experience at all possible levels of interpersonal relationships.

Recommendations

Based on the research executed for this study, I advance the following recommendations that could prove useful to the church:

1. Attempts must be made at reeducation aimed at emphasizing the positive potentials of conflict to church and community life.
2. Members should be taught the necessity of initiating conciliatory and peacemaking activities to encourage the ministry of reconciliation.
3. Practical methods should be used by qualified personnel (e.g., attorneys) to educate the membership about the destructive and often expensive method of settling differences through litigation.
4. Greater emphasis and encouragement should be placed on the utilization of institutionalized processes (policies) of conflict management at all levels of church and family life. Careful encouragement should be given to trust and relationship building, thus providing the environment for safe confrontation and assertive communication.
5. Pastors should continue to use self-help learning skills to improve their listening, assertion, collaborative problem-solving, mediation, and third-party intervention skills in their intervention in domestic conflicts.
6. There should be an intelligent and intentional involvement in community disputes to lend expertise to recover dislocation and bring reconciliation to community life.
7. Priority should be given by conference administrators to the in-service training of pastors in the field of conflict management.
8. Conferences should designate pastors for districts whose skills are appropriate for the congregation's needs.
9. Formal training in conflict management should be instituted as required courses in college or seminary, especially in the business, education, nursing, and theology curricula. Introductory courses on *problem-solving* should be introduced in academy or within the home-management or citizenship curricula.
10. Each church district should endeavor to secure and maintain resource personnel to aid third-party intervention and conciliation processes. This resource personnel may be voluntary (ad hoc) or on a retainer fee basis.

11. Emphasis should be placed on conflict management as an aspect of church growth, where qualitative and quantitative relational growth may be achieved and defensiveness be reduced, recognizing conflict as a process and not an event.

12. Finally, based on the principles of andragogy, more intentional processes and procedures *should* be initiated to make adult learning involvement and participation more meaningful and purposeful than presently experienced. This kind of seminar could be used to introduce members to continuing or lifelong learning in the trusting environment of their own education buildings.

Creative conflict management as an administrative skill may hold the key to a pastor's assessment of his/her pastoral efficiency and capability in dealing with conflicts. Mutual cooperative approach to conflict can demonstrate to the world the results of vertical and horizontal reconciliation as evidenced in Christian reciprocity.

APPENDIXES

APPENDIX 1

Survey Instrument Information

Questionnaire

ATTITUDES TOWARD CONFLICT
A SURVEY OF SEVENTH-DAY ADVENTIST MINISTERS

Your response will help in developing a more conscious approach to handling differences and conflicts in the church. Circle the number of the answer that most nearly represents your thinking.

A. To what extent for you is each of the following issues a source of conflict with others. Circle the appropriate answer.

		NEVER/	SELDOM/	SOMETIMES/	OFTEN/	VERY OFTEN
1.	Church & Conference Promotions	1	2	3	4	5
2.	Building Programs	1	2	3	4	5
3.	Union/Conference/ Mission/Decision- Making Process	1	2	3	4	5
4.	Members' Leisure Time Activities	1	2	3	4	5
5.	Church Music	1	2	3	4	5

		None/	Very Little/	Little/	Much/	Very Much
6.	Social Concerns (e.g.) Politics, Teenage Pregnancy	1	2	3	4	5
7.	Church Standards	1	2	3	4	5
8.	Church Board Decisions	1	2	3	4	5
9.	Church Disciplinary Matters	1	2	3	4	5
10.	Pastor's Family Life	1	2	3	4	5
11.	Minister's Remuneration & Benefits	1	2	3	4	5
12.	Pastor's Leadership Styles	1	2	3	4	5
13.	Pastor/Pastor Relationships	1	2	3	4	5
14.	Job Satisfaction	1	2	3	4	5
15.	Theological/Biblical Differences	1	2	3	4	5
16.	Pastor-Laity Relationships	1	2	3	4	5
17.	Time Management	1	2	3	4	5
18.	Other	1	2	3	4	5
		1	2	3	4	5
		1	2	3	4	5

B. On a scale of 1–5 circle the level of discomfort, pain and conflict you experience in arguments, disruptions, and quarrels with:

		None/	Very Little/	Little/	Much/	Very Much
1.	Spouse (or ex-spouse)	1	2	3	4	5
2.	Parents	1	2	3	4	5
3.	Children (stepchildren)	1	2	3	4	5
4.	Other Relatives	1	2	3	4	5
5.	Boss (e.g., Conf. pres.)	1	2	3	4	5

6.	Close Friends	1	2	3	4	5
7.	Coworkers (peers)	1	2	3	4	5
8.	Subordinates	1	2	3	4	5
9.	Others	1	2	3	4	5

C. Circle the method you most often use when you are in a conflict situation.
1. To win at all cost
2. To yield or to accommodate
3. To confront
4. To avoid or to withdraw
5. To compromise

D. How capable are you in the following areas?

		NOT GOOD ENOUGH/	FAIR/	QUITE COMPETENT/	EXCELLENT
1.	Negotiating	1	2	3	4
2.	Problem-solving	1	2	3	4
3.	Mediating as a third party	1	2	3	4
4.	Listening (as in counseling)	1	2	3	4
5.	Introducing changes & innovations	1	2	3	4
6.	Being assertive	1	2	3	4
7.	Being diplomatic	1	2	3	4

E. On a scale of 1–5 indicate your level of agreement or disagreement to the following statements by circling a number as follows:

		Strongly Disagree/ 1	Disagree/ 2	Don't Know/ 3	Agree/ 4	Strongly Agree 5
1.	Suppression of conflict leads to peace and harmony in the long term	1	2	3	4	5
2.	Conflict is neither negative nor positive	1	2	3	4	5
3.	Real growth occurs through properly confronting differences	1	2	3	4	5
4.	Many church conflicts are protests against the abuse of power	1	2	3	4	5
5.	When trust in our integrity is lost, it is hard to regain	1	2	3	4	5
6.	Pastors often lack the skills to resolve differences with creative and productive results	1	2	3	4	5
7.	Church members often express their hostilities in ways which hinder and disrupt the work of the church	1	2	3	4	5
8.	The win/lose method is the chief way most churches use in settling disputes	1	2	3	4	5

9.	Conflict and reconciliation are incompatible	1	2	3	4	5
10.	Reconciliation and forgiveness do not aid conflict management	1	2	3	4	5
11.	Conflict over facts is generally easier to manage than conflict over values	1	2	3	4	5
12.	Conflicts can be handled in a way that all parties can win, and the church be stronger for it	1	2	3	4	5
13.	If Christians care about the church, they will disagree on how to operate it	1	2	3	4	5
14.	A simple majority vote is often enough to decide important matters in the church	1	2	3	4	5
15.	The way some people behave in conflict situations leads to sinful acts	1	2	3	4	5
16.	Conflict management styles cannot be replaced by new styles	1	2	3	4	5
17.	Self-esteem often determines the method one uses or adopts in a conflict	1	2	3	4	5

18.	Most church conflicts involve reason rather than emotions	1	2	3	4	5
19.	Many misunderstandings are simply the result of language usage	1	2	3	4	5
20.	The most effective organizations are the ones that develop processes for managing conflict	1	2	3	4	5
21.	Proper conflict management requires unanimity for its existence	1	2	3	4	5
22.	Hope and expectation are not necessary to handle conflict well	1	2	3	4	5
23.	I do not feel myself confident in dealing with conflicts in the church	1	2	3	4	5
24.	Overall, members share a healthy pride in belonging to our church	1	2	3	4	5
25.	There is a disturbing amount of conflict in my church/district/ conference	1	2	3	4	5
26.	There is frequently a small group of members who opposes what the majority wants to do	1	2	3	4	5

27. In important   1   2   3   4   5
    discussions in our
    church, adequate
    opportunity for
    consideration of
    different approaches
    is generally not
    provided

F. Complete the statement by circling the one correct number.

I work in or study at

1. Caribbean Union	2. West Indies Union	3. East Caribbean Conference
4. Guyana Conference	5. West Jamaica Conference	6. North Caribbean Conference
7. Surinam Field	8. Bahamas Conference	9. South Caribbean Conference
10. West Indies College	11. Cayman Island Mission	12. Central Jamaica Conference
13. Grenada Mission	14. East Jamaica Conference	15. Caribbean Union College

G. Circle your present marital status.
   1) Single
   2) Married (living with spouse)
   3) Separated
   4) Divorced
   5) Widowed
   6) Other

H. What is your age range? Circle answer.
   1) 20–30 years
   2) 31–40 years
   3) 41–50 years
   4) 51–60 years
   5) 61–70 years
   6) 70 and over

167

I. Circle your highest level of education completed.

1. Senior Ministerial Student
2. Bachelor's
3. Master's
4. M. of Div.
5. Doctorate

J. Circle the year of your graduation (Bachelor's)

1. 1945–1949
2. 1950–1960
3. 1961–1970
4. 1971–1980
5. 1981–1986

K. Circle how many persons are in your household including yourself who are

1. 0–5 years	0	1	2	3	4 or more
2. 6–12 years	0	1	2	3	4 or more
3. 13–18 years	0	1	2	3	4 or more
4. 19–24 years	0	1	2	3	4 or more
5. above 25 years	0	1	2	3	4 or more

L. Circle the topics you would attend if a Conflict-Management Seminar were held in your area. You may add any other.

1. How to Resolve Quarrels
2. Decision-Making Strategies
3. The Pastor as a Party in Conflict
4. Basic Principles of Conflict Management
5. Diagnosing and Averting Conflict
6. How to Work with an Adversary
7. Effective Communications Technique
11. Competition & Cooperation in Conflict Management
12. Introducing Changes and Innovations Creatively
13. How to Identify Conflict Management Styles
14. Theology of Conflict
15. When the Majority Prevails
16.
17.

8.	How to Help Others Handle Conflict	18.
9.	Christian Assertiveness	19.
10.	Forgiveness & Reconciliation in Conflict Management	20.

M. Write the first thoughts that enter your mind as you read the following statements:

1) The greatest source of conflict for me in my family right now is

2) The greatest source of conflict for me in my work right now is

3) There would be less conflict in my life if

4) I am most likely to get into verbal disagreements when

Appendix 2

Creative Conflict-Management Seminar Modules

Understanding Conflict

A. Session 1 (90 Minutes)
    Icebreaker
    Definitions
    History
    Handout 1: Principles and Assumptions
    Exercise 1: Resignation or Option
    Break
B. Session 2 (75 Minutes)
    Types of Conflict
    Early Signs of Conflict
    Some Prescriptions for Reaction to Early Signs
    Exercise 2: Reasons for Conflict
    Causes of Conflict
    Conflict Cycle
    Exercise 3: Abram and Lot or Option
    Break
C. Session 3 (75 Minutes)
    Exercise 4: Functional or Dysfunctional
    Possible Negative and Positive Results of Conflict
    Barriers to Creative Conflict Management
    Handout 2: Prevention, Control, Stimulation
    How to Tell whether Conflict Is Constructive
    Handout 3: For Further Reading
    Feedback and Summary

===

Icebreaker

1. Greet the participants, introduce self, and write each participant's name on a card. Later, shuffle the cards and distribute them in pairs. Hand out Survey Exercise to be done individually.
2. Have the participants in each twosome interview each other to find out their seminar expectations etc.
3. After the interview, each participant introduces his partner, telling what his partner's expectations for the seminar are. (This free exchange of information helps to put goal expectations in focus and provide opportunity for renegotiation and self-directedness. It will give the facilitator opportunity to integrate interests of participants and of facilitator.)
4. Discussion of survey.

Introduction of Seminar Goals

The Creative Conflict-Management Seminar will seek to develop

1. knowledge of the modern findings of research regarding conflict management and resolution;
2. an understanding of how this knowledge may be used or transferred in certain practical situations to church settings;
3. skill in planning group activities and innovating changes;
4. attitudes of concern, understanding, and sensitivity to people demonstrating dysfunctional behavior response to conflict situations;
5. knowledge and practice in some communication skills;
6. awareness of some principles of reconciliation, restitution, forgiveness, confrontation, and third-party intervention;
7. knowledge about pamphlets, books, films, associations, and other resources available for aiding conflict management and reconciliation; and
8. improvement in personal competencies, movement toward self-actualization, and encouragement into future private investigation of the subject.

Facilitator's Goal: Understanding Conflict

The goals of this learning module will include the following:
1. To develop in each pastor an awareness of some behavioral science theory relevant to conflict management and group life
2. To help pastors relate or transfer information and new skills to their job situations
3. To help pastors become more acquainted with some common concepts and assumptions associated with conflict and conflict-management theories

Pastors' Terminal Objectives for Module 1

Upon completion of this learning module, the pastors will be able to
1. define conflict in their own words;
2. explain the three philosophies of conflict management;
3. correctly identify the conflict cycle in order of its presentation in real-life situation;
4. identify some early warning signs of conflict and some prevention methods;
5. analyze and recognize the various stages one may experience while in a conflict situation;
6. identify at least five positive and five negative results of conflict;
7. reflect orally on one experience of stress, power, and conflict;
8. identify some principles and assumptions about conflict management; and
9. use prevention and control techniques in conflict management.

Focus of Module 1

General introduction to conflict.

Conflict
Definitions

Conflict is a relationship between two or more parties who believe they have incompatible goals.

Conflict exists whenever an action by one person or group prevents, obstructs, or interferes with or in some way makes less likely the desired action of another party or group.

Conflict is all kinds of opposition or antagonistic interactions.

Conflict refers to any perceptual and/or behavioral incongruences within a person or between people or groups.

Conflict management is the process that regulates or controls the convergence of aims, methods, and behaviors.

Conflict resolution is the total convergence of aims, methods, and behaviors that returns relationships to a state of trust and informality.

Creative conflict management is the intentional use of skills and processes that tend to encourage and maintain positive responses to conflict situations.

History

Three philosophies characterize attitudes to conflict, and this attitude often influences one's perception about conflict management. However, these three philosophies are sometimes integrated in the process of handling differences and must not be perceived as exclusive of one another. These philosophies are
1. traditional—bad, destructive, should be eliminated;
2. behavioristic—accepted, try to avoid, resolve; and
3. integrative/interactionist—conflict must be intentionally handled.

Discussion of Handout 1

Exercise 1: Resignation or Option (Group Discussion)

Break

Conflict is an inevitable experience of church life and should be intentionally managed rather than overtly or covertly discouraged or denied. It can be made a source of congregational cohesiveness and growth or a source of congregational disintegration and decline. Either result may be influenced by one's perception of conflict in the ecclesiological context. To the question, can anything good come out of conflicts? The answer is yes, if you manage it instead of allowing it to manage you.

Types of Conflict

A. Constructive and Destructive
   Realistic and Unrealistic
   Substantive and Emotional
   Distributive and Integrative
B. Interpersonal and Intrapersonal
   Intergroup and Intragroup

Any type of conflict may escalate because of one or a combination of three reasons: (1) competitive processes involved in the attempt to win the conflict, (2) processes of misperception and biased perceptions; and (3) processes of commitment arising out of pressures for cognitive and social consistency.

Early Signs of Conflict

Knowledge of the sources of conflict will not guarantee the absence of conflict, but it can serve to aid identification of the onset of conflict. Several signs are available to the careful manager of conflict that indicate appropriate action should be taken to make successful intervention possible. They include
- continued fierce expressions of competition;
- inability or unwillingness to agree on purpose or goals;
- unbridled jealousy;
- expressions of unwillingness or resistance to communicate;
- repeated generation of negative feelings;

- different role perceptions;
- ineffective communication, identity crises, and intransigence;
- sudden drop in attendance, particularly of long-established members;
- an increase in telephoning among the various members;
- frequent resignations from positions of leadership;
- voting patterns indicating the rise of opposition to the leadership; and
- withdrawal of support by some of the power structure.

Some Prescriptions for Reaction to Early Signs
1. Increase pastoral calling and visitation
2. Slow down simultaneous innovations
3. Increase dialogue between groups, old and new members, and young and old members
4. Renew institution of long-range planning

Exercise 2: Reasons for Conflict

Causes of Conflict
Various sources contribute to the origin of conflict, and knowledge of these sources can aid with the handling of imbalances or differences. At least four sources are identified:
1. Communication problems—semantic, noise, lack of clarification
2. Structural factors—line authority, specialization, essential services
3. Human factors—personality, self-esteem, budgets, we-they dichotomy
4. Conflict-promoting interactions—experiences that lead to competition, domination, and/or provocation

Conflict Cycle
The etiology of conflict is action, threat, and reaction and may be perceptual or behavioral. Conflict generally follows a pattern and, once begun, completes the cycle if not resolved. It can take minutes, months, or years to be solved but may be terminated at any stage of its existence. The various stages are as follows:

1. Tension development — precontemplation — potential opposition
2. Role dilemma — cognition
3. Injustice collection — contemplation — personalization

178

4.	Confrontation	— intervention	— behavior
5.	Adjustments	— maintenance	— outcome

How these stages are handled can determine whether the conflict experience becomes a source of growth or of retardation.

During the conflict cycle or process, people may differ over four aspects of an issue:

- Facts — What is the situation? Data? What is going on?
- Goals — Where are we headed? What of the future?
- Methods — What is the best, easiest, most efficient, and most Christian way to do what we want to do?
- Values — What has priority? What is most important? What long-range beliefs should affect decisions?

Factual differences are those easiest to work with, and value differences are usually the most difficult. Persons often have varying levels of commitments to these issues and should be handled differently.

Reasons for Differences

Here are the common reasons for differences:

1. *Information* available to the parties may be different. One party may have more, less, or different information. Also, it may be from a different source or perspective.
2. *Perception* of the data can be different for different persons even though the later are the same. Each person relates to data from his or her own unique history of experiences.
3. *Role often causes persons to take very different positions.* The pastor, board chairperson, custodian, or committee member all have different roles.

Differences can be handled when each party tries to understand the frame of reference and limitations of the other's position.

Exercise 3: Abram and Lot or Option

Break

Exercise 4: Functional or Dysfunctional

Possible Negative and Positive Results of Conflict
Conflict can be both dysfunctional and functional, and the result may depend on *how* the conflict situation is managed.

Some Negative Results
- People feel more distant.
- The disruption may cause some people to leave.
- Distrust and suspicion may develop.
- Some persons will feel defeated.
- Cooperation may diminish, and self-interest take priority.
- Persons may develop passive and active resistance to each other rather than work in team spirit.
- Blaming, generalizing, and distorted and interrupted communication.
- Reduced job satisfaction.
- Personal hurt, unnecessary rigid structures, and wasted energies.
- Loss of momentum, motivation, relationships, and self-esteem.

Some Positive Results
- A greater diversity of viewpoints is heard.
- Innovation and creativity are encouraged.
- Persons are forced to state their positions and views more clearly.
- Motivation and energy are increased.
- There is a greater sense of genuineness in relationships.
- There is more commitment to improving relationships.
- Conflict allows members to express hostility that otherwise might lead to withdrawal and explosion.
- Conflict allows the group to get a clear picture of its own needs and to adjust itself accordingly.
- Conflict creates new groups, e.g., new church, new departments, etc.
- Conflict helps to provide group identity and internal cohesion.
- Conflict binds antagonists together.

- Conflict strengthens the democratic philosophy of pluralism.
- During the competitive period, levels of work and corporation within each group are high.

Barriers to Creative Conflict Management

Several barriers exist that may serve to inhibit the positive utilization of conflict, and being sensitive to them can help overcome them. Some barriers include the following:

- Fear of disruption
- Group norms
- Tradition
- Fear of vulnerability—mine/yours
- Fear of worsening the situation
- Power differences
- Formal structure of organization

Most, if not all, of these barriers appear to be related to anticipated negative results of conflict.

Handout 2: Prevention, Control, Stimulation

How to Tell Whether Conflict Is Constructive

1. If the relationships among group members are stronger and the members are better able to interact and work with each other, the conflict has been constructive.
2. If the group members like and trust each other more, the conflict has been constructive.
3. If all the members of the group are satisfied with the results of the conflict, the conflict has been constructive.
4. If the members of the group have improved their ability to resolve future conflicts with one another, the conflict has been constructive.

Effectiveness and productivity often suffer when emphasis is placed on avoiding conflicts, resolving them prematurely, or stifling any discussion of difference. In such situations, serious difficulties often arise within the relationship among group members.

Handout 3: For Further Reading

Feedback and Summary (Include Transparencies T-1 and T-2)

Resource Material

Dailey, C. A. "The Management of Conflict." *Chicago Theological Seminary Register* LIX (May 1969): 1–7.

Deutsch, Morton. *The Resolution of Conflict.* New Haven: Yale University, 1973.

Hill, Barbara J. "An Analysis of Conflict Resolution Techniques: From Problem-Solving Workshop to Theory." *Journal of Conflict Resolution* 26 (March 1982): 109–138.

Johnson, David W., and Frank P. Johnson. *Joining Together.* Englewood Cliffs, NJ: 1982, 1975.

Nebgen, Mary K. "Conflict Management in Schools." *Administrator's Notebook* 26 (1977–78): 7–10.

Leas, Speed B., and Paul Kittlaus. *Church Fights.* Philadelphia: Westminster Press, 1973.

Robbins, Stephen P. *Managing Organizational Conflict: A Non-Traditional Approach.* Englewood Cliffs, NJ: 1974.

Conflict Survey Exercise

Circle the correct responses.

True   False   Lack of conflict is a sign of a healthy group.

True   False   A conflict exists whenever incompatible activities exist.

True   False   Conflicts are usually destructive to a group.

True   False   Conflicts that are not openly expressed and constructively resolved will be expressed indirectly and persist.

True   False   Conflict can and should be avoided whenever possible.

True   False   It is not possible to teach people how to deal with conflicts effectively.

True   False   Conflicts are valuable and even necessary to a group.

True   False   Conflicts are destructive to relationships.

True   False   Conflicts promote higher levels of cognitive and moral reasoning.

True False Conflicts help you understand what you are like as a person.

True False Ignoring conflicts usually causes them to dissipate and go away.

True False A conflict uses up energy and thus decreases a group's ability to work effectively.

Conflict has been constructive if (tick four):

a. Relationships are stronger.
b. The group has dissolved.
c. Group members like and trust each other more.
d. Most group members are satisfied with the results.
e. All group members are satisfied with the results.
f. Future conflict resolution ability is improved.

Adapted from David W. Johnson and Frank P. Johnson, *Joining Together* (1982), pp. 232–233.

Exercise 1: Resignation

Situation:

The superintendent of a large church resigned her post in May, giving the unhappy working conditions of the Sabbath School council and other unfavorable remarks about her and the Sabbath School as reasons for her resignations. She felt she could no longer endure the pressure and stress of the post. She also felt she had no option but to resign.

Examination:

- What could she otherwise have done?
- What other options did she have before she resigned?
- Assuming she did not tell the pastor about her feelings, how could telling her pastor influence the decision?

Exercise 2: Reasons for Conflict

Brainstorm:

With the use of a flip board, give some reasons why there are conflicts in the church.

Optional:

In groups of four (4) give some reasons for and against this statement: "All babies should be dedicated in the main sanctuary of the church, whether illegitimate or not." In full group, try to identify some sources of conflict evident in the responses.

Abram and Lot

Now Lot, who was moving about with Abram, also had flocks and herds and tents. But the land could not support them while they stayed together, for their possessions were so great that they were not able to stay together. And quarrelling arose between Abram's herdsmen and the herdsmen of Lot. The Canaanites and Perizzites were also living in the land at that time.

So, Abram said to Lot, "Let's not have any quarreling between you and me, or between your herdsmen and mine, for we are brothers. Is not the whole land before you? Let's part company. If you go to the left, I'll go to the right; if you go to the right, I'll go to the left."

Lot looked up and saw that the whole plain of the Jordan was well watered, like the garden of the Lord, like the land of Egypt, toward Zora. (This was before the Lord destroyed Sodom and Gomorrah.) So, Lot chose for himself the whole plain of the Jordan and set out toward the east. The two men parted company. (Gen. 13:5–11 NIV)

Questions
1. What factors contributed to this conflict situation?
2. Who were the disputants?
3. How was the conflict dealt with?
4. What was the short-term effect of the resolution?
5. What was the long-term effect of dealing with conflict in this way?

Optional Exercises (using similar questions)
1. The three temptations of Jesus
2. Cain and Abel
3. David and Goliath
4.
5.

In pairs, try to break up this conflict into the five conflict stages.

———

185

Conflict: Functional or Dysfunctional?

Circle the response you would take in each situation.

Situations

1. A group of your friends is watching a television program in your home. Two of the people are having an argument, which becomes so loud that the rest of the group cannot hear the television. How would you react to this situation?
   a. Tell the two people to leave the room or tell them to be quiet.
   b. Tell the two people to lower their voices or ask them to quit arguing or ask them to leave the room.
   c. Ask them to lower their voices.
   d. Ask the group to move closer to TV or turn up the volume.
   e. Do nothing, turn off the TV or leave the room yourself.

2. You are the moderator in a group session with five other people. The purpose of the session is to formulate a plan that requires consent from all participants. One of the participants is so involved with the important details of the plan that he is delaying the group from reaching agreement. As moderator, what would you do in this situation?
   a. Tell him to be quiet or tell him to leave the group.
   b. Ignore him or persuade him to ignore the details.
   c. Postpone the discussion of the details until a later time.
   d. Allow limited discussion.
   e. Try to understand what the participant should say or let the person have the floor and explain his position.

3. Your boss (president) has called you into his office, and you discover he wants your opinion about the performance of a coworker (fellow pastor). The coworker is your best friend and neighbor, but you

are inclined to believe that his performance is substandard. What would you tell the boss (president)?

    a. Request that the boss (president) ask the coworker to join the discussion.

    b. Explain to the president that you understand the situation, but he is your best friend and you could not be unbiased in your opinion.

    c. Give no opinion.

    d. In the discussion, point out the coworker's good and poor work habits.

    e. Talk around the issue.

4. You are a staff specialist and have been assigned two projects: one by your immediate supervisor and one by the supervisor of another department. There is adequate time to complete both projects by the deadline date. However, neither project would be completed with the degree of excellence required by your organization. What would you do?

    a. Ask one or another of the supervisors for assistance.

    b. Tell only one of the supervisors about the problem.

    c. Contact both supervisors involved and tell them about your problem.

    d. Do either one or the other of the projects first without contacting either of the supervisors.

    e. Do nothing about problem or complete both projects within the deadline date.

Facilitator's Guide

Goal: To compare functional and dysfunctional forms of conflict.

Group size: Three to five persons (several groups may be directed simultaneously).

Process

1. Each participant analyzes the four conflict situations on an individual basis and circles the response to each situation that he believes represents the most effective solution. (Individual.)

2. The group then analyzes the various responses made to each question. In which situations is the conflict functional? Dysfunctional? (Group work.)
3. What choice or choices should the effective conflict manager have chosen/avoided? (Large group activity.)

Optional
1. Introduce the exercise as you (I) see fit.
2. Ask the participants to think back to a bad conflict experience. Ask them to jot down a few notes (phrases, words) about why it was a bad experience. (Allow 3 minutes)
3. Ask the participants to repeat the same *procedure* for a particularly good conflict experience they recall. (Allow 3 minutes.)
4. Have the participants pair up. Then give them these instructions:
   a. Share your experiences and your interpretations of why they are good or bad.
   b. What are some similarities and differences?
   c. What makes for productive and nonproductive conflict experiences for both persons?
   d. Try to stay with only personal experiences. (Allow 10–15 minutes.)

5. On return to full group setting, record the items in two columns on the easel, chalkboard, or flip board.
6. The facilitator summarizes the emerging concepts and enters Presentation.

Source: Stephen P. Robbins, *Managing Organizational Conflict.* (Englewood Cliffs, NJ: Prentice-Hall, 1974), pp. 142–144.

Principles for Conflict Management

1. Help others feel better about themselves.
    Persons and organizations manage conflict best when they are feeling good about themselves.
    Lowered psychological power base creates poor managers of conflict. Ways of affirming people: listen to another person, take seriously the goals of others as significant to them, and look for and appreciate the strengths and gifts of others.
2. Strive for effective communication.
    Effective communication consists of in-depth and reflective listening and sending with the knowledge that one's perceptions and messages are uniquely one's own.
3. Examine and filter assumptions.
    Unexamined assumptions contribute to destructive conflict.
4. Identify goals, what is wanted (Ask *what*, not *why*, questions).
5. Identify the primary issue.
6. Develop alternatives for goal achievement.
    Search for alternatives that will allow all parties to achieve what is important and fulfilling to them.
7. Institutionalize conflict-management processes.
    To be effective, conflict-management processes must be institutionalized and not created solely for special occasions. That is why churches need policies to direct action.

Adapted from G. Douglas Lewis, *Resolving Church Conflicts* (1981), pp. 47–73.

Conflict Management
Insights from the Behavioral Sciences
Miscellaneous Assumptions about Conflict
(From *Church Fights* by Speed Leas and Paul Kittles, pp. 43 ff.)

1. *"Conflict is possible where relationships are not tenuous.* Where interpersonal relationships are not firm, where people don't know each other, where they have a minimum amount of trust, and little feeling for how others operate, the very strong tendency will be to suppress any conflict. On the other hand, when people care about one another and what the other does, then there can be conflict."

2. *"The elimination of the personal motives from conflict tends to lead toward sharper conflict.* . . . What this proposition asserts are that when you are in touch with what your motives are, you will tend not to idealize or dehumanize the battle, you will be less likely to carry it on as if it were a crusade for the *true*, *right*, and *just*. Lewis Closer in his book on social conflict writes: 'Conflicts in which the participants feel that they are merely the representatives of collectivities and groups, fighting not for self but only for the ideals of the groups they represent, are likely to be more radical and merciless than those that are fought for personal reasons.'"

3. *"Conflict is less sharp in those groups which appeal to the periphery of one's personality.* Again, Closer says: 'In groups in which relations are functionally specific and affectively neutral, conflicts are apt to be less sharp and violent than in groups wherein ties are diffuse and affective, engaging the total personality of their members.'"

4. *"The larger the number of conflicts, the greater the stability of the organization.* . . . Behavioral scientists have been able to show that where there are only a few conflicts in an organization— and especially where there is only one—the organization tends to become more and more polarized. That is, every important decision to be made tends to be made only in relation to the major conflict."

5. *"The closer the group personally, the greater the threat the conflict poses.* When conflict does occur in close groups, it tends to be more

threatening because people care more about one another and the effect of the other's response will be more deeply felt."

6. *"Where groups tend to suppress conflict, there will be an accumulation of feeling, leading toward a potentially dangerous conflict. . . .* Pressure can build up causing a large explosion over a rather minor conflict."

Prevention and Control Techniques

A. Much needless strife can be averted by personal conflict prevention and control methods.
   1. Use fewer roadblocks (ordering, threatening, judging, name-calling) that sometimes encourage conflict-promoting interactions.
   2. Reflective listening helps reduce or eliminate negative emotions and/or may help solve the problem.
   3. Assertion skills help the persons get their needs met with minimum strife and often prevent the buildup of emotions that so often causes conflict.
   4. Awareness of which behaviors are likely to start a needless conflict can help eliminate some confrontation.
   5. Constructive release of personal tension like walking, gardening, and exercises.
   6. Increased emotional support from family and friends can decrease one's proneness to unnecessary conflict.
   7. Heightened tolerance and acceptance of others also tends to diminish unrealistic conflict. (Incorporating some of the wisdom of rational-emotive therapy can increase one's tolerance and acceptance.)
   8. Issues control aids conflict prevention and control.
   9. A careful appraisal of the full consequences and cost of a conflict may deter you from involving yourself in needless disputes.

B. Group/organization prevention and control.
   1. Centralized, bureaucratic organizations can tend to generate conflict. The structure of the group can escalate or discourage conflict. Rigid structures have less effective communication and are less adept at managing conflict.
   2. The personality and methods of the leader are also important. Managers who have low levels of defensiveness and who are

192

supportive tend to help people in their organizations avert unnecessary strife.

3. The climate of a group also influences the amount of conflict it generates. Win-lose situations continue to foster competition.
4. Well-conceived and clearly stated policies and procedures that have the understanding and support of the relevant persons create orderly processes, which can help mitigate unnecessary chaos and conflict.
5. The degree of change and the methods by which change is introduced influence the amount and severity of disputes in the institution.
6. Mechanisms to settle grievances need to be established.
7. Training for conflict management is necessary for the prevention of needless conflict and for the resolution of inevitable conflicts.

Source: Robert Bolton, *People Skills* (1979), pp. 210–215.

When to Stimulate Conflict?

Since change and conflict tend to enhance growth and progress, when low levels of conflict exist, the alert pastor may need to stimulate conflict. One or more affirmative answers to the following questions suggest, according to Robbins, that stimulation is needed.

1. Are you surrounded by yes-men?
2. Are subordinates afraid to admit ignorance and uncertainties to you?
3. Is there so much concentration by decision makers on reaching a compromise that they may lose sight of values, long-term objectives, or the company welfare?
4. Do managers believe that it is in their best interest to maintain the impression of peace and cooperation in their unit, regardless of the price?
5. Is there an excessive concern by decision makers for not hurting the feelings of others?
6. Do managers believe that popularity is more important for the obtaining of organizational rewards than competence and high performance?

7. Are managers unduly enamored with obtaining consensus for their decisions?
8. Do employees show unusually high resistance to change?
9. Is there a lack of new ideas forthcoming?
10. Is there an unusually low level of employee turnover?

Three basic stimulation techniques are readily available to managers (pastors).
1. Manipulate communication channel
—Deviate messages from traditional channels
—Repress information
—Transmit too much information
—Transmit ambiguous or threatening information

2. Alter the organization's structure (redefine jobs, alter tasks, reform units or activities, reorganize committees)
—Increase a unit's size
—Increase specialization and standardization
—Add, delete, or transfer organizational members
—Increase interdependence between units

3. Alter personal behavior factors
—Change personality characteristics of leader
—Create role conflict
—Develop role incongruence

Although these techniques apply to intentional stimulation of conflict, a new pastor in a district can unintentionally stimulate conflict by unwise introduction of early changes and modification of existing structures. Any one or combination of these points could influence the onset of an experience, which could be extremely psychologically damaging to both the church and the pastor.

==

Handout 3
Source: Speed Leas, *Moving Your Church through Conflict* (Washington, DC: Alban Institute, 1985), pp. 17–22.

CHAPTER III

When conflict occurs in a local parish, the church leadership is often in disagreement not only about the issues involved, but also about the degree of conflict. Some will say that it is trivial; it will blow over; if no attention is paid, it will go away. Others will be greatly concerned about any tension and will complain that it is just terrible; if something isn't done right away, the church will be split down the middle and will lose members and income.

> The material in this book is based on three assumptions:
> Not all conflict is the same;
> One's "gut reaction" is not a reliable indicator of the actual level of difficulty;
> Response to conflict should be adjusted to the level of difficulty.

Determining the severity of conflict is not much helped by the literature. Much of the organization development literature on conflict management suffers from the same problems that the leader of the local church experiences. Organization development approaches to conflict management assume only three possibilities: no conflict; win/lose conflict; and win/win conflict. Win/win is a so-called cooperative or constructive approach, and win/lose, destructive or competitive. Here is the way Johnson and Johnson[1] differentiate between the two:

CONSTRUCTIVE (Win/Win)
Defining the controversy as a mutual problem.
Participation by all group members.
Open and honest expression of ideas and feelings.

Everyone's contributions listened to, given attention, taken seriously, valued, and respected.

Quiet members encouraged to participate.

Effective sending and receiving communication skills used.

Differences in opinions and ideas sought out and clarified.

Underlying assumptions and frames of reference brought out into the open and discussed.

Disagreement not taken as personal rejection by some or all group members.

Adequate differentiation of positions; differences clearly understood.

Adequate integration of positions; similarities clearly understood, and positions combined in creative syntheses.

Emotions responded to with involvement and other emotions.

Equal situational power among all members.

Moderate level of tensions.

DESTRUCTIVE (Win/Lose)

Defining the controversy as a "win/lose" situation.

Participation by only a few group members; self-censorship and withdrawal.

Closed or deceitful expression of ideas and feelings.

The contribution of many members ignored, devalued, not respected, and treated lightly.

Quiet members not encouraged to participate.

Effective sending and receiving communication skills not used.

Differences in opinions and ideas ignored or suppressed.

Underlying assumptions and frames of reference not brought out into the open and discussed.

Disagreement taken as personal rejection by some or all group members.

Inadequate differentiation of positions; differences not clearly understood.

Inadequate integration of positions; similarities not clearly understood, and positions not combined in creative syntheses.

Emotions responded to by uninvolved understanding or ignored.

Unequal power among group members.

Tension level too low or too high for productive problem-solving.[2]

As this list indicates, there either is conflict or there isn't. Conflict is either "on" or "off;" there doesn't seem to be any "in-between." Further, much of the current literature on conflict management assumes that conflict, even when "on," is within manageable limits. Differentiating between those conflicts which are easy, those which are tough and those which are impossible has rarely been addressed in organization development literature. There are some conflicts in which the standard, organization development approach to conflict management proposed by such practitioners as William Dyer, Alan Filly, Joyce Hocker, Frost and William Wilmot, Rensis and Jane Gibson Likert,[3] and others simply are not appropriate because they assume that the parties to the conflict are going to have the best interests of the organization at heart and will play according to the rules of the Marquis of Queensberry. For example, the methods proposed by Likert and Likert in their book, *New Rules of Managing Conflict*,[4] assume that the game will be played fairly: valuing differences between persons in the organization; using supportive listening skills; working for consensus; deemphasizing status; and depersonalizing problem-solving.

The appropriateness of these methods for approaching institutional conflict need to be questioned when not all the parties have the best interests of the relationship or the organization at heart or when they are unwilling or unable to keep their behavior within the bounds of reasonable and ethical behavior. This is just as true within the local church as in business or government. Sometimes church fights are low level affairs which can be worked out between the parties involved with little or no "outside" assistance. Other difficulties can escalate into very difficult situations indeed: groups or individuals "take matters into their own hands," taking the church's financial records, changing the locks on the doors, barring entrance to meetings, started competing congregations, disrupting meetings, suing the congregation in civil court, etc.

The question, then, for churches—as well as other systems—is, "How bad is the conflict?" Can it be handled internally, with little loss to the congregation and leaders? Is outside help needed? Will collaborative (win/win) approaches be appropriate? Will active listening skills help? Or, will stronger interventions be needed?

To deal with these concerns I have built on the theories of Malcolm Leary,[5] which assume that there are stages of conflict, that one can distinguish between them and that different strategies should be used with each stage. (I am indebted to Mel Hensey for calling this article to my attention.) I have substantially changed Leary's premise so that I doubt that he would recognize it. First, I have avoided the use of "stages" to describe the levels of conflict. Theories which describe human behavior or thought development stages are now criticized and might be particularly awkward in conflict theory. Stage theory assumes an orderly progression of emotions, behavior or thought as in Kubler-Ross' progression from denial to anger, etc., in the grief process. Fowler's stages of faith development or Kohlberg's stages of ethical development. I doubt that future researchers will be able to show a predictable pattern of conflict development from easy to difficult. Depending on what is at stake, the level of fear in the system (or individual), the skill with which people manage differences, and other such factors, conflict may begin at high levels without going through easier, lower "stages." Further, it is not unusual to see de-escalation from high level to low level conflict, with discontinuity between what started out very difficult and miraculously ended up almost sanguine.

Second, Leary's nine-stage theory is far too complex for actual conflict management, differentiating between so many levels that its utility is lost on the practitioner. Finally, I have attempted to be rigorous in using behavioral categories for discriminating between what I call levels of conflict. These behavioral categories are my own and come from my experience in working with conflicted religious organizations.

In any organization, whether it is religious or secular, voluntary or paid, small or large, not all the people will be at the same level in any given conflict. In each congregational conflict some of the people may be severely exercised, others mildly upset and others (there are always some) who think the thing is a tempest in a teapot and are unconcerned.

It will be critical for the pastor, lay leader, consultant or executive working with the congregation to know how many people are at what level of conflict. If only one or two are having difficulty, they can be dealt with individually and the larger organization not brought into the conflict management. If a larger group is involved, then more comprehensive strategies should be used. The trick will be to respond to individuals and groups at their level and not to assume that, because certain individuals are experiencing high level conflict, the rest of the organization is also at that place. The conflict does not need to be dealt with as if it were organization-wide.

Identifying Levels of Conflict

I have identified five levels of conflict which I designate both with numbers and titles in order of ascending difficulty. They are:

I   Problems to Solve;
II Disagreement;
III Contest;
IV Fight/Flight;
V   Intractable Situations;

Level I: Problems to Solve

This first level of conflict describes real conflict; that is, differences. Level 1 does not describe a "problem of communication" or misunderstanding where parties, who have interpreted something incorrectly, feel uncomfortable. Actual differences exist, people understand one another, but have conflicting goals, values, needs, action plans or information.

At this level, parties to the conflict feel discomfort in one another's presence. There may be short-lived anger or a denial of hostile feelings. Feelings, however, are not the key indication of the level of conflict. Anger may flare at any level. At Level I the anger will be short-lived and quickly controlled; sustained anger is an indicator of higher levels of conflict (especially III and IV).

The two key identifying characteristics of each level of conflict are the parties' objectives and the way they use language. At Level I conflict, the objective of the key actors is to fix the problem, to use rational methods to determine what is wrong. At this level the parties will be problem-oriented and not person-oriented. They will be quick to move to rational problem-solving techniques and will be optimistic about working through the difficulty as they confront it (not the person). Usually people at Level I believe collaborative methods are available and choose to engage the conflict openly, fully sharing information and allowing participation by everyone involved (everyone, that is, who is at Level I).

Language at Level I tend to be clear, specific, oriented to the here and now, not loaded with innuendo, not blaming and, to use a Berne[6] category, in the "adult." Persons at Level I am likely both to invite others to describe the difficulty or what they want, and to contribute, as fully as necessary, descriptive and specific information about what is or is not happening which is creating the problem.

Level II: Disagreement

This second level of conflict, disagreement, is more difficult than Level I, though not yet at the degree of win/lose. In Level I, parties are concerned about solving problems. In Level II their objectives are less concerned with problem-solving than with self-protection. At Level II a new concern enters: me. I would like to solve the problem, but I don't want to get hurt or be besmirched in the process. In short, I want to come out looking good.

At Level II a new element of shrewdness and calculation enters. The parties call on friends to discuss the problem and ask for advice, planning strategies to deal with the conflict when it is next expressed in a meeting or relationship.

The language used to describe the problem at Level II shifts from specific to general. The parties stop naming individuals with whom they are having difficulty and allude to "some people;" each is more protective of the self and of others. Instead of describing who is doing or not doing what, participants report, "There is no trust," "We have a communication problem," "We need more openness," or "People should act more like Christians around here." Behind each of these generalizations is a specific, factual happening; but those involved distance themselves from this reality and each other by generalizations. At Level II they are not hostile, just cautious. This caution can keep people from getting close enough to each other to work through their differences.

Other behaviors also characterize Level II conflict. Parties are cautious about sharing all that they know about the difficulties; they tend to withhold information that might enhance the other or hurt themselves. Compromise is a commonly proposed strategy for dealing with the differences, although it may not be appropriate or possible. The idea of compromise doesn't last long and is difficult to revive at Levels III and IV.

Hostile humor, the barbed, distancing gibe that does nothing to relieve tension, but puts down or derides the other and what she or he believes to be important, also is a part of Level II conflict.

Level III: Contest

Win/lose dynamics are not encountered until one reach Level III; win/lose is a fairly high level of conflict but falls short of the hostilities and agonies of fight/flight dynamics. It is a pity that much of the literature on conflict (some of which I have written myself) is unable to help the person in conflict recognize that although win/lose is tough, it is not at the level of fight/flight dynamics which are destructive of organizational tissue and individual integrity.

As the name suggests, the objectives of the parties in Level III have shifted from self-protection to winning. At this point, what is important to the actors is not hurting or getting rid of one's opponent. Many at Level III are stimulated and exhilarated by a worthy opponent and disappointed when the opposition folds without putting up an interesting challenge. The objectives of the Level III protagonists are usually more complex than those of Levels I and II. There is often more than one problem to "fix." Factions often emerge and several or many problems cluster into issues and causes. For example, one concern may be about male-oriented language in worship, but there may also be questions whether to hire a male or female assistant pastor, and whether there is a disproportionate number of women on the church board. As these problems cluster and individuals find allies who think the same as they do on all or most of the questions, the group talks of women's issues, *takes sides*, and forms factions which support positions consistent with the interests of their constituency. These emerging factions are looking for victories, for evidence their group is in the ascendancy, that they have more power or control than others. The win/lose dynamic is in effect.

Language shifts from that used at Levels I and II; at Level III distortion becomes a problem. Whether the person perceives, or only describes, the world in a distorted way, is a chicken and egg problem beyond the scope of this book. However, it is clear from research on conflict and perceptions,[7] and from theories of psychological intervention (especially Transactional Analysis, Rational-Emotive Therapy, and Neuro-Linguistic Programming) that perceptual distortions are a serious problem, especially in individuals and groups in moderate or high conflict with themselves, others or the world about them. Several key distortions occur at Level III as well as at IV and V: magnification, dichotomization, over-generalization, and assumption or arbitrary inference.

201

Magnification is the tendency to see oneself as more benevolent than one is and the other as eviler than he or she is.

Dichotomization is the tendency to divide everything and everybody into neat dual, but separate packages: us or them, right or wrong, stay or leave, fight or flee, etc. In dichotomization, it is almost impossible to see shades between extremes or to find more than two alternative choices.

Over-generalization. In Level II there is a tendency to see specific behavior as an example of a category of events or attitudes (trust, friendly communication, etc.); in Level III generalization takes on an out of control and/or pernicious quality: "You always," "He never," "Everybody."

Assumption. At Level III the contestants delude themselves, believing that they are excellent mind readers, students of their opposition's subtlest motives. They often believe they know the other's mind better than he or she does: "You're just trying to wreck the church." Note this not only describes (perhaps wrongly) the consequences of the other's behavior, but purports to be keen insight into the reasons for the behavior.

Another very helpful list of categories of distorted thinking, which often occurs at Level III and higher, was developed by the school of thought called Rational-Emotive Therapy. Here is the list from Goodman and Maltby's *Emotional Well-Being through Rational Behavior Training*.[8]

Types of Irrational Thinking
1. Inconsistency: The person expects high standards from himself or others sometimes, and not at others.

2. The Non Sequitur: His reasoning has gaps in it––hence the use of the term *non sequitur*, Latin for "it doesn't follow." He concludes that he will not believe what someone says because they have long hair or are late for an appointment.

3. Generalizing from a Few Particulars: The person makes general conclusions based on a few isolated facts, as in the case of deciding that all people belonging to a certain group have qualities that he has found in one or two members of that group.

4. Exaggeration: The person describes a moderate failure as a catastrophe or an inconvenience as a terrible problem.

5. Building a Case: The person selects only those observations about someone or something that fits his preconceived conclusion—favorable or unfavorable.

6. Shifting Responsibility: Instead of assessing responsibility for a given situation to one or more possible causes, the person arbitrarily assigns it to a person he has selected or a condition he has decided, in advance, is the cause.

7. Viewing Feelings as Facts: The person believes that because he reacts to something or someone in a certain way that is emotional, this means, therefore, that something or someone is the way he views them.

8. Viewing Memories as Present-Day Realities: The person persists in thinking, feeling, and acting today as if certain past events or conditions were still in effect and still governing his behavior.

9. Perceiving Remote Possibilities as Imminent Probabilities: The person fails to distinguish between these two very different situations. He cannot see the difference between "could" and "is likely to."

10. Trying to Reconstruct Reality: The person thinks in the "as if" mode, declaring that a person or situation "should" be different than it is, simply because he wants it to be that way, failing to recognize the antecedents for something being the way it is.

11. Expecting Immediate or Rapid Change: Impatience can lead to irrational conclusions about the speed of changes in situations or other's or one's own behavior. The emotional desire for change interferes with clear perception as to its feasibility and its speed.

12. Following Established Habit Patterns: The satisfaction derived from repeating behavior interferes with clear perception as to

whether the behavior is personally or socially desirable. The person reasons that because a behavior was gratifying in the past, therefore, it deserves to be repeated in the future, regardless of consequences.

13. Assuming One's Behavior is Externally Caused: This assumes a direct relationship between outside events and one's own feelings, thoughts or actions, ignoring one's own role in creating behavior.

14. Assuming One is Responsible for Whatever Happens: This is the opposite of No. 13 above and is based on the arbitrary concept of self-blame, rather than an objective weighing of various causes. This is also the opposite of No. 6, wherein one shifts responsibility to others arbitrarily, resulting in "other-blame," and ultimately to paranoia.

15. Perfectionism: The person thinks in terms of "always," "never," "have to" and "must not" with respect to his own behavior and that of others, or regarding conditions and situations he either insists be achieved or demands be maintained. He does not recognize fallibility as an inescapable quality of human beings.

16. Magical Thinking: The person believes that something will or might happen because he dreams, feels, or thinks that it should, according to some preconceived "system" of ideas he has adopted. Astrology, superstition, witchcraft, and other arbitrary ideologies are classic examples of the magical way of perceiving and interpreting the world.

17. Mindreading: The person believes he can "feel" what other people are thinking or that they can feel what he is thinking. He thus imagines many reactions that may be totally at variance with reality.

In addition to the language and objectives criteria for identifying Level III behavior, other behaviors are common indicators at this level. For example, it is likely that there will be resistance to making peace overtures on the part of individuals at Level III. Somehow the idea of "winning" seems contradictory to inviting others to try to work out a solution or resolution to the problems or issues; the parties each hang back waiting for others to show "weakness" by admitting there is a problem rather than asking them to join in taking steps to end the tension.

Personal attacks are endemic at this level and are often mixed up with problem identification. In informal settings the parties are uncomfortable with each other and not likely to continue conversations beyond what is required by social probity. Further, at Level III, the parties are being torn between using rational argument and appealing to emotions. Although emotional appeals ("How could you go against us when we are so much for you?") usually have little or no impact on either neutral audiences or partial contestants, they seem to increase at this level of conflict.

Level IV: Fight/Flight

At Level IV the objectives of the parties change from wanting to win to wanting to hurt and/or get rid of the others. This behavior differs from Level III behavior in that changing the others or the situation is no longer enough; in fact, parties do not believe the others can or will change. Therefore, they believe their only option is removal of the others from their environment. Examples of Level IV conflict include attempts to get the pastor fired, trying to get those with whom one doesn't agree to leave the church and/or attempting to get people to join oneself in leaving. Here the objectives have shifted significantly. Rather than the good of the organization, the good of a subgroup (which can either be a minority or a majority group) becomes the central concern. Being right and punishing become predominant themes.

It is at this level that factions solidify. Clear lines mark who is in and who is out of each of the camps. Strong leaders emerge, and members of factions conform to the wishes of the leaders and the will of the group. Subgroup cohesiveness is more important than the health of the total organization.

Not only does factional membership solidify, but language jells into ideology. Members of factions talk about principles more than issues; they refer to eternal verities such as truth, freedom and justice; they speak of incontrovertible rights: property rights, the right to life, the right to bear arms, etc. These principles are used to sanctify the Level IV combatants and

---

make it possible for them to be less concerned with the ethics of means and to believe with Saul Alinsky, "If the ends don't justify the means, what does?"

Level IV conflict is designated as Fight/Flight because it brings out the primitive survival responses of both defendants and proponents. There is no middle ground between running or attacking, and the attacker cannot differentiate persons attacked from the ideas proposed or defended.

Other behaviors common to this level include a detachment of the parties from one another, which prevents awareness of the pain they cause the others, and an unforgiving, cold, self-righteousness. The parties at this level attempt to enlist outsiders in their cause—outsiders, that is, who will join with them, not outsiders who are neutral and will help manage the conflict, outsiders who will help them punish or get rid of the "bad people." Further, when the parties are in the same room, they will not speak to one another and will only be seen together on unfriendly and hostile terms.

Level V: Intractable Situations

I have titled this level with a word which means unmanageable. Level V conflicts are not within the control of the participants; they are conflict run amok.

While the objective of the participants in Level IV conflict is to punish or remove the others from the organization, in Level V the objective of each party is to destroy the others. The opposition is seen not only as anti-functional to the organization, but harmful to society at large and therefore to be removed. An example of this kind of behavior in churches is where members of a church which has dismissed a pastor feel constrained to see that the pastor does not get another church position and hinder the pastor's search.

At Level V parties usually perceive themselves as part of an eternal cause, fighting for universal principles. Since the ends are all-important, they believe they are compelled to continue to fight; they cannot stop. Indeed, the costs to society, truth and God of withdrawal from the fight are perceived as greater than the costs of defeating the others even through prolonged conflict. Therefore, continuing the fight is the only choice; one cannot choose to stop fighting.

Speed Leas

1. David W. Johnson and Frank P. Johnson. *Joining Together-Group Theory and Group Skills* (Englewood Cliffs-Prentice-Hall, 1975) 157.
2. Adapted from above.
3. William G. Dyer. *Team Building, Issues and Alternatives* (Reading Addison-Wesley, 1977) Alan Filly, *Inter-Personal Conflict Resolution* (Glenview Scott-Foresman, 1975) Joyce Hacker Frost and William W. Wilmot. *Interpersonal Conflict* Dubuque: Wm C. Brown, 1978). Resins Likert and Jane Gibson Likert, *New Ways of Managing Conflict* (New York: McGraw-Hill, 1976).
4. Ibid.
5. Malcolm Leary, Association of Teachers of Management, "Handling Conflict: Dealing with differences––creatively and constructively" Published by the Association of Teachers of Management.
6. For a discussion of Eric Berne's theory see Thomas a Harris, *I'M OK––You're OK* (New York Harper, 1967).
7. A description of each of these theories of cognitive therapies can be found as follows. Transactional Analysis, Eric Herne, *What Do You Say After You Say Hello* York Bantam, 1972). Rational Emotive Therapy, Ruth Wissler & Richard Wissler, *The Principles and Practice of Rational Emotive Therapy* (San Francisco: Jossey-Bass, 1980), Neuro-Linguistic Programming. Richard Bandler and John Grinder, *The Structure of Magic* (Palo Alto: Science and Behavior Books, 1975).
8. David S. Goodman and Maxie C. Maltby Jr., *Emotional Well-Being Through Rational Behavior Training* (Springfield Charles C Thomas Publisher, 1978) pp. 41–42.

Forgiveness, Reconciliation, and Restitution

A. Session 1 (75 Minutes)
   Focus, Facilitator's Goals, and Pastor's Terminal Objectives
   Theology of Conflict
   Why People Quarrel or Fight?
   Christian's Roles in Conflict
   How Differences May Be Resolved
   Reconciliation
   Basic Steps to Reconciliation
   Exercise 1: Private Meditation and Group Activity
   Break
B. Session 2 (60 Minutes)
   Theology of Forgiveness
   Forgiveness
   Steps in Forgiveness
   Obstacles to Forgiveness
   Some Misunderstandings about Forgiveness
   Asking Forgiveness Is Difficult
   Restitution
   Handout 1: Cycle of Forgiveness/Unforgiveness
   Exercise 2: Asking for Forgiveness
C. Session 3 (45 Minutes)
   Review of Handout 2 (Guidelines for Christians in Conflict)
   Exercise 3: Peacemaking Qualities Inventory
   Exercise 4: Key Qualities of a Peacemaker
   Summary and Feedback

Focus of Module 2

An understanding of forgiveness, reconciliation, and restitution can aid creative conflict management and preserve good interpersonal relationships.

Facilitator's Goals

The goals of this learning module include the following:

1. To demonstrate from Scripture that the Christian is to engage in the work of reconciliation
2. To help pastors reflect on the forgiveness-restitution concept in reconciliation
3. To share some views about steps and obstacles to forgiveness
4. To give pastors the opportunity for personal reflection and the examination of their attitude to church discipline and three steps of Matthew 18:15–18 and the admonition of 1 Corinthians 6
5. To show that this triad can serve to prepare members for the task of ministries of reconciliation and intervention

Pastors' Terminal Objectives

Upon the completion of this learning, module the pastors will be able to:

1. indicate from Scripture (Matt. 5:43–48) the roles that determine how a Christian view an antagonist,
2. explain how reconciliation relates to conflict management,
3. explain some practical steps of forgiveness,
4. recognize some obstacles to forgiveness and reconciliation,
5. identify some qualities of the peacemaker,
6. identify five clusters of skills associated with interpersonal relationships, and
7. recognize and explain the principle of reconciliation from 2 Corinthians 5:17–21.

Theology of Conflict

Conflict: A Certainty
1. John 16:33
2. 1 Corinthians 10:13
3. 2 Timothy 3:1–4
4. 1 Peter 4:12

Biblical Reasons for Existence of Conflict
1. Pride (James 4:1–3, 6; Prov. 13:10)
2. Self-centeredness (Isa. 53:6)
3. Deceitfulness (Jer. 17:9; Rev. 12:9)

God's Intention for Man (1 Cor. 14:33)

Christian's Roles in Conflict
1. Give gentle answers (Prov. 15:1)
2. Be merciful; peacemaker (Matt. 5:7–9)
3. Do not be judgmental; be self-examining (Matt. 7:1–5)
4. Show love for neighbor (Luke 10:27)

Why People Quarrel or Fight?
1. To win rewards or maintain possessions
2. To establish a desired position or goal
3. To experience psychological release; catharsis
4. To escape inevitabilities

How Differences May Be Resolved
1. Forgiveness
2. Negotiation and problem-solving
3. Examining personal investment and involvement in the situation and taking appropriate action(s)
4. Biblical concept of reconciliation

Reconciliation

Meanings
1. To exchange enmity for friendship
2. To remove any impediment to unity and peace
3. To remove mutual hostility by mutual concession

Basic Steps to Reconciliation
1. Reconciliation with God
2. Confession, repentance, and forsaking
3. Giving and accepting forgiveness
4. *Learn the spiritual truth of reconciliation*

       1 Corinthians 6:1–11
       Matthew 7:1–3
       Galatians 6:1
       John 17:21
       Acts 2:1–4

Reconciliation is not just settling disputes. It is to bring about healing and restoration between disputing parties. Biblical examples of reconciliation between persons include the following:
1. Jacob and Esau (Gen. 25, 27, 32, 33)
2. Joseph and his brothers (Gen. 37, 39, 50:15–23)
3. The prodigal son (Luke 15:11–31)

Reconciliation does not begin at the church headquarters but in the heart of each believer, each minister of reconciliation.

(Make further comments on ministry of reconciliation.)

The church has failed in initiating reconciliation because
1. it has defaulted to secular institutions,
2. it has defaulted to privates rather than community (church) responsibility, and
3. it has been unwilling to risk confrontation, intimidated by conflict.

What Can the Church Do?
1. Teach
2. Train
3. Identify the gifted
4. Intervene in conflict

Large Group Discussion
What concepts come to mind when you think of
- Matthew 5:23–25,

- Romans 5:9–11,
- 2 Corinthians 5:17–20, and
- Colossians 1:19–20?

Exercise 1: Private Meditation and Group Activity

Break

Forgiveness and Restitution

Theology of Forgiveness

1. God's forgiveness is a gift. Accept it.
2. God's forgiveness involves repentance. Repentance realigns destructive energies into more constructive ways.
3. God's forgiveness involves confession (1 John 1:9).
4. God's forgiveness is powerful (Mic. 7:18–19).
5. God's forgiveness is ours to share. Mediate forgiveness to others.

Forgiveness

Forgiveness basically means to send away and remit. It implies complete cancellation of debts, the remission of the punishment due to sinful conduct, or the complete removal of the cause of the offense (*aphiemi*). Forgiveness also means to bestow a favor unconditionally and is often used to refer to both divine and human forgiveness (*charizomai*).

God is willing to forgive human beings of their sins.

> 2 Chronicles 7:14
> Proverbs 28:13
> Isaiah 55:7
> 1 John 1:9

God also is willing to forget man's past life of sin, whereby he no longer recognizes the sinful conduct as having occurred.

Psalm 103:12	Micah 7:19
Isaiah 38:17	Hebrews 8:12
Isaiah 43:25	Jeremiah 31:34

When a person forgives another, he/she subsequently submits to the consequences of injustices. (God's willingness to forgive man cost him the

---

death of his Son.) Forgiveness of others has moral obligations and is not optional or conditional.

Steps in Forgiveness

1. Acknowledge the hurt. Affirm the pain.
2. Decide to forgive. It takes an act of the will for the spirit to forgive.
3. Remember that forgiveness is a process and that it will take time (sometimes).
4. Remember that forgiveness is not easy.
5. Gather the testimonies and witnessing of people who have forgiven and listen to their experiences.
6. Forgive yourself.
7. Try to see the one who hurts you in a newer light.

Obstacles to Forgiveness

Forgiveness is not always a two-way street. Five major obstacles that repeatedly hinder the act of forgiveness include the following:

1. *The person you need to forgive does not want to be reconciled.* Forgiveness does not have to be reciprocal to be real to you especially when it is followed by *your* changed attitude and behavior. You no longer carry a grudge or resentment and have begun the reconciling process.
2. *The person from whom you need forgiveness is withholding it.* So long as you are not obstructing the forgiveness process, you are doing all that you can. Forgiveness takes time, and not everyone works on your time table of readiness.
3. *The person you need to forgive is dead.* One sincere prayer of forgiveness can cut through time and effect reconciliation beyond the grave. You may also need some catharsis—touching base with painful past experiences can heal memories.
4. *The person you need to forgive does the hurtful thing repeatedly.* Certain situations demand our efforts at forgiveness because the relationships represent a significant instrument in our lives.
5. *You need to forgive an institution, a society, or an organization.* This may be by accepting the forgiving gesture of a representative of the organization (even though compensation is not offered).

Some Misunderstandings about Forgiveness

1. Forgiveness is not easy—not instinctive, but intentional.
2. Forgiveness takes time (ability to forgive cannot be rushed).

3. Forgiving does not mean forgetting. (Here, forgetting is the intentional decrease in negative memories; don't call to memory the injury or *dismiss it when it knocks*.)
4. The ability to forgive is a strength. It breaks the cycle of violence.
5. Forgiveness has great benefits for you—the one doing it. It promotes hope, peace, and positive expectation.

Asking Forgiveness Is Difficult

Here are four of the most unpleasant aspects of forgiveness:
1. *Remembering* the hurt, the people, the events, the pain, the powerlessness, the hopelessness—reliving it all again.
2. Asking forgiveness may indicate admission of wrong, confessing guilt.
3. Asking forgiveness is a humiliation.
4. Fear of rejection (insult, slammed door).

Restitution

The understanding of restitution is dependent upon the understanding of forgiveness, mercy, and justice. The wronged person must be concerned about justice. Application of restitution also involves the ability to repay or inability to pay back. The concept of forgiveness as a gift nullifies compulsory restitution, but it may initiate in the wrongdoer a desire to restore.

Forgiveness by God is dependent upon repentance and not upon restitution. Restitution is never the measure of forgiveness but may prove itself the fruit of repentance. It is an act of peacemaking (Rom. 14:7; Isa. 32:17). God can use the inability of a wrongdoer to repay to teach lessons of stewardship and dependence (on him) to the wronged one and the wrongdoer. God can utilize every problem situation as a growing experience for all persons involved. There is a balance between the obligation of restitution by the wrongdoer and the expectation of restitution by the one who is wronged.

Handout 1: Cycle of Forgiveness/Unforgiveness

Exercise 2: Asking for Forgiveness

———

Review Handout: Guidelines for Christians in Conflict

Exercise 3:   **Peacemaking Qualities Inventory (Private)**
Exercise 4:   **Large group work together on "Key Qualities of a Peacemaker"**
Facilitator: Develop the concept of peacemaking and peacekeeping and its possible effect on conflict management.

Vocabulary of Forgiveness

Positive	Negative
I am sorry.	I am not sorry.
Let us make up.	It will never be the same again.
There is still hope for us.	It is hopeless.
I did not mean to hurt you.	You do not deserve an apology.
Let us be friends again.	I do not need you.
Let us forgive and forget.	It is too hard to forgive you.
Let us start over again.	It won't work.
I love you.	Goodbye.

Five Sets of Skills

Five clusters of skills critical to satisfying interpersonal relationships are as follows:
- Listening skills
- Assertive skills
- Conflict-resolution skills
- Collaborative problem-solving
- Skill selection

Summary and Feedback (Include Transparencies T-3, T-4)
Resource Material

Augsburg, David. *Caring Enough to Forgive: Caring Enough Not to Forgive.* Ventura, CA: Regal Books, 1981.

_____

Buzzard, Lyn, and Lawrence Eck. *Resolving Our Differences.* Elgin, IL: Daniel C. Cook, 1982.

Cook, Jerry, and Stanley C. Baldwin. *Love, Acceptance and Forgiveness.* Ventura, CA: Regal Books, 1981.

Davis, Ron Lee. *A Forgiving God in an Unforgiving World.* Eugene, OR: Harvest House, 1984.

Donnelly, Doris. *Putting Forgiveness into Practice.* Allen, TX: Argus Communications, 1982.

Senior Peacemaker's Handbook, Christian Conciliation Service of Atlanta. 1984.

Swedes, Lewis B. *Forgive and Forget.* Philadelphia, PA: Harper & Row, 1984.

A. Private Meditation (10 Minutes)

Reflection 1

Read Matthew 5:38–42 and Luke 6:27–36, 41–42.

What influence should the actions of others have on your conduct? Can you use the sins of others to justify your sins? How does Jesus's teaching in this area compare with the corresponding worldly principles? Whose principals have you been following in this matter, those of Jesus or those of the world?

Reflection 2

Read Ephesians 4:1–3 and Romans 12:17–21.

How hard should a Christian work to maintain peace? How hard have you worked to maintain peace in this situation (of conflict)? How should you treat someone with whom you are having a dispute? How could you apply this principle in your situation?

Reflection 3

Read Matthew 18:21–25 and Ephesians 4:32. Are you as eager to forgive and to be reconciled as you are to assert your rights?

B. Group Discussion (20 Minutes)

1. Read Matthew 5:43–48 (Discuss the attitudes one should have to wrongdoers.)

2. Read Matthew 18:15–18. (Discuss steps to handling differences.)

What are the implications for church discipline, visitation, etc.?

Exercise 2: Asking for Forgiveness (Private)

Four of the most unpleasant aspects of forgiveness are as follows:

1. Remembering
2. Confessing of guilt
3. Humiliation
4. Afraid (the other will say no)

If you were to rank these statements in order of unpleasantness, which would come first, second, third, and fourth?

1.
2.
3.
4.

Has any one of these unpleasantries stood in the way of your exercising forgiveness? Does any one of these obstacles represent a reason why you are having trouble asking for forgiveness now?

Remember these signs of forgiveness and peace:

handshake	telephone call
truce	dinner with an adversary
gift	kiss

Source: Doris Donnelly, *Putting Forgiveness into Practice*. (Allen, TX: Argus Communication, 1982), p. 44.

===

Peacemaking Qualities Inventory

A. Directions: Pretend you are asked to answer the following twenty questions. Circle *Y* (yes), *N* (no), or *M* (maybe). Skip those that you feel do not apply to you.

Are you a person who

1.	will initiate forgiveness?	Y	N	M
2.	demands an apology before you will grant forgiveness?	Y	N	M
3.	frequently has a running feud going with someone?	Y	N	M
4.	gossips, thereby starting arguments between people?	Y	N	M
5.	thinks some deeds are unforgiveable?	Y	N	M
6.	thinks it's harder for men to forgive?	Y	N	M
7.	holds grudges?	Y	N	M
8.	gets angry easily?	Y	N	M
9.	loves a good fight?	Y	N	M
10.	avoids conflict?	Y	N	M
11.	believes in capital punishment?	Y	N	M
12.	thinks admitting fault is for losers only?	Y	N	M
13.	fakes reconciliations; pretends everything is OK when it isn't?	Y	N	M
14.	provokes conflict?	Y	N	M
15.	is merciful and compassionate?	Y	N	M
16.	believes in an eye for an eye?	Y	N	M
17.	believes only God forgives?	Y	N	M
18.	has experienced being forgiven (by anyone)?	Y	N	M
19.	thinks governments are strongest when they don't show mercy?	Y	N	M
20.	equates strength with nonforgiveness?	Y	N	M

B. Go back over your maybes and check whether they are maybes or yes or no. Ask someone to guess what answers you made on those maybe questions.
C. What does this inventory tell you about yourself?

Source: Doris Donnelly, *Putting Forgiveness into Practice*. (Allen, TX: Argus Communication, 1982), p. 16.

===
Source: Lynn R. Buzzard and Juanita Buzzard, *Resolving Our Differences* (Elgin, IL: David C. Cook, 1982), Transparency 14.

Instruction: Fill in description from texts.

Key Qualities of a Peacemaker

QUALITY	DESCRIPTION	JESUS—OUR EXAMPLE
1. ACTIVE LISTENER		Matthew 19:13–15
2. TRUSTWORTHY		John 17:4
3. NONJUDGMENTAL		John 8:1–11
4. SPIRITUAL PERSPECTIVE		John 17
5. CONSCIENCE		Mark 3:1–6; 10:17–23
6. PATIENT PERSISTENCE		John 12:27
7. PEOPLE-CENTERED		John 11:33–35
8. VULNERABILITY		Philippians 2:4–8

===

Source: Lynn R. Buzzard and Juanita Buzzard, *Resolving Our Differences* (Elgin, IL: David C. Cook, 1982), Transparency 6.

Cycle of Forgiveness	Cycle of Unforgiveness

To Forgive

Reconciled — Forgiven
Forget — Confess
Healed — Guilty
START HERE

Results of Forgiveness:

Reconciliation—II Cor. 5:18-20

Forgiven—free from guilt—Mt. 18:21,22

Severed friendships mended—Mt. 18:15

Heals wounds of others—Jas. 5:16

Clear conscience—Jer. 31:34

Not to Forgive

More Hatred
Savage Response — Violence
Revenge — Hatred
Retaliate — Hostility
START HERE

Results of Unforgiving Heart:
Anger
Bitterness
Loss of faith in justice and authority
Faith in humanity ends
Anger at world and life
Paralysis of mind and soul
Medical and psychological problems
Irresponsible behavior
Faith in God affected

==
Guidelines for Christians in Conflict

1. *Have the mind of Christ* (Phil. 2:5). Live with his spirit and message as they come to us through the New Testament. (If Jesus were here in my place, what would he think? What would he do? Answers here will set the right direction.)

2. *Speak the truth in love* (Eph. 4:15). Speak not in angry denunciation or in querulous faultfinding, but in love. This positioning would prompt individuals to see the other person's point of view and understand why he thinks as he does, even if we were not led to agree with or excuse him. There will be deceit, but we should neither be taken in by it nor call bad names or impute evil motives simply because of a differing opinion.

3. *Be aglow with the Spirit* (Rom. 12:9–12). To be content in prayer is to live and do our work in responsiveness to God's Spirit (CHF Quakers' method). The Quakers have a practice when "the sense of the meeting is not clear because of differing views of entering into a period of silence. Within the silence, it usually follows that the Holy Spirit speaks in such a way that when human speaking is resumed, there is agreement. CHF Lk 6:27, 28—pray for those who abuse you.

4. *Test everything: hold fast what is good* (1 Thess. 5:19–22). This appears in the context of other wise counsel about respecting authority, living peaceably, encouraging the fainthearted, being patiently helpful, doing good to one another instead of trying to get even for an injury.
   Test everything—get the facts and don't jump to conclusions based on misinformation
      —see the whole situation (gestalt)
      —see the consequences of every decision
      — judge how it will affect our own future serving, not our comfort or income or easy living or pleasure, but our serving

5. *All things are not expedient* (1 Cor. 6:12). RSV says not all things are helpful (modify freedom [of choice]). Don't let zeal outrun our wisdom (CHF Mt 10:16). Improve our strategy, be alert to caution and restraint.

Harkness, p. 139.

"Gradualism" ought never to be a substitute for action or a cover for cowardice, but in many circumstances, it is the part of Christian wisdom to be clearsighted about what can be accomplished and not expect everything to be done at once.

6. *Do not be conformed to this world* (Rom. 12:2; John 7:12).

7. *We must obey God rather than men* Acts 5:29 (12–41). One must be sure disobedience is according to principles and not preferences.

And so with a future filled with Christian potentialities, the church, the individual, and the pastor must stand up like the brave and fulfil that divine call, divine mandate to carry out the task of reconciliation.

Quote 1 Corinthians 5:17–21 ("Therefore . . .")

Examine for Process

_____

Source: Georgia Harkness, *The Ministry of Reconciliation* (Nashville, TN: Abingdon Press, 1971), pp. 38–39.

Communicating in Conflict Situations

A. Session 1 (2 hours)
   Focus, Facilitator's Goals, Pastors' Terminal Objectives
   Exercise 1: Survey Inventory (Discussion)
   Some General Concepts of Communication and Transactional Analysis
   Handout 1: Barriers to Communication
   I-Messages
   Listening Skills
   Exercise 2
   Break (15 minutes)
B. Session 2 (2 Hours)
   Emotions and Rational-Emotive Therapy
   Assertive Messages and Behavior
   Exercise 3: Role Play and Evaluation Confrontation
   Exercise 4: Confrontation
   Summary: Review of Exercise 1, Feedback

Communicating in Conflict Situations

Focus

Improved communication skills can aid conflict management and reduce perceptual and behavioral incompatibilities.

Facilitator's Goals

The goals of this learning module include the following:

1. To review some general concepts of communication
2. To help pastors understand four key concepts in rational-emotive therapy (RET) and how feelings can influence conflict management.
3. To explain transactional analysis and barriers to good communication.
4. To help pastors recognize the advantages of confrontation in conflict management, and
5. To explain I-messages and you-messages.

Pastor's Terminal Objectives

Upon completion of this learning module, the pastors will be able to

1. demonstrate skills in the affirmative/assertive techniques as means of deepening relationships and regulating conflict's progress,
2. identify barriers to communication and the five levels of communication,
3. demonstrate some listening skills,
4. recognize the use of verbal and nonverbal communication,
5. explain four key concepts of RET and recognize some effects of emotions or conflict management, and
6. distinguish between I-messages and you-messages.

Introduction

Exercise 1: Survey Inventory

Communication involves what you say and how you say it. Speaking effectively and listening carefully are equally important processes in communicating. The use of verbal and nonverbal messages aids the communication process, but they can also impair communication if incongruences exist between them. True communication is achieved when the sender and receiver understand the same intended message. Communication breaks down when messages are misunderstood or misused completely. This can be adjusted by three steps: hearing the message, restating the message, and securing confirmation of the accuracy of the listener's interpretation. Sometimes the strength of the relationship determines the interpretation of the message content.

Some General Concepts of Communication

Essentials of Effective Communication

There are three key qualities that foster improved communication: genuineness, nonpossessive love, and empathy.

Genuineness means being honest and open about one's feelings, needs, and ideas.

Nonpossessive love involves accepting, respecting, and supporting another person in a nonpaternalistic and freeing way.

Empathy refers to the ability to really see and hear another person and understand him from his perspective.

Basic Elements of the Communication Process

1. Source/encoder
2. Message
3. Channel (verbal or nonverbal)
4. Receiver/decoder
5. Feedback
6. Barriers
7. Context in situations

Characteristics of Effective Communication

A.1. Clearly own your messages by using personal pronouns such as *I* and *me*.
7. Make your messages complete and specific.
8. Make your verbal and nonverbal messages congruent with each other.
9. Be redundant.

10. Ask for feedback concerning the way your messages are being received.
11. Make the message appropriate to the receiver's frame of reference.
12. Describe your feelings by name, action, or figure of speech.
13. Describe other members' behavior without evaluating or interpreting.

B. Effective communication is aided in cooperative orientations as seen by behavior characteristics below:

Competitive Orientation	Cooperative Orientation
Evaluation	Description
Control	Problem orientation
Strategy	Spontaneity
Neutrality	Empathy
Superiority	Equality
Certainty	Provisionalism

Levels of Communication

Level 1	Cliques (shallow talk)
Level 2	Third-person conversation (speak about others)
Level 3	Ideas, philosophy
Level 4	Feelings (affective response to needs)
Level 5	Total, peak (full freedom and exposure)

Christians should find level 4 particularly helpful in developing close relationships in the body of Christ. They should not deny or repress feelings, for feelings are real and natural. Instead, they should recognize feelings, admit them, and deal positively with them. Some people deal with conflicts productively while some do not.

> Emotions respond
> Intellect evaluates (Ps. 119:9)
> Will chooses

Immature behavior—when the process of evaluation is carried out and decision is made on feelings.

Mature behavior—when the process of evaluation is carried out and decision is made for the right things. One *wills* to do right.

C. Some Functions of Nonverbal Communication

People communicate either verbally or nonverbally or both verbally and nonverbally.

Verbally—words (speaking, singing, laughing, etc.)

Nonverbally—touching, looking, smiling, listening, gestures, etc.

1. Repetition/redundancy
2. Substitution (hand clasp at a funeral)
3. Contradiction (poor gesticulation)
4. Complementation (congruence with verbal message)
5. Regulation

Nonverbal Codes

1. Kinesics (bodily movements)
2. Physical (appearance)
3. Haptics (touching behavior)
4. Paralanguages (vocalics—the range of vocal cues that accompany the words of our messages)
5. Proxemics (territory, space)
6. Chronemics (use of time—being early to meetings)
7. The environment and its objects (what the churchyard tells about the church!)

D. Transactional Analysis

Personality (according to Berne) is divided into three ego states: parent, adult, and child.

The adult is the rational aspect of personality.

The child is the immature, irrational aspect of personality.

The parent is the moralizing, power-protective conscience of personality.

The purpose of transactional analysis is to get the three states working.

Illustration and Explanation

Cycle of Forgiveness	Cycle of Unforgiveness

Handout 1

To Forgive

Reconciled — Forgiven

Forget — Confess

Healed — Guilty

START HERE

Results of Forgiveness:

Reconciliation—II Cor. 5:18-20

Forgiven—free from guilt—Mt. 18:21,22

Severed friendships mended—Mt. 18:15

Heals wounds of others—Jas. 5:16

Clear conscience—Jer. 31:34

Not to Forgive

More Hatred

Savage Response — Violence

Revenge — Hatred

Retaliate — Hostility

START HERE

Results of Unforgiving Heart:
Anger
Bitterness
Loss of faith in justice and authority
Faith in humanity ends
Anger at world and life
Paralysis of mind and soul
Medical and psychological problems
Irresponsible behavior
Faith in God affected

© 1995 David C. Cook Publishing Co. Printed in U.S.A.

Buzz Session

What effect can these responses have on communication?

Does your president speak to you as an adult or as a parent?

Can you perceive communication breakdown if you respond to a person as a parent rather than as an adult, especially over an extended period?

Transactional adult stimuli/responses can reduce conflict. Interpersonal conflict often develops out of crossed transaction.

Levels of Conflict in the Church

Example 1

Adult S: What caused you to come so late to the meeting?

Adult R: Because the car broke down on my way.

Example 2:

Adult S: What caused you to come so late to the meeting?

Adult R: I tried so hard, yet you always criticize me. (This is a child response.)

0

Handout 1: Barriers to Communication (Discussion)

Transactional analysis paves the way for understanding the barriers to communication. Barriers to communication threaten self-esteem and encourage defensiveness, resistance, and resentment. They can also lead to despondency, withdrawal, feelings of defeat or of inadequacy. Barriers serve as a feeling-blocker and extended use of them can permanently damage a relationship.

Break

(Presentation)

I-Messages and You-Messages

You-messages constitute the blaming type of message and are generally discouraged.

I-messages normally have three components and are generally honest, clear confessionals.

1. Condition resulting from the behaviors of the other or from the specific behavior of the other.
2. The tangible, concrete effect *you* experience from that behavior.
3. The feelings generated within *you* by the behavior.

*Give examples.

The sequence in I-message (behavior-effect-feeling) suggests that the feeling is being blamed on the possible effect, *not* on the other person's behavior. I-messages meet three important criteria for effective confrontation:

1. They have a high probability of promoting a willingness to change.
2. They contain minimal negative evaluation of the other person.
3. They do not injure the relationship.

Listening Skills

Most persons spend an average of 70 percent of their waking hours in communicating—writing (7 percent), reading (16 percent), talking (30 percent), and listening (45 percent). Listening is the process by which the human organism selects, processes, and stores aurally.

Skill Clusters	Specific Skills
Attending skills	A posture of involvement
	Appropriate body motion
	Eye contact
	Nondistancing environment
Following skills	Door openers
	Minimal encourages
	Infrequent questions
	Attentive silence
Reflecting skills	Paraphrasing
	Reflecting feelings
	Reflecting meaning (tying feelings to content)
	Summative reflections

Active listening involves the doing, saying, and observing aspects of communication that motivate others into providing further information to aid the communicative process.

What to Do During Active Listening
1. Assume an active listening posture (head, arms, and feet).
2. Maintain eye contact.
3. Make active listening facial expressions
4. Make nonverbal encouragements

What to Say during Active Listening
1. Make verbal encouragements ("I see," "Yes," "Yeah," "I understand," etc.).
2. Use good verbal quality.

What to Observe during Active Listening
1. Identify the content of the person's verbal statements.
2. Identify the person's feelings.
3. Identify the feelings of the person's verbal behavior.
4. Identify the feelings of the nonverbal behavior.

Why Reflective Responses Work

Reflective listening makes more sense to some people when they consider six peculiarities of human communication.

1. Words have different meanings for different people (semantic cause of conflict).
2. People often *code* their messages.
3. People frequently talk about "presenting problems" when another topic is of greater concern to them. Active listening aids the defiltering process and hidden agendas.
4. The speaker may be blind to his/her emotions or blinded by them.
5. Listeners are often easily distracted.
6. Listeners hear through filters that distort much of what is being said.

Reflective listening provides a check for accuracy and a channel through which warmth and concern can be communicated.

1. Listening and hearing are not the same thing.
2. Listening is not a natural process.
3. All listeners do not receive the same message.
4. Listening is a learned response, a behavior.
5. The decision to listen resides with the listener.
6. Listening and reading are not identical processes.

Faulty Listening Behaviors

Pseudo-listening
Stage hogging (one-way listening)
Selective listening
Filling in gaps
Assimilation to prior messages
Insulated listening
Defensive listening
Ambushing
Insensitive listening

Reasons for Poor Listening

Message overload
Preoccupation
Rapid thought

Physical "noise"
Hearing problems
Faulty assumptions
Lack of training

Listening Process
1. Hearing
2. Attention
3. Understanding
4. Remembering
5. Evaluating
6. Responding

Types of Listening
1. Active listening versus passive listening
2. Social listening versus serious listening
   —Informal social listening: appreciative, conversational, and courteous listening
   —Critical listening
   —Discriminative listening

How to Become a Better Listener

A pastor's basic tendency toward prescription of solutions can impede his listening skills. Several steps can be taken to help pastors become better listeners.

1. Develop a determination to listen.
2. Use listening time wisely. Use lag time wisely.
3. Determine the speaker's purpose for communicating and your purpose for listening early in the interaction.
4. Recognize that words may have multiple referents.
5. Control emotions and biases.
6. Be a reflective listener.
7. Do not dismiss a subject as disinteresting.
8. Do not use the speaker's appearance or delivery as an excuse for not listening.
9. Listen for the whole story.
10. Watch for verbal and nonverbal cues.
11. Take notes judiciously.

12. Remember, speed of speech and speed of thought allows for lag time, which often impedes listening. Use lag time for listening, not for responding. It is the quality or nature of the communication that promotes effective conflict management.

Exercise 2: Listening

Break

Emotions and Rational-Emotive Therapy

(Presentation)

Emotional components of conflicts include anger, distrust, defensiveness, scorn, resentment, fear, and rejection. When feelings are strong, it is usually best to deal with the emotional aspects of conflict first. Real issues can be best handled constructively when the emotions have been removed or reduced. Rationality is often reduced in the presence of feelings. Only if emotions are managed appropriately can the conflict-management process continue along lines that encourage a systematic, noninjurious, and growth-producing experience.

During a conflict, always focus on the emotions first. One way of doing this productively is to use the conflict-resolution method:

- Treat the other person with respect.
- Listen and restate to the other's satisfaction your perception of the message.
- Briefly state your point of view.

This method can be used individually or by agreement with another, or it can be facilitated by a neutral third party. By using this method, people can agree to disagree and experience good human relationships after the conflict has been concluded.

Rational-Emotive Therapy (RET)

This therapy started about 1955 with Dr. Albert Ellis and can be particularly useful to the one not necessarily interested in protracted counseling. RET argues that there are irrational beliefs that have been reinforced in such a way that unconsciously the person sees himself as unworthy and no good. One's irrational behavior is conditioned by one's illogical thoughts about self. RET believes in prescription rather than long-term counseling.

To Ellis, man is both uniquely rational and irrational, and humans experience emotional disturbances through thinking illogically and irrationally. The therapy is built on an ABC frame: A, behavior; B, thoughts about it; and C, consequence of the behavior. The key point: it is not what happened that disturbs, but it is one's views, perception, and interpretation of the behavior (action) that causes disturbance. In this therapy, the facilitator unmasks the illogical thoughts and self-defeating verbalizations. This method strives on the collaborative, integrative problem-solving method.

Irrational beliefs (IBs) have been categorized as follows:

1. *Awfulizing statements.* These statements evaluate situations as awful, could not be worse.
2. *Mustabation* (*should*s, *ought*s, and *must*s). RET says, "It is," so *you* work on it. "The church ought to look after my parents." RET says, "But the church is not doing it," so *you* do it.
3. *Globalizing* (evaluations of human worth). All global evaluations of persons are counterproductive and illogical (e.g., all good pastors have interns).
4. *Need statements* (making wishes, absolute need, or demand).

Remedy for Irrational Beliefs

1. Emotional disturbances are caused by irrational thoughts.
2. Talking ourselves out of believing those irrational ideas reduces or removes those disturbances.
3. Nothing else is required—not even RET.

Assertive, Nonassertive, and Aggressive Behavior

Question (straw vote):

You are at a workers' meeting with eighty other pastors. The president speaks softly, and you, as well as others, have trouble hearing him. What would be your response?

Responses:

    a. You raise your hand, get his attention, and ask if he will mind speaking louder.

    b. You yell out "Speak up."

    c. You continue to strain to hear but say nothing about his too-soft voice.

Definitions

Nonassertive behavior: Inhibition from expressing own actual feelings; others make decisions, and own rights are suppressed.

Aggressive behavior: Own feelings are expressed, but in so doing, others' feelings are hurt and their rights may be infringed upon.

Assertive behavior: Allows for honest expression of feelings of all parties in situation and negotiation to accommodate the rights of all.

Types of People

Passive   —Rarely take initiative

                     —Afraid to upset friends

                     —She/he is a doormat

Aggressive   —Not very popular

                     —People tend to avoid them

                     —Needs to be more sensitive

Assertive   —Well-adjusted

                     —Well-developed sense of self-esteem

                     —Wide range of social skills

Assertive Messages

A very good means of asserting oneself is to use messages that contain three parts:
- A nonjudgmental description of the behavior to be changed
- A disclosure of the asserter's feelings
- A clarification of the concrete and tangible effect of the other person's behavior on the asserter

Effective assertion is firm yet without domination. The formula for an assertion message is this:

When you (state the behavior nonjudgmentally), I feel (disclose your feeling) because (clarify the effect on your life).

The assertive message prescribes no solution, and the recipient of the message can respond appropriately and thus preserve self-respect.

Examples of Assertive Messages

1. When you use my car and do not refill the gas tank, I feel unfairly treated because I must pay more money for gasoline.
2. When you are often late to pick me up after work, I feel frustrated because time is wasted while I wait for you, and I must rush dinner to be on time for seven o'clock.

Exercise 3: Role Play—Types of Behavior

Confrontation

What is confrontation? It is offering the maximum of useful information with the minimum of threat and stress.

Goals of Confrontation

1. To help the person expose areas of feelings, experiences, and behavior that he has so far been reluctant to expose
2. To help the person understand modes of self-destructive behavior and unused resources
3. To help the person learn how to confront himself

What Should Be Confronted?

1. Discrepancies
2. Distortions
3. Games, tricks, and smoke screens
4. Evasions
5. Behaviors versus values

The Manner of Confronting

1. In the spirit of accurate empathy
2. Tentatively
3. With care
4. Involvement
5. Motivation
6. Relationship between parties
7. The state of the person

Potential Response by a Person to Confrontation

1. Discredit the confronter (counterattack)
2. Persuade the confronter to change his views
3. Devaluate the importance of the topic being discussed
4. Seek support for one's own views elsewhere, i.e., seek out other third-party interveners
5. Change cognition to correspond to that of the confronter (i.e., to agree with the pastor)
6. Examine his behavior with the help of the pastor (or another person)

Exercise 4: Assertive, Nonassertive, and Aggressive Behavior
Key Tests of Confrontation
1. To make visible the issues involved
2. To examine the assumptions
3. To explain the alternatives
4. Unmask and explore defenses
5. Mistimed confrontation can be a disaster, although a caring confrontation can aid conflict management and make it possible for each part to level with the other.

Guidelines for Confrontation
1. Focus your feedback *not* on the actor *but* on the action.
2. Focus your feedback *not* on your conclusions *but* on your observations.
3. Focus your feedback *not* on judgments *but* on descriptions.
4. Focus your feedback *not* on quality *but* on quantity.
5. Focus your feedback *not* on advice and answers *but* on ideas, information, and alternatives.
6. Focus your feedback *not* on the amount available within you as giver *but* on the amount useful to the receiver.
7. Focus feedback *not* on the easiest time and place to suit your own schedule *but* on the best time and the optimal situation for the receiver.
8. Focus feedback *not* on why *but* on what and how.

By putting these eight guidelines together, five basic principles can be deduced:
1. Confront caringly
2. Confront gently
3. Confront constructively
4. Confront acceptingly
5. Confront clearly

Summary
Review of Exercise 1
Include Transparency T-5
Feedback

241

Resource Material

Adler, Ronald B., and George Rodman. *Understanding Human Communication*. 2nd ed. New York: Holt, Rinehart & Winston, 1985.

Augsburg, David. *Caring Enough to Confront*. Ventura, CA: Regal Books, 1985.

Bolton, Robert. *People Skills*. Englewood Cliffs, NJ: Prentice-Hall, 1979.

Egan, Gerard. *The Skilled Helpers*. Monterey, CA: Brooks Cole, 1982.

Floberg, Jay, and Alison Taylor. *Meditation*. San Francisco, CA: Jossey-Bass, 1984.

Johnson, David W., and Frank P Johnson. *Joining Together*. Englewood Cliffs, NJ: Prentice-Hall, 1982.

Whitman, Richard F., and Paul H. Boise. *Speech Communication*. New York: Macmillan, 1983.

Communication Survey Inventory

Circle the Correct answer.

1. T F Prejudice can be a noise in the communication process.
2. T F Noise is any element that interferes with the communication process.
3. T F Good sending skills require the sender not to be redundant.
4. T F Only when emotions are rising should one confront the other.
5. T F Confrontation often leads to stronger relationships.
6. T F Nonverbal communication hinders good verbal communication.
7. T F Learning the rational-emotive therapy process can aid the busy pastor in conflict management.
8. T F An example of noise with a group could be how trustworthy a member is seen to be.
9. T F Personal relationships have little influence on communication within a hierarchical organization.
10. T F Two-way communication is when the leader gives instruction and members listen.

Instructions
1. Hand out survey and explain exercise.
2. Each participant answers statements.
3. At the completion of the inventory, direct participants to look for the answers in the presentations. (Communication Survey Inventory will be reviewed during the summary and feedback period.)

Multiple Choice: Circle the correct responses.
1. When speakers receive feedback indicating that messages have not
    been understood correctly, it is called

    a.   deferred feedback   c)   ambiguous feedback
    b)   negative feedback   d)   positive feedback

2. The speaker usually focuses the most attention on the

    a)   message   c)   receiver
    b)   feedback   d)   situation

3. Approximately how much of our waking day is spent communicating?

    a)   30 percent   c)   70 percent
    b)   90 percent   d)   50 percent

4. The most serious barrier to listening is the

    a)   speaker   c)   message
    b)   situation   d)   listener

5. The most important responsibility of a listener is to
    a) search for the speaker's purpose and intent
    b) pay attention as an active listener
    c) listen without evaluation until the speaker is finished
    d) repress the tendency to respond emotionally

6. Listening
    a) is relatively unimportant to the communication process
    b) occupies about 50 percent of our daily lives
    c) is easy for most people
    d) is about the same thing as hearing

7. The stage of listening during which the listener weighs evidence
    and determines the presence or absence of bias is

    a)   attention   c)   evaluating
    b)   understanding   d)   responding

8. It is a good communication practice when sending messages to (choose three)
   a) use more than one way of getting the message across
   b) ask the receiver to give feedback on the content and intention of the message
   c) make evaluations and inferences when listening to other group members
   d) describe your feelings
   e) speak for others in the group who are too shy to speak for themselves

9. The major barrier to effective communication is the tendency most people must
   a) talk too much
   b) talk too little
   c) judge and evaluate
   d) not listen

10. Peter wants to sit where he can have the most influence on the decision-making and has the most contact with his president, who always sits at the head of a rectangular table. Where should he sit?
   a) at the end of the table
   b) at the side of the table next to the president
   c) at the side of the table far from the president

Exercise 2: Listening (Optional)
Person A
1. Give the relationship of the person who knows you best and describe yourself as that person would describe you.
2. Listener restates what he heard.
3. Person A makes confirmation or correction.

Person B
1. Relates some specific experiences such as a joyful experience, a formative decision, a successful experience, or a significant person in your life.
2. Listener restates the experience.
3. Person B makes confirmation or correction.

Exercise 3: Role Play—Three Types of Behavior
Exercise 3.1: Two Senior Pastors
Another pastor who is known to have a bad driving record requests you to lend him your car to go to a funeral at which he is officiating. You are in the third week of a six-week evangelistic series of meetings, and you just cannot afford to be without your car—just in case he meets an accident. How would you react?

Exercise 3.2: Intern and a Senior Pastor
Situation 1
You try to explain to your senior pastor the reason why you were late for an appointment, but he starts screaming at you for being unreliable. (You have been with him three months and may be with him another three months.)

Situation 2
Same situation, but you have already been assigned a district of your own that you will take up full responsibility in three weeks' time. What would be your reaction in this case?

Process:
1. Each role play takes five minutes.
2. Group comments occur after the role plays.
3. Slips of paper are given if observations may be written, or group may be allowed to discuss each role play so that the next one benefits from comments.

Exercise 4: Assertive Behavior
1. Develop a conflict situation on the supplied paper.
2. Give three potential responses to it to show your understanding of assertive, nonassertive (passive), and aggressive behavior.
3. Discuss answers in pairs:
   —Which type is most comfortable for you?
   —When and with whom are you most likely to behave differently?

Conciliatory Communication Strategies

(Examples from Thomas Gordon, *Parent Effectiveness Training* [NY: Peter H. Wyden, 1970] and *Teacher Effectiveness Training* [NY: David McKay, 1977].)

1. **Ministry When the Other Person Has the Problem**

   Active Listening vs. Unacceptance Responses

   Twelve ineffective communication responses (language of unacceptance, putdowns)

   Solution responses:

   1. *Ordering, commanding, or directing.* Example: "You stop complaining and get your work done."
   2. *Warning or threatening.* Example: "You'd better get on the ball if you expect to get a good grade in this class."
   3. *Moralizing, preaching, or giving* shoulds *and* oughts. Example: "You know it's your job to study when you come to school. You should leave your personal problems at home where they belong."
   4. *Advising or offering solutions or suggestions.* Example: "The thing for you to do is to work out a better time schedule. Then you'll be able to get all your work done."
   5. *Teaching, lecturing, or giving logical arguments.* Example: "Let's look at the facts. You better remember there are only thirty-four more days of school to complete that assignment."

   Judgment, evaluation responses:

   6. *Judging, criticizing, disagreeing, or blaming.* Examples: "You're just plain lazy" or "You're a big procrastinator."
   7. *Name-calling, stereotyping, or labeling.* Example: "You're acting like a fourth-grader, not like someone almost ready for high school."
   8. *Interpreting, analyzing, or diagnosing.* Example: "You're just trying to get out of doing that assignment."

   Others that may prove ineffective:

   9. *Praising, agreeing, or giving positive evaluations.* Example: "You're really a very competent young man. I'm sure you'll figure how to get it done somehow."
   10. *Reassuring, sympathizing, consoling, or supporting.* Example: "You're not the only one who has ever felt like this. I've felt that way about tough assignments too. Besides, it won't seem hard when you get into it."

---

11. *Questioning, probing, interrogating, or cross-examining.* Examples: "Do you think the assignment was too hard?" "How much time did you spend on it?" "Why did you wait so long to ask for help?" "How many hours have you put in on it?"

12. *Withdrawing, distracting, being sarcastic, humoring, or diverting.* Examples: "Come on, let's talk about something more pleasant." "Now isn't the time." "Let's get back to our lesson." "Seems like someone got up on the wrong side of the bed this morning."

How these twelve responses may affect me if I have a problem:
- They make me stop talking, shut me off.
- They make me defensive and resistant.
- They make me argue, counterattack.
- They make me feel inadequate, inferior.
- They make me feel resentful or angry.
- They make me feel guilty or bad.
- They make me feel I'm being pressured to change—that I'm not accepted as I am.
- They make me feel the other person doesn't trust me to solve my problem.
- They make me feel I'm being treated paternalistically, as if I were a child.
- They make me feel I'm not being understood.
- They make me feel my feelings aren't justified.
- They make me feel I've been interrupted.
- They make me feel frustrated.
- They make me feel I'm on the witness stand being cross-examined.
- They make me feel the listener is just not interested.

An example:

JOHNNY: Tommy won't play with me today. He won't ever do what I want to do.

MOTHER: Well, why don't you offer to do what he wants to do? You've got to learn to get along with your little friends. (Advising, moralizing.)

JOHNNY: I don't like to do things he wants to do, and besides, I don't want to get along with that dope.

MOTHER: Well, go find someone else to play with then if you're going to be a spoilsport. (Offering a solution; name-calling.)

JOHNNY: He's the spoilsport, not me. And there isn't anyone else to play with.

MOTHER: You're just upset because you're tired. You'll feel better about this tomorrow. (Interpreting, reassuring.)

JOHNNY: I'm not tired, and I won't feel different tomorrow. You just don't understand how much I hate the little squirt.

MOTHER: Now stop talking like that! If I ever hear you talk about one of your friends like that again, you'll be sorry. (Ordering, threatening.)

How to Identify Conflict Styles

A. Session 1 (2 hours)
   Focus, Facilitator's Goal, Pastor's Terminal
   Objectives
   Assumptions
   Terms of Modal Choices
   Handout 1: Testing Mode (Leas's Survey)
   Exercise 1: Taking of Survey to Determine Modal Preference
   (Follow Instructions)
   Modal Styles and Criteria for Use
   Handout 2: Summaries to Conflict-Styles Review
   Exercise 2: Conflict-Management Styles Exercise
   Strategies for Dealing with Conflict
   Break

B. Session 2 (1 hour)
   Exercise 3: Case Study
   Conflict Situations
   Management Approaches to Conflict
   Steps to Changing Modal Preferences
   Mention: Alternative Conflict-Management Surveys
   Summary and Feedback

C. Session 3: Optional
   This period will be used to makeup or complete or explain anything
   discussed in modules 1–4 so far.

How to Identify Conflict Styles

Focus

Various conflict reactions lead to either cooperative or competitive behavior, which can be changed according to desired outcome or more productive results.

Facilitator's Goals

The goals of this learning module include the following:

1. To demonstrate from conflict theory the outcomes and approaches to conflict
2. To help pastors identify their own preferred conflict-management styles
3. To encourage the development of a repertoire of conflict-management styles.

Pastor's Terminal Objectives

Upon the completion of this learning module, the pastors will be able to

1. identify and evaluate their preferred conflict-management style in terms of its effectiveness in resolving conflict and maintaining interpersonal relationships,
2. explain three approaches and three outcomes to conflicts,
3. use the win-win problem-solving option whenever possible, and
4. identify instruments available for analyzing conflict styles and situations.

Assumptions

Various styles of conflict management exist, and all have uses, limitations, and consequences. No one style is appropriate in every situation, and the advantages and disadvantages of all styles should be known to conflict managers. Conflict-management styles are learned behaviors and can be changed if so desired. At least four assumptions have been developed concerning modal choices.

1. People have characteristic approaches to conflicts.
2. People develop conflict styles for reasons that make sense to them.
3. No one style is automatically better than another.
4. Peoples' styles undergo changes to adapt to the rationality demands of new situations.

Together, the styles taken in conflict will take four directions: (1) avoidance, (2) maintenance, (3) reduction or de-escalation, and (4) escalation. Successful conflict management is aided by following a process of strategic planning as follows:
1. Choose strategies and tactics based on goals.
2. Gather the available information.
3. Make tactical choices.

This success can be further aided by the use of appropriate communication skills, power, or a combination of both.

Various Modal Choices (Three Typologies)

• Withdrawing	Avoiding	Avoiding
• Forcing	Competing	Win
• Smoothing	Accommodating	Yield
• Compromising	Compromising	Compromising
• Confronting	Collaborating	Problem-solving

Handout 1: Testing Mode (Leas's Survey)

Exercise 1: Taking of Survey to Determine Modal Preferences

Modal Styles
- The five conflict-handling modes based on the assertiveness/cooperativeness matrix are as follows:
- A competing style is high on assertiveness and low on cooperativeness. The party is concerned with achieving his own outcomes/goals without concern for the other and typically engages in tactics (force, argumentation, and so on) to achieve his goals.

- An accommodating style is low on assertiveness and high on cooperativeness. The party is purely concerned with helping the other achieve his outcomes without regard to his own goals
- An avoiding style is low in assertiveness and cooperativeness and is exemplified by a party who prefers to manage a conflict by withdrawing from it, postponing the decision, and so on.
- A collaborative style is both assertive and cooperative and is demonstrated by a party who seeks to achieve both his own objectives and the other's objectives generally through some problem-solving process.
- Then there is the compromising style, which shows a preference for moderate levels of assertiveness and cooperativeness. It is a median style between the collaborative style on the one hand and the competitive or accommodative style on the other hand. It involves exchanging concessions.

Criteria for Modal Choice

Avoidance

Many conflict situations can be avoided because they are low priority in terms of organizational functioning or when it just isn't worth your time and effort to get involved.

- Sometimes a situation is in the developmental stages and needs time to mature, or you may want to collect more information and others' perception before acting.
- When you are convinced that active confrontation can produce nothing but negative results for you or the organization, avoidance is a wise choice.
- If the power dynamics of the situation are such that you can't imagine a positive outcome for the organization, avoid the situation.
- Avoidance is a good choice when it is more appropriate for others to manage a conflict situation.

Accommodation

- Accommodation is a good choice when building relationships is more important than the conflict.
- When your investment in the conflict is not high, accommodate.

- When the power dynamics are against you, accommodation is a way to minimize your losses and to maintain a climate of cooperation with the other party.

Competition
- When speed and decisiveness are at a premium, as they are in emergencies, competition is called for.
- When you conflict with parties who will not cooperate and who attempt to capitalize on your collaborative behavior, stay competitive. (Be certain to test carefully your perceptions before you compete on this basis.)
- When organizational functionality is at stake and an unpopular decision needs to be made, and/or you are certain you are correct and the other is in opposition, maintain your competitive stance.
- When your investment is high, it is important to be assertive about your position. At first, this may be competitive behavior or may be perceived as such; however, your assertive stance is necessary to preserve interaction. As interaction proceeds, you may work toward collaboration, if you choose.

Collaboration
- This mode is important if your investment in the situation is high and you value the other party's viewpoint and relationship.
- When you desire the participation of all parties and you have a strong commitment to the management solution, use the collaborative mode.
- A collaborative mode is appropriate when your rational goals are high and team development is as important as the management of an organizational concern.
- The collaborative mode is the best choice when you have a high investment in creativity and maximum use of people's resources in managing a problem situation.

Compromise
- From our viewpoint, compromise has little to recommend as an opening strategic modal choice. Choosing to do so limits the creativity of the management process.

- Compromise becomes a choice when expediency becomes a priority, time is running out, or collaboration and/or competition have failed.
- Compromise can provide temporary management solutions to a conflict, while interaction continues to seek more satisfying ones.

Handout 2: Summary to Conflict Styles or Optional (Review)

Exercise 2: Testing Preference

Regardless of the modal choice, five considerations are generally made before entering a conflict:

1. Stakes (are the stakes high or low?)
2. Conflict of interests
3. Social pressure (self-esteem)
4. History of interaction
5. Time pressure

Strategies for Dealing with Conflict

Three major strategies for dealing with conflict include the following:

1. The win-win strategy
2. The lose-lose strategy
3. The win-lose strategy

Categories 2 and 3 are most often used; although collectively, they are least effective. They always provide winners and losers.

Win-Lose and Lose-Lose Strategies

Common characteristics of win-lose and lose-lose methods are as follows:

1. There is a clear we-they distinction between the parties rather than a "we versus the problem" orientation.
2. Energies are directed toward the other party in an atmosphere of total victory or total defeat.
3. Each party sees the issue only from its own point of view rather than defining the problem in terms of mutual needs.
4. The emphasis in the process is upon attainment of a solution rather than upon a definition of goals, values, or motives to be attained with the solution.
5. Conflicts are personalized rather than depersonalized with an objective focus on facts and issues.

6. There is no differentiation of conflict-resolving activities from other group processes, nor is there a planned sequence of those activities.

7. The parties are conflict-oriented, emphasizing the immediate disagreement, rather than relationship-oriented, emphasizing the long-term effect of their differences and how they are resolved.

Win-Win Methods

Win-win methods strive on the consensus and integrative decision-making models. The success of these models depends on participants doing at least five things:

1. Focus upon defeating the problem rather than each other
2. Avoid voting, trading, or averaging
3. Seek facts to resolve dilemmas
4. Accept conflict as helpful, providing it does not elicit threats or defensiveness
5. Avoid self-oriented behavior when it portends the exclusion of others' needs or positions

A person using the win-win strategy says at least three things:

1. "I want a solution that achieves your goals and my goals and is acceptable to both of us."
2. "It is our collective responsibility to be open and honest about facts, opinions, and feelings."
3. "I will continue the process by which we arrive at agreement but will not dictate content."

In this kind of strategy, the effective decision is the product of quality and acceptance. Consequently, four options exist to this orientation:

1. High concern for quality, low concern for acceptance
2. High concern for acceptance, low concern for quality
3. High concern for quality, high concern for acceptance
4. Low concern for quality, low concern for acceptance

It must be noted that there are three levels of acceptance or lack of acceptance for ranking all possible solutions to a problem: some alternatives will be supported by each member, some alternatives will not be unacceptable to each member (don't care), and some will be personally opposed by each member.

Conflict Situations

Exercise 3: Case study

At least three situations exist that may create conflict:

1. Approach-approach
2. Approach-avoidance
3. Avoidance-avoidance

Approach-Approach

This situation refers to a conflict in which two options for resolving a situation are equally attractive but mutually exclusive—the person can have only one (option) but wants both. The value of the alternatives, the probability of recurrence, and the number of alternatives may determine the choice made under the approach-approach situation. The more alternatives, the higher the potential for conflict. (If a pastor has three calls pending, he is likely to have more conflict than if he has only one conflict to decide on.) This type is probably the easiest to solve.

Approach-Avoidance

This situation refers to settings where a decision must be made that has desirable and undesirable outcomes that occur simultaneously. Questions of principle and pragmatics often end in this category. (An example would be a board's desire for high-quality decisions [approach], but they are not willing to spend the time necessary for this desire [avoidance]). When ambivalence exists over a long time, withdrawal usually results.

Avoidance-Avoidance

This situation exists when a group or individual is forced to make a decision that is undesirable to avoid another undesirable outcome.

The conference committee that must decide between reducing staff or reducing base salary or reducing expansion when expansion is the only way to survival and progress is in an avoidance-avoidance situation. One thing to do with avoidance-avoidance situations is to plan *never* to be in that kind of situation again. Have alternatives. People terminate their relationships when forced into repeated avoidance-avoidance decisions.

Conflict frustration—frustration that results from conflict—is a product of three major types of conflicts: approach-approach conflict, approach-avoidance conflict, and avoidance-avoidance. Approach-avoidance conflict is the most difficult to resolve since the goal or object has both positive and negative qualities for the person. He is attracted to it and repelled by it at the same time, and it generally causes the greatest amounts of frustration.

Management Approaches to Intergroup Conflicts

Management has traditionally employed a variety of approaches to intergroup conflicts:

1. *Separation*. This strategy rests on the notion that the conflict between the groups can be minimized if the contact between is minimized.
2. *Affiliation*. In this approach, the assumption is that if the two (or more) groups are united into one, the conflict is likely to dissipate.
3. *Annihilation*. In this strategy, management employs the notion that conflict is best settled when the groups go at it; the more powerful group will prevail.
4. *Regulation*. Management established strong sanctions and legal procedures for dealing with intergroup conflicts.
5. *Interaction*. This approach seeks to resolve the conflict through discussion while maintaining the identity of each group and the functional relationship between them.

Recommendations: Plan to Change Modal Choice?

If you observe that your preferred style is proving dysfunctional and are thinking of changing your mode, try following these steps:

1. Identify your current conflict-management styles and how you use them in different settings. Are you satisfied with them?
2. Identify which style it is you want to change and to what.
3. Identify what behaviors would be characteristic of the new styles. What actions would enable you to do and be who you want to be?
4. Practice these behaviors first in settings that have lower risk and are supportive.

5. Practice these behaviors in daily settings. Develop means of getting feedback on the impact of your actions.
6. Are you satisfied with the results? If so, reinforce or support these new behaviors so that they become natural patterns of action.

Mention: Alternative Conflict-Management Surveys

Summary and Feedback (Include Transparency T-5)

Session 3: Optional (Makeup of Former Sessions)

Resource Material

Burke, R. J. "Methods of Resolving Superior-Subordinate Conflicts." *Organizational Behavior and Human Performance* 5 (1970): 31.

Filley, Alan C. *Interpersonal Conflict Resolution.* Glenview, IL: Scott, Foresman, 1975.

Folberg, Jay, and Alison Taylor. *Mediation: A Comprehensive Guide to Resolving Conflicts without Litigation.* San Francisco, CA: Jossey-Bass, 1984.

Hocker, Joyce L., and William W. Wilmot. *Interpersonal Conflict.* 2nd. ed. Dubuque, IA: Wm. C. Brown, 1985.

Leas, Speed B. *A Lay Person's Guide to Conflict Management.* Washington, DC: Alban Institute, 1979.

Lewis, G. Douglas. *Resolving Church Conflicts.* San Francisco, CA: Harper & Row, 1981.

Pneuman, Roy, and Margaret E. Bruedhl. *Managing Conflict.* Englewood Cliffs, NJ: Prentice-Hall, 1982.

Conflict-Management Styles Exercise

A. Match the following styles of conflict management with their characteristics.
   A. Withdrawing/avoiding
   B. Forcing/competing
   C. Smoothing/accommodating
   D. Compromising/compromising
   E. Confronting/collaborating/problem-solving

1. _____ The goals are important; the people are not.
2. _____ The people are important; the goals are not.
3. _____ Neither the goals nor the people are important.
4. _____ Both the goals and the people are important.
5. _____ The goals and the people are moderately important.
6. _____ Stay away from the issues and people in a conflict.
7. _____ Conflicts are problems to be solved.
8. _____ Conflicts should be avoided in favor of harmony.
9. _____ Sacrifice in part to find a common agreement.
10. _____ Win by attacking and overpowering.

B. What two major concerns should you consider when engaged in a conflict? Circle the answers.
1. Where and when to fight
2. The importance of the goals
3. The importance of the relationship
4. The importance of winning

Adapted from D. Johnson and Frank P. Johnson, *Joining Together*, 1982, p. 286.

Exercise 3: Case Study

Your wife complains that you are always busy with church work and have no time for her. Three days later, you both agree to go on a dinner date the following week, Thursday. Two other couples—friends of both of you—are invited to make an evening of it so that all three couples can spend a well-deserved evening together. You both discussed it again on Wednesday night before going to bed and are looking forward to it and expecting to have a great time together.

You call her from your vestry telling her how you love her and that you were looking forward to tonight. She sounds equally anticipatory. You take her to her favorite restaurant, and she orders her special dish. Everything seems to be working to schedule, and all three couples are talking and enjoying the evening.

An hour later, she requests to go home as she is having a severe headache. You say to her, "Every time we are having fun, you have a headache." She replies, "Just take me home, honey, and you can come back. I will be okay." You take her home and volunteer to support or help to make her comfortable. She tells you thanks and reports she is okay.

You then tell her you are leaving to return to the restaurant. Your wife asks where you are going and appears about ready to cry. She then says to you, "Are you leaving me alone?" You now remind her she said you could return after she got home.

Process: Each participant answers the following questions privately:
A.1. How do you think you would respond to this situation? What do you think would happen? Will you go or stay?
5. When did this conflict begin? At the dinner or a week ago, when the complaint was made? Or even before that?
6. What do you think is the problem, and what can you do to improve the situation?
7. Will your actions lead to avoidance, maintenance, escalation, or de-escalation?

8. How could active, reflective listening and confrontation help this situation or avoid a repetition? Was there one-way nonverbal communication going on for weeks (months) that was not recognized?

(Is the stage set for the twenty-fifth wedding anniversary or for the divorce court?)

B. As an entire group, get five teams (2) to role play the five modal choices of conflict management for this case (five minutes per choice).

Handout 1: Testing Mode

Source: Speed Leas, *A Layman's Guide to Conflict Management* **2** (Washington, DC: Alban Institute, 1979), pp. 2–4, 6.

Instructions

Choose a conflict "setting" in which you are sometimes or often in conflict. You should not attempt to think of yourself "in general" or in a variety of settings, but in one environment. A "setting" is an environment, or organization, or relationship that has significance for you as distinct from other settings or relationships. For example, a setting might be your relationship with your spouse as distinct from your relationship with your children; it might be your relationships with your coworkers or with your boss; it might be your relationships at church, or on a community board.

We have found people tend to get different scores as they think of themselves in each setting. So if you want to reflect on your conflict behavior at work, and you have filled out this instrument using your understanding of yourself at home, you'll need to do it a second time to discover whether you read yourself differently in the two environments.

It is not a good idea to choose one conflict that may have occurred in a setting. Rather, let yourself be reminded of several conflicts that may have occurred in that setting. Moreover, don't choose the worst conflicts that you may have experienced in this setting. Try to reflect on yourself in the usual and regular situations that you get into, as well as those which may have been particularly tough or easy.

Answer each question with a response that is as close as it can be to how you usually respond in this conflict setting. Each question contains a pair of statements describing possible behavior responses. For each pair, *circle the "A" or "B" statement which is most characteristic of your own behavior.*

In many cases, neither "A" nor "B" may be very typical of your behavior; nonetheless, please select the response that you would be more likely to make.

Instrument

1. A. Using logic, I try to convince the other of the value of my position.
   B. I use whatever authority I must convince the other of my position.

2. A. I let others take responsibility for solving the problem.
   B. I seek the other's help in working out a solution.

3. A. I try to find a compromise solution.
   B. I actively listen to the other.

4. A. I try to get my way.
   B. I will try to go along with what the other wants.

5. A. I don't let others abuse my rights.
   B. I show empathy about his/her plight.

6. A. I try to surface all his/her concerns.
   B. If I give up something, I expect the other to give up something.

7. A. I press my argument to get points made.
   B. I attempt to work on all concerns and issues in the open.

8. A. I assert my rights.
   B. I will give up some points in exchange for others.

9. A. I might try to soothe the other's feelings to preserve our relationship
   B. I encourage the other to act for himself/herself.

10. A. I tell him/her my ideas.
    B. I propose a middle ground.

11. A. I remind the other I am an authority on the subject we are dealing with.
    B. To keep the peace, I might sacrifice my own wishes for those of the other.

12. A. I invite the other to join with me to deal with the differences between us.
    B. I assume that giving advice creates dependence on me.

13. A. I try to show him/her the logic of my position.
    B. I usually repeat back or paraphrase what the other has said.

14. A. I use the constitution or policy icy manual as a backup for my position.

B. I encourage the other to stay with me in the conflict.

15. A. I try to do what is necessary to avoid useless tensions.
    B. If it makes the other happy, I might let him/her retain some of his/her views.

16. A. I subtly threaten our relationship if I don't get my way.
    B. I am firm in pursuing my argument.

17. A. I am concerned with satisfying all our wishes.
    B. I try to avoid unpleasantness for myself.

18. A. I don't try to persuade another about what should be done. I help him/her find his/her own way.
    B. I try to find a fair combination of gains and losses for both of us.

19. A. I try to postpone the issue until a later time.
    B. I try to show the logic and benefits of my position.

20. A. I am nonjudgmental about what the other says or does.
    B. I call in an authority who will support me.

21. A. I try to find an intermediate position.
    B. I usually seek the other's help in working out a solution

22. A. I tell the other about the problem so we can work it out.
    B. I propose solutions to our problems.

23. A. I usually ask for more than I expect to get.
    B. I offer rewards so the other will comply with my point of view.

24. A. I try not to give advice, only to help the other find his/her own way.
    B. Differences are not always worth worrying about.

25. A. I calculate about how to get as much as I can, knowing I won't get everything.
    B. I try to gain the other's trust to get him/her on my side.

26. A. I sometimes avoid taking positions that would create unpleasantness.
    B. I pout or withdraw when I don't get my way.

27. A. I help the other take care of his/her own problems.
    B. When someone avoids conflict with me, I invite him/her to work it out with me.

28. A. I try to put as little of myself forward as possible, attempting to utilize the strengths of the other.

___

B. I point out the faults in the other's arguments.

29. A. When someone threatens me, I assume we have a problem and invite him/her to work it out with me.

B. When I am right, I don't argue much; I just state my position and stand firm.

30. A. I will give in a little so everybody gets something he/she wants.

B. I try not to hurt the other's feelings.

31. A. I carefully prepare my case before joining the argument.

B. I admonish the other to do as I say.

32. A. I try to be considerate of the other's wishes.

B. If we are at a loss as to how to work an issue through, we ask for a third party.

33. A. To succeed, one needs to be flexible.

B. In a conflict, one should focus on fact-finding.

34. A. I evaluate the positives and negatives of the other's argument.

B. If the other's position is important to him/her, I would try to meet those wishes.

35. A. It is more important to be right than to be friendly.

B. I try to help the other feel courage and power to manage his/her own problems.

36. A. I assume that in a conflict, we will all be able to come out winners.

B. I assume conflict management is the art of attaining the possible.

37. A. When opposed, I can usually come up with a counter-argument.

B. I assume we can work a conflict through.

38. A. I clearly prescribe my goal and expectations.

B. In a conflict, everybody should come out with something though not everything that was expected.

39. A. I prefer to postpone unpleasant situations.

B. I support the other in trying to find his/her way.

40. A. I defend my ideas energetically.

B. I only share that which is helpful to my case.

41. A. I let others know whether my requirements are being met.

B. I try not to hurt the other feelings.

_____

42. A. I attempt to define our mutual problems jointly.
    B. I sympathize with the other's difficulties but don't take responsibility for them
43. A. I put together a logical argument.
    B. I express a lot of caring toward the other.
44. A. If it is important, I will put pressure on the other to get what is needed.
    B. I join with the other to gather data about our problem.
45. A. I assume relationships are more important than issues.
    B. I assume that each of us must give up something for the good of the whole.

Scoring the Conflict-Strategy Instrument

Circle the letters below which you circled on each item of the questionnaire.

	Persuade	Compel	Avoid/ Accommodate	Collaborate	Negotiate	Support
1.	A	B				
2.			A	B		
3.					A	B
4.	A		B			
5.		A				B
6.				A	B	
7.	A			B		
8.		A			B	
9.			A			B
10.	A				B	
11.		A	B			
12.				A		B
13.	A					B
14.		A		B		
15.			A		B	
16.	B	A				
17.			B	A		
18.					B	A

19. B		A			
20.	B				A
21.			B	A	
22. B			A		
23.	B			A	
24.		B			A
25. B				A	
26.	B	A			
27.			B		A
28. B					A
29.	B		A		
30.		B		A	
31. A	B				
32.		A	B		
33.				A	B
34. A		B			
35.	A				B
36.			A	B	
37. A			B		
38.	A			B	
39.		A			B
40. A				B	

41.	A	B			
42.			A		B
43. A					B
44.	A		B		
45.		A		B	

Total number of items circled in each column:

Source: Alan C. Filley, *Interpersonal Conflict Resolution* (Dallas, TX: Scott, Foresman, 1985), pp. 48–55.

Personal Styles of Conflict Resolution

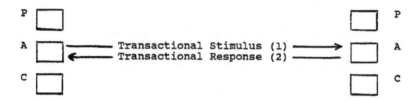

Handout 2

People learn behavior in different ways. Much learning occurs through trial and error as an individual discovers that one behavior leads to reward or pleasure and another behavior leads to punishment or pain. People also learn behavior by patterning themselves after models. One individual behaves like another because the other seems to have gained reward or satisfaction through a behavioral style. Still another method for learning calls for the individual to make a conscious choice regarding behavior. This process involves establishing possible alternative behaviors, determining the likely consequences of those behaviors, computing the odds that the costs or benefits associated with the different behaviors will take place, and selection of the best behavior.

The effect of these different methods of learning on supervisory training is illustrated in a study by Couch (1965), who compared incidents from which two groups of supervisors reported that they learned supervisory techniques. One group had a high degree of training related to supervisory practices; the other group had little or no training in such practices. Both groups, it should be pointed out, had the same degree of overall education. Couch's results indicated that both groups learned principally through personal experience. However, the well-trained group learned by reasoning processes and by observation, while the poorly trained group learned by trial and error. The well-trained group gained information from peers, subordinates, and superiors, while the poorly trained group often simply imitated the behavior of an immediate superior. Thus, supervisory training apparently gave the well-trained group the means to analyze information gained through their own experience.

Regardless of the source of learning, however, behavior eventually becomes fixed and resistant to change; once we are comfortable with a pattern of behavior, there are costs associated with changing a practiced and familiar style. A different style is unfamiliar, perhaps uncomfortable, and might lead to unpredictable outcomes. This chapter focuses on the patterns of behavior which individuals utilize for conflict resolution and provides a model for analyzing the consequences of different styles.[290] In a later chapter, we shall address the problem of changing one's pattern of behavior.

STYLES OF CONFLICT

As the axes in Figure 4-1 indicate, there are at least two major concerns in a conflict situation. One concern involves the extent to which an individual wish to meet his own personal goals. In the present discussion we shall take *goals* to mean either *means* or *ends*, since a person may see his goal as that of doing the task the way he wants to do it or of accomplishing an end which he personally values. Another concern is the extent to which an individual wants to maintain a relationship with another individual or group and to be accepted by that individual or group. For the sake of convenience, in Figure 4-1 concern for personal goals is scaled from 1 to 9, representing the increasing degree of importance in the mind of the individual; similarly, concern for relationships is scaled from 1 (low concern) to 9 (high concern). Given this scaling, we may identify the following approximate types or styles: High concern for personal goals and low concern for relationships (9, 1); low concern for personal goals and high concern for relationships (1, 9); low concern for personal goals and low con-

FIGURE 4-1. A Model of Conflict Management Styles. Special permission for reproduction of the material below is granted by the author, Jay Hall, Ph.D., and publisher. Teleometrics International. All rights reserved and no reproductions should be made without express approval of Teleometrics International.

---

290 This chapter is based on Robert R. Blake and Jane S. Mouton's "The Fifth Achievement," *The Journal of Applied Behavioral Science*, Vol. 6, No. 4, 1970, pp. 413–26; and Jay Hall's *Conflict Management Survey*, Houston, Texas: Teleometrics, 1969.

Differences only serve to drive people apart; their "personal" implications cannot be ignored. Realistically, to differ is to reject. Maximum attention to the needs and desires of others is required if relationships are to endure. Conflict requires self-sacrifice and placing the importance of continued relationships above one's own goals. It is better to ignore differences than to risk open combat by being oversensitive; one must guard against causing irreparable damage to his relationships.

Differences are a natural part of the human condition. In and of themselves, they are neither good nor bad. Conflict is usually a symptom of tensions in relationships, and should be treated accordingly. When accurately interpreted, they may be resolved and serve to strengthen relationships, rather than to divide. Conflict requires confrontation and objective problem-solving, often of a type that goes beyond the apparent needs and opinions of the parties involved. Not only are people brought more closely together when conflicts are worked through, but creativity may be achieved.

Differences should be treated in the light of the common good. At times some parties are obliged to lay aside their own views in the interest of the majority; this allows the relationship to continue to function, however imperfectly, and affords a basis for redress later. Everyone should have an opportunity to air his views and feelings, but these should not be allowed to block progress. It is never possible for everyone to be satisfied and those who insist on such an unrealistic goal should be shown the error of their way. Resolution requires a good deal of skill and persuasive ability coupled with flexibility.

1/1	9/1
Differences simply reflect the more basic attributes which distinguish among people: past experiences, irrational needs, innate limitations and potentials and levels of personal aspirations. As such, they are essentially beyond the influence of others. They constitute necessary evils in human affairs, and one must either accept them or withdraw from human contacts. Impersonal tolerance is the most enlightened approach to handling conflicts.	Differences are to be expected among people for they reflect the nature of the species: some have skills and others have none, and some are right and some are wrong. Ultimately right prevails, and this is the central issue in conflict. One owes it to himself and those who rely on his judgment to prevail in conflicts with others whose opinions and goals are in doubt. Persuasion, power, and force are all acceptable tools for achieving conflict resolution; and most people expect them to be employed.

Concern for Personal Goals

cern for relationships (1,1); moderate concern for personal goals and moderate concern for relationships (5,5); and high concern for personal goals and high concern for relationships (9,9). Let us consider each style.

The (9, 1) win-lose style—"the tough battler"

One who seeks to meet his own goals at all costs, without concern for the needs or the acceptance of others, engages in tough battles. For such an individual, winning or losing is not merely an event; instead, he views losing as reduced status, weakness, and the loss of his self-image. On the other hand, to win gives the (9, 1) person a sense of exhilaration and achievement. There is no doubt in his mind that he is right; he stands by his convictions and defends his position, expressing anger and frustration when others do not accede to him. He feels that if there is a winner there must be a loser and that he must be the winner, whatever the cost. The (9, 1) person is quite willing to sacrifice individuals in a group if they refuse to go along with his desires. For him, conflict is a nuisance which occurs only because others do not see the correctness of his own position. He

———

demonstrates to those with whom he disagrees that they are wrong with facts that support his own position.

The (1, 9) yield-lose style—"the friendly helper"

This type of person overvalues maintenance of relationships with others and undervalues achievement of his own goals. He desires acceptance by others and gives in to their desires where they conflict with his own. He is the kind of person who might say, "Well, yes, there are some things I would like to have accomplished, but it's OK, I don't want to make trouble." He feels differences can't be discussed or confronted to any extent without someone getting hurt in the process. Conflict, he feels, grows out of the self-centeredness of individuals and should be avoided in favor of harmony. He seems to feel that anger is bad and that confrontation is destructive; he may try to redirect potential conflict by breaking the tension with humor or suggesting some non-conflictive activity. Mutuality of interests and harmony of relationships are paramount in his approach.

The (1, 1) lose-leave style

The person using this style sees conflict as a hopeless, useless, and punishing experience. Rather than undergo the tension and frustration of conflict, the person using the (1, 1) style simply removes himself either mentally or physically. Encounters with others are kept as impersonal as possible, and in case of disagreement, the (1, 1) person will withdraw. He will comply to avoid disagreement and tension, will feel little commitment to the decision reached, and will not openly take sides in a disagreement among others.

The (5, 5) compromise style

The basis of this approach is that half a loaf is better than none. One using this style seeks to find a position which allows each side to gain something. The (5, 5) person enjoys the maneuvering required to resolve conflict and will actively seek to find some strong middle ground between two extreme positions. He may vacillate between expressing anger and

---

then trying to smooth things over and may seek to use voting or rules as a way of avoiding direct confrontation on the issues. If he is confronted with a serious disagreement, he will suggest some mechanism for finding a "workable" solution (such as voting or trading) rather than working out the disagreement to find the best solution.

The (9, 9) integrative style—"the problem solver"

The individual employing the (9, 9) style actively seeks to satisfy his own goals as well as the goals of others. The (9, 9) person does not see the two sets of objectives as mutually exclusive and feels that no one's goals need be sacrificed if the appropriate conflict resolution is achieved. The (9, 9) person (1) sees conflict as natural and helpful, even leading to a more creative solution if handled properly; (2) evidences trust and candidness with others and recognizes the legitimacy of feelings in arriving at decisions; (3) feels that the attitudes and positions of everyone need to be aired and recognizes that when conflict is resolved to the satisfaction of all, commitment to the solution is likely; (4) sees everyone as having an equal role in resolving the conflict, views the opinions of everyone as equally legitimate; and (5) does not sacrifice anyone simply for the good of the group.

RELATIONSHIP OF CONFLICT STYLES AND OTHER RESEARCH

As just described, Hall (1969) has identified five different behavior styles. Of these five, we shall consider the three—which research describes in more detail. They are: (1) the "tough battler," who seeks his own goals and is willing to sacrifice the goals of others; (2) the "friendly helper," who gives in to the goals of others even at the cost of his own desires; and (3) the "problem solver," who seeks to find an outcome that meets both his goals and the goals of others.

Bargaining styles like these three have recently been investigated by Cummings and his associates (Cummings et al., 1971; Harnett et al., 1973). They adapted a scale developed to measure personality and attitudes in experimental bargaining situations originated by Shure and Meeker (1965) and correlated the three bargaining styles with four dimensions from the Shure-Meeker questionnaire (Cummings et al., 1972). The personality dimensions in the questionnaire are as follows:

1) Conciliation versus belligerence in interpersonal relations. Conciliators advocate responding to the needy or less fortunate with understanding, help, and friendliness. They admit their own wrongs and are not motivated by revenge.
2) Risk avoidance versus risk taking. Risk avoiders are on adventurous, have a low activity level, and will not expose themselves to dangers or hazardous risks.
3) External versus internal control. Externally controlled persons believe that events are controlled by external forces over which they have no control; that is, by fate or chance
4) Suspiciousness versus trust. Suspicious persons are characterized by quasi-paranoid traits of selfishness, projection of hostility, excitability, tenseness, and the lack of trust.

By combining these personality dimensions with various forms of bargaining behavior, we can present a typology of such behaviors and the personality correlates of each. Cummings and his associates identified three types of bargainers, the "tough bargainer," the "soft bargainer," and the "equalizer." For our purposes, the "tough bargainer" is equivalent to what we have called the "tough battler" (9, 1); the "soft bargainer" is our "friendly helper" (1, 9); and the "equalizer" is our "problem solver" (9, 9). These three bargaining styles, it will be noted, also exhibit similarities to the Parent, Adult, and Child behaviors described in Chapter 3.

Cummings and his associates found that "tough bargainers" were high in internal control, risk taking, and belligerence. The style is unrelated to measures of trust or suspiciousness. The relationships are quite consistent with those posited for the win-lose battlers, since they believe strongly in their own rightness and will do almost anything to avoid losing the battle and destroying their egos.

The win-lose battling style is also consistent with the "Parent" behavior of the transactional analysis model proposed by Eric Berne (1961). The Parent is normative, controlling, and judgmental in his statements and behavior. Like the win-lose battler, he makes sharp distinctions between right and wrong and is unconcerned with the gray area between the two extremes. The Parent thinks in terms of fixed rules and values and will probably elicit either Parent behavior (counter-dependence) or Child behavior (dependence) from those with whom he or she interacts.

The second style to be considered is the helping or yielding approach. The soft bargainer actively seeks acceptance and affiliation with others and maintains relationships by yielding to the demands or goals of others, since he feels that interpersonal relations are too fragile to withstand direct confrontations on differences. Such a person complies with the wishes of others at the cost of personal goals.

The Cummings data indicate that the soft bargainer is high in external control, low in risk taking, and high in trust. The style is unrelated to conciliation or belligerence. Thus, the soft bargainer might be expected to give in to the demands of others and to avoid the risks of damaging interpersonal relationships. Trust and optimism may help to make this dependent position more tenable.

The soft style reminds us of the "Child" behavior in the transactional analysis model. The Child is subordinate, dependent, and characterized by emotionalism and fantasy. This orientation is certainly antithetical to conflict resolution based on mutual understanding of facts and mutual respect for the needs of others.

The third style to be considered is that of the problem solver, which Hall calls "the dominant style for conflict management." The problem solver believes that his goals and the goals of others are not mutually exclusive and seeks to maintain the relationship and to meet his own goals by searching for solutions which are mutually acceptable. He believes that more can be achieved with two parties working together than when a single party dominates and acknowledges the reality of facts and feelings as a necessary ingredient for the resolution of conflict. He deals with others in a trusting, open, and candid way.

There is a problem-solving style, identified by Cummings as that of the "equalizer," which is fact oriented rather than defeat-oriented and which seeks a fair outcome for both parties. The equalizer is found to be high in internal control, high in trusting behavior, high in conciliation, and unrelated to the measure of risk taking. Other research (Zend, 1972) has shown that trusting behavior is displayed when one does not avoid stating facts, ideas, or feelings that might make him vulnerable to others. One exhibiting trusting behavior does not resist or deflect attempts of others to exert control over him and is responsive to their suggestions. That is, he can work interdependently with others rather than seeking to dominate or to control.

The problem solver is explicitly associated with the "Adult" style in the transactional analysis model. The Adult deals with facts and reality, does not dominate or impose arbitrary rules as does the Parent, and is not involved in fantasy as is the Child. The Adult deals with a problem descriptively and concentrate on giving and receiving information. There is no automatic right or wrong or good or bad but, rather, a need to solve problems objectively.

How to Make Good Decisions and Introduce Changes

A. Session 1 (2 Hours)
    Focus, Facilitator's Goals, Pastors' Terminal Objectives
    Exercise 1 and 2 (Individual and Group Work)
        Power: Overview
    Handout 1: Discussion
        Decision-Making
        Methods of Decision-Making
        Handout 2: Discussion
        Handout 3: Discussion
        Characteristics of Effective and Ineffective Decision-Making
        Obstacles to Effective Decisions
    Exercise 3: To Be Handed Out
        What Is a Good Decision?
    Exercise 4
        Quality of Decision
        Criteria for Choosing a Method
    Break

B. Session 2 (1 Hour)
    Exercise to Review Exercise 1
    Collaborative Problem-Solving Method
    Brainstorming
    Handout 4
        What Goes Wrong with Decision-Making?
        When the Process Fails
    Exercise 5
        Introducing Change
        How to Promote New Ideas and Change for Adoption: Some
        Principles
    Review: Transparency and Rediagnosis

How to Make Good Decisions and Introduce Changes

Focus

Change and decision-making processes can influence the conflict process and conflict management.

Facilitator's Goals

1. The goals of this learning module include the following:
1. To identify certain concepts associated with power and authority as they may influence the conflict process
2. To help pastors become more acquainted with principles and types of decision making and some of their potential consequences
3. To help pastors become more acquainted with proven principles of introducing and selling change
4. To help pastors recognize trouble and to deal with it efficiently
5. To help pastors recognize some obstacles and characteristics of effective decision-making.

Pastors' Terminal Objectives

Upon the completion of this learning module, the pastors will be able to

1. identify some aspects of good decision-making,
2. identify various sources of decision-making,
3. select right criteria for selecting appropriate decision-making methods,
4. recognize some pitfalls causing failure in the collaborative problem-solving method,
5. identify five to seven steps to effective problem-solving, and
6. recognize the various sources and bases of power at work in their interpersonal relationships.

Power: Overview

Power, as the ability to influence, has often proven a source of conflict even in the church. Four areas where power contributes to conflict-creating situations include (1) the abuse of power, (2) the assignment of power, (3) the assumption of power, and (4) the absence of power.

- *Abuse of power.* Conflicts arise whenever there is an abuse of relationships and responsibilities. Power is sometimes preserved by domination by the status quo and by withholding of information.
- *Assignment of power.* Because authority is often carelessly assigned, the result is often excessive power, ambiguous power, and exclusive power.
  - Excessive power—too much responsibility, too many positions to one person.
  - Ambiguous power—not clearly defined authority in the position; little or no job description.
  - Exclusive power—power that does not pursue reconciliation and is generally fear motivated.
- *Assumption of power.* This creates clash of power. It assumes authority and position and must be challenged, lovingly.
- *Absence of power.* Vacations, resignations, attending meetings and conferences can leave the church without effective leadership and in chaos and conflict. Indifference about responsibility can lead to absence of power. The effective use of power involves restraint to ensure its continuity.

The sources of power are where you get power. The basis of power is what you manipulate.

Where do I get power?	What tools do I have to influence others?
Sources:	Bases:
Position	Coercion
Personal characteristics	Reward
Expertise	Persuasion
Opportunity to control information	Knowledge

Coercive power is the ability to deprive or punish for noncompliance with demand and depends on fear.

Reward power is the ability to reward, that is, to give desired rewards in return for compliance.

Persuasive power is the ability to allocate or manipulate symbolic rewards, e.g., to give awards or to highlight the favorable behavior of a member to a deviant member.

Knowledge, or access to information, is the final base of power, e.g., being on Conference committee or able to take advantage of a situation because of one's closeness to that situation.

Position power is due to structural or organizational status.

Personal power is based on personality traits and charisma. It is sometimes called referent power.

Expert power is the ability to control specialized information and is a powerful source of influence.

Opportunity power is to be in the right place at the right time (so you have been able to accept a call). With this overview, it can be safely observed: power can be used to influence decision-making.

*Handout/Review—to be discussed.

Decision-Making

Church problems come in three categories and demonstrate correlated relationships.

1. The outcome problem: What outcome (future condition) do you see as important to bring to pass?
2. The blockage problem: What blockage will you address as the main thing preventing that desired from happening?
3. The action problem: What action will you take to change the blockage situation so that the desired outcome can be achieved?

These three problems correlate with three types of problem solvers.

1. *Idealists* focus on the outcome problems. They are good at stretching out a vision of how the future should be, but they tend to lose interest in the means of achieving it.
2. *Observers* focus on the blockage problems. They understand well why things are the way they are, but they are reluctant to define a desired outcome and take responsibility for bringing it about.

3. *Doers* focus on action problems. They want to get busy with the action and are impatient with discussions of outcomes and blockages.

Methods of Decision-Making

1. The member with the most authority, without a group discussion.
2. The member with the most expertise, without a group discussion.
3. Averaging the opinion of individual group members, without a group discussion.
4. The member with the most authority, following a group discussion.
5. A minority of group membership, without the consultation of the entire group.
6. A majority vote following a group discussion.
7. Consensus or agreement of the entire group following a group discussion.

Reaction to decisions are affected by who makes them, as well as by what the decisions are and the process.

Generally, the pastor should take into consideration more than just the effective solution choice to a problem. The following questions should be considered:

1. Does the solution violate biblical truth or principle?
2. Does this solution meet the needs of those affected?
3. Will people support the implementation of this solution?
4. Will this solution create other problems?
5. Will this solution help avoid problems in the future?
6. Why should this solution be selected over the others?

Handout 2: Advantages and Disadvantages of the Decision-Making Process

Decision by Consensus

In consensus, all members understand the decision and are prepared to support it. Although consensus implies unanimity, it is not dependent on it since the process allows members to have enough time to state their views and their opposition to other members' views. Group members must listen carefully and communicate effectively. In reaching consensus, group members need to see differences of opinion as a way of (1) gathering additional information, (2) clarifying issues, and (3) forcing the group to seek better alternatives.

Basic Guidelines for Consensual Decision-Making
1. Avoid arguing blindly for your own opinions.
2. Avoid changing your mind only to reach agreement and avoid conflict.
3. Avoid conflict-reducing procedures such as majority voting, tossing a coin, averaging, and bargaining.
4. Seek out differences of opinion. They are natural and expected. Try to involve everyone in the decision process.
5. Do not assume that someone must win and someone must lose when discussion reaches a stalemate.
6. Discuss underlying assumptions, listen carefully to one another, and encourage the participation of all members.

Handout 3: Suggestions for Arriving at Consensus
Characteristics of Effective and Ineffective Decision-Making
Most decisions that affect people are made by small groups and the effectiveness of the decision may depend upon how effective the group is. Five major characteristics of an effective decision are as follows:
1. The resources of group members are fully utilized.
2. Time is well spent.
3. The decision is correct or of high quality.
4. The decision is implemented fully by all the required group members.
5. The problem-solving ability of the group is enhanced or at least not lessened.

A decision is effective to the extent that these five criteria are met; if all five are not met, the decision has not been made effectively.

Remember, three modes of resolution to post-decisional conflict exist. One mode is undoing or reversing a decision. Another mode, at the opposite pole from undoing, is reaffirming the decision, with full implementation. A third mode, intermediate between the first two, is that of curtailing implementation so that partial adherence is combined with partial reversal.

Obstacles to Effective Decisions
1. Fear of consequences
2. Conflicts and cliques in the congregation
3. Inadequate and fixed leadership styles
4. Too little knowledge about the effects of inappropriate decisions on the climate of the group
5. Inappropriate transfer of parliamentary procedures to the church (a congregation of volunteers)

Exercise 3: Personal Reflections (Some Observations)
What Is a Good Decision?
1. Inspires initial confidence.
2. You based your decision on an adequate amount of information.
3. The decision was clearly necessary and directed to the *real* issue.
4. It coincides with what you believe the Bible teaches and with your overriding priority to worship God and serve him.
5. The decision will better accomplish the goals than the other options.
6. It is a well-balanced decision (without major risks), and it will not create additional problems.
7. You can support it objectively and defend it logically.
8. You are confident it will be implemented by those on whom its success depends.

Exercise 4: Cash Register Worksheet
Quality of Decision
Studies have shown that decisions made by many persons are generally superior to an individual decision. The reasons are given as follows:
1. A person working around other people acts somewhat differently than he would if he were working at the same task alone.
2. Group interaction pools the resources of the group.
3. An expert is likely to be in a group.
4. Mistakes are likely to be cancelled out by other members.
5. Blind spots are often corrected in a group.
6. Group discussion often stimulates ideas.
7. Groups offer more security in risk-taking than in individual decision-making.

Right Criteria of Method

Each method has uses, limitations, and consequences, and each can be desirable under certain circumstances. Each method of decision-making should be based on the following:

1. The type of decision to be made
2. The amount of time and resources available
3. The history of the group
4. The nature of the task being worked on
5. The kind of climate the group wishes to establish
6. The type of setting in which the group is working

Break

Exercise to Review Exercise 1

Problem-solving and decision-making are two sides of a coin and sometimes are used as synonyms.

Collaborative Problem-Solving Method
1. Define the problem in terms of needs, not as solutions.
2. Brainstorm possible solutions.
3. Select the solution that will best meet both parties' needs (after having checked out possible consequences).
4. *Plan who will do what, where, and by when. (Very important.)
5. Implement the solutions.
6. Evaluate how you worked the problem-solving process and, later, how well the solution turned out.

Brainstorming is the listing of potential solutions or ideas without clarification, fine-tuning, or evaluation with interest being on quantity, not quality.

Guidelines: Don't evaluate

Don't clarify or seek clarification

Go for every idea

Expand on each other's ideas

List every idea

Avoid attaching people's names to the ideas they suggest or listing each person's contribution separately.

Solution rigidity should be avoided.

*Handout 4: Decision-Making Rationale and Aid
What Goes Wrong with Decision-Making?

Four basic coping patterns can appear when people are faced with challenges that require decisions:
1. Active cooperative strategy in search of answers
2. Complacency (nonresponse)
3. Defensive avoidance

Rationalization—"It can't happen to me."
Procrastination—"I can take care of it later."
Buck passing—"Let George do it."
4. Panic

When the Process Fails
Even with the best of intentions, something will fall apart. However, be sure to follow certain guidelines to reduce failure.
- Avoid the traps in the process.
- Handle emotions first.
- Define the problem properly.
- Don't evaluate or clarify during brainstorming.
- Work out the nitty-gritty details.
- Follow up to see that action steps are carried out.
- Smoke out hidden agendas.
- Recycle the process (in case of stalemate).

Exercise 5: Change Reflection

Introducing Change
Introducing and dealing with change is among the most common of pastoral problems. Pastors need to interest themselves not only with the technical aspects of a change but also to consider the *human relations* problems that a change can generate. Often people resist change because it may hurt them economically, psychologically, socially, and morally. Prestige and self-esteem may also be involved in defensive reaction to change introduction.

Seemingly, irrational attitudes and behavior are symptoms of deeper problems, and these problems must be brought to the surface if they are not to undermine the change. Real problems must be brought out into the open, and pastors must level with members. The objective of leveling is to provide members with complete background information that leads to change, share the details of the change, and establish two-way communication rather than attempt a one-way sale of the change. Elicit questions, concerns, objectives, and suggestions for implementing the change. It is always advisable to be sensitive to the self-esteem issues that typically surround change.

How to Promote New Ideas and Change for Adoption: Some Principles
1. Be aware of the acceptance stages.
   a) *Awareness*—Knowledgeable but not interested.
   b) *Interest*—Wants to know who, where, what, how.
   c) *Evaluation*—What are the benefits for me? Can I do it?
      i) To get a benefit I don't have.
      ii) To protect a benefit I have.
      iii) To replace a benefit I lost.
      iv) Don't be general in listing benefits—be specific.
   d) *Trial* (Expect opposition here)
      i) I'm sold on the benefits.
      ii) There will be reasons why he can't.
      iii) Emphasize the positive.
      iv) Ignore the negative.
      v) Stress as leader that you will help.
      vi) Be sure to follow through with support at this stage.
   e) *Adoption*—The more complex the change, the more difficult to make the change. Four types of changes may occur:
      i) Equipment and material
      ii) Improved practice
      iii) Innovation
      iv) Enterprise level (expertise success)
2. Understand differences among individuals.
   a) Innovators—7 percent of the average group
      i) They like seminars and conventions.
      ii) They like looking for new ideas.
      iii) They feel secure.
   b) Early Adopters—15 percent
      i) They are in the leadership position.
      ii) They are generally below forty-five years old.
      iii) They have more formal education.
      iv) They trust the establishment.
      v) They latch on to new ideas with minimum investigation.
      vi) They are willing to participate in training sessions.
   c) Early Majority—30 percent
      i) Above average in age, education, and experience.
      ii) They tend to wait until idea is proved before adopting.
      iii) They are not opposed to change.

---

iv) They are not risk oriented.

v) They fear failure.

vi) Some hold leadership positions.

vii) Others are informal leaders.

viii) Generally, they are quite active.

d) Majority—25 to 30 percent

i) They are irregular in participation.

ii) They do not hold key leadership posts.

iii) Their needs are generally met outside the community of believers.

e) Nonadopters—10 percent

i) They never accept new ideas.

ii) They are inactive.

iii) They are suspicious of change.

iv) They do not participate in decision-making.

3. Develop strategy for change.

a) State your objectives specifically.

i) Make them realistic.

ii) Make them reachable.

iii) Make them measurable.

b) Identify the features and benefits of the idea.

c) Analyze the positive and negative forces.

d) Plan actions to relate to the adoption process and individual differences.

e) Check up on your effectiveness.

f) Be willing to modify.

Introducing Change

1. Be prepared for some serious questions, even opposition to any new ideas.

a. Opposition.

b. Not a bad idea but wrong timing.

c. Right time—won't work.

d. I was always in favor of this idea.

2. Provide short historical background that shows need for project then show what is being suggested relates to the need.

3. Present both sides of the picture.

4. Give strongest arguments last.
5. Check reasons for opposition.

Behavior in the Midst of Conflict and Change
1. Win at all cost
2. Withdrawal
3. Compromise
4. Yielding
5. Resolving in constructive ways (*listen*)

Pastors need to
- know what the institution (or person) is all about (philosophy);
- know its line chart, its table of organization; and
- know the formal and informal structure and use it.

Summary and Feedback

Review (Include Transparencies T-6, T-7)

Resource Material

Deutsch, Morton. *The Resolution of Conflict*. New Haven: Yale University, 1973.

Filley, Alan C. *Interpersonal Conflict Resolution*. Glenview, IL: Scott, Foresman, 1975.

Johnson, David W., and Frank P. Johnson. *Joining Together*. Englewood Cliffs, NJ: Prentice-Hall, 1982, 1975.

Lindgren, Alvin J., and Norman Shewchuk. *Let My People Go*. Nashville, TN: Abingdon, 1980.

Lueckle, David. "Problem-Solving in the Church." Pasadena, CA: Charles E. Fuller Institute of Evangelism and Church Growth, 1982.

Robbins, Stephen P. *Essentials of Organizational Behavior*. Englewood Cliffs, NJ: Prentice-Hall, 1984.

Rush, Myron. *Management: A Biblical Approach*. Wheaton, IL: Victor Books, 1984.

Wheeler, Daniel D., and Irving L. Janis. *A Practical Guide for Making Decisions*. New York: The Free Press, 1980.

———

Decision-Making and Power Survey

Circle T if it is true, and F if it is false.

T   F   The more people involved in decision-making, the longer it takes to reach a decision.

T   F   The fewer people involved in decision-making, the higher the quality of the decision.

T   F   For decisions to be made effectively, the group members should have highly developed interpersonal and group skills.

T   F   Groups should be solution rather than problem oriented.

T   F   The credibility of a communicator depends on his/her perceived expertise and reliability.

T   F   Forewarning receivers of an intention to convert them decreases their resistance to the message.

T   F   Basically, power is bad and should not be used.

T   F   The successful use of power can end a conflict.

T   F   A central strategy to resolve a conflict is to establish mutual influence in the group.

T   F   The use of coercive power lessens the conflict.

Match the following decision-making methods with their definitions.

_____	1 Consensus . . .	a)	Leader makes decision
_____	2 Majority vote . . .	b)	Everyone must agree
_____	3 Minority vote . . .	c)	At least 51 percent of the members must agree
_____	4 Averaging . . .	d)	Leader makes decision after listening to group
_____	5 Expert . . .	e)	The one who knows the most makes the decision

	6	Authority with discussion . . .	f)	Leader polls members; decision is the most popular response.
	7	Authority without discussion . . .	g)	A small subgroup makes the decision.

Adopted from David W. Johnson and Frank P. Johnson, *Joining Together* (Englewood Cliffs, NJ: Prentice-Hall, 1982, 1975).

Exercise 2: Power Review

"He is a powerful pastor."

Questions:

What do you understand by this statement?

What is power? What makes him powerful?

What personal characteristic(s) of the pastor makes him powerful?

Process:

1. Using the flip board or chalkboard, list the answers.
2. Categorize answers with help of the group under what may be considered bases of power.
3. Use this exercise to introduce presentation on *power*.

Exercise 3.1: Personal Reflection

Reflect on your usual mode of making decisions by circling the appropriate word.

Fast	slow
feeling	factual
intuitive	impulsive
calculated	spontaneous
relaxed	anxious
thinking-oriented	action-oriented
indifferent	overly concerned
self-sufficient	dependent on others
procrastinate/delay	eager/initiative

Exercise 3.2: Value Decisions

Which of the following kinds of decisions are most difficult for you to make?

1. Disciplining of children
2. How and where to spend money
3. Relationship with in-laws

4. Religious or church involvements
5. Planning vacations or how to spend leisure time

How does Exercise 3.1 influence your answers in Exercise 3.2?
Process for Both Exercises 3.1 and 3.2:
1. Allow five minutes for private quiet reflection.
2. Question the group to see whether their decision-making process focus was on outcome problems, blockage problems, or action problems.

Cash Register Worksheet[291]

The Story

A businessman had just turned off the lights in the store when a man appeared and demanded money. The owner opened a cash register. The contents of the cash register were scooped up, and the man speed away. A member of the police force was notified promptly.

Statements about the Story

1. A man appeared after the owner had turned off his store lights. T F ?

2. The robber was a man. T F ?

3. The man did not demand money. T F ?

4. The man who opened the cash register was the owner. T F ?

5. The store owner scooped up the contents of the cash register and ran away. T F ?

6. Someone opened a cash register. T F ?

7. After the man who demanded the money scooped up the contents of the cash register, he ran away. T F ?

8. While the cash register contained money, the story does not state how much. T F ?

9. The robber demanded money of the owner. T F ?

10. The story concerns a series of events in which only three persons are referred to: the owner of the store, a man who demanded money, and a member of the police force. T F ?

11. The following events in the story are true: someone demanded money, a cash register was opened, its contents were scooped up, and a man dashed out of the store. T F ?

---

291 Adopted from J. William Pfeiffer and John E. Jones, *A Handbook of Structural Experiences for Human Relations Training*, vol. V (La Jolla, CA: University Associates Press, 1970), p. 12.

Cash Register Worksheet
Group Decision-Making
Goals:

A. To demonstrate how decision-making is improved by consensus seeking.

II. To explore the impact that assumptions have on decision-making.

III. To compare the results of individual decision-making with decisions made by groups.

Group Size: 5–7
Time Required: Approximately thirty minutes.
Process:

B. Give each participant a copy of the Cash Register Worksheet. Allow five minutes to read "The Story" paragraph and then to indicate whether each of the "Statements about the Story" is true, false, or unknown (indicated by a question mark).

II. Form groups of five to seven members each. Give each group one copy of the Cash Register Worksheet and indicate that each group has approximately ten minutes to reach consensus on whether each statement is true, false, or unknown.

III. Announce the correct answers. (Statement 3 is false, statement 6 is true, and all other statements are unknown).

IV. Have a discussion on the exercise, eliciting comments about making assumptions and about the values of group decision-making versus individual decision-making.

NB V.   Each participant writes down two implications of this experience to real-life ministry.

— How does assumptions affect visitation, evangelism, goal setting, church discipline, and planning?

— How does it feel to give up points of views?

Optional Exercise: Problem-Solving
1. Think of a problem in your conference.
2. Suppose you have been told to solve this problem.

3. Write out six to ten steps that you would probably take in trying to deal with this problem.
4. Check whether your list agrees with the format for problem-solving to be presented.

Exercise 5.1

C. By yourself.

Reflect on some *change* you introduced and recall what made it successful. What words describe that experience?

> D. Think of some *change* that was introduced into your church, business, or school, and it had bad results. Relive that episode. What *words* describe that experience? (15 minutes)

Exercise 5.2

E. Group in full.

Identify the words identified in numbers 1 and 2. Identify which were positive or negative.

4. Identify what could have been done.
5. Try to develop (together) a step arrangement for introducing changes, based on number 4 (15 minutes).

Power Currencies

Several kinds of power exist. The eight currencies of power listed below have been identified by Lasswell and Kaplan (*Power and Society*, Yale Univ. Press, 1968) as universal. They maintain that the *real* currencies of power are the *real* values of persons and systems. You probably deal in several of these currencies every day.

Power Currencies

Power Currencies	Description
Wealth:	Control of money, property, budgets. You may give, share, bargain with, or deny to others these elements of wealth-power. Others may do the same to you.
Respect:	Status, honor, recognition, and prestige that may come from accomplishing goals, your own or society's. Respect may be awarded to others or denied to others. Self-respect comes from achieving your own self-interests.
Information:	Ability to gather, analyze, share, or distort and withhold information. This includes controlling the introduction of new ideas. Information-power is the power of the press and a form of power most used by clergy.
Rectitude:	Often called rectitude power, this includes the ability to appeal to others, confer on others, or deny righteousness, goodness, and virtue. Clergy trade on their own rectitude power and appeal to others to act in a righteous manner.

Affection:	Power to create a climate of caring, kindness, giving affection, friendship, neighborliness—all the things that go into loving relationships and reconciliation. Of course, you can also withhold and undermine these.
Influence:	Capitalizing on friendships, other people's feelings of indebtedness to you, leverage of some sort that enables you to affect the behavior of others. Other people attempt to use their influence-power on you too.
Skills:	Proficiency in your profession: in counseling, preaching, teaching, empowering others, planning, problem-solving, collaborative decision-making, social change, interpretation, listening, group work, etc. Most clergy have their skill-power as their greatest and most attractive currency of power, which often leads to increased income (wealth-power) and recognition (respect-power).
Well-Being:	Sense of security, safety, knowing the rules and living within them, expecting others also to live within them (law and order), health of mind, body, and spirit, an inner sense of spiritual certainty about one's own life and the future, including after death.

Advantages and Disadvantages of Decision-Making Methods

Method of Decision-Making	Disadvantages	Advantages
1. Decision by authority without discussion	One person is not a good resource for every decision; advantages of group interaction are lost; no commitment to implementing the decision is developed among other group members; resentment and disagreement may result in sabotage and deterioration of group effectiveness; resources of other members are not used	Applies more to administrative needs; useful for simple, routine decisions; should be used when very little time is available to make the decision, when group members expect the designated leader to make the decision, and when group members lack the skills and information to make the decision any other way.
2. Expert member	It is difficult to determine who the expert is; no commitment to implement the decision is built; advantages of group interaction are lost; resentment and disagreement may result in sabotage and deterioration of group effectiveness; resources of other members are not used.	Useful when the expertise of one person is so far superior to that of all other group members that little is to be gained by discussion; should be used when the need for membership action in implementing the decision is slight.

3.	Average of members' opinions	There is not enough interaction among group members for them to gain from each other's resources and from the benefits of group discussion; no commitment to implement the decision is built; unresolved conflict and controversy may damage group effectiveness in the future.	Useful when it is difficult to get group members together to talk, when the decision is so urgent that there is no time for group discussion, when member commitment is not necessary for implementing the decision, and when group members lack the skills and information to make the decision any other way; applicable to simple, routine decisions.
4.	Decision by authority after discussion	Does not develop commitment to implement the decision; does not resolve the controversies and conflicts among group members; tends to create situations in which group members either compete to impress the designated leader or tell the leader what they think he or she wants to hear.	Uses the resources of the group members' more than previous methods; gains some of the benefits of group discussion.

5. Majority control	Usually leaves an alienated minority, which damages future group effectiveness; relevant resources of many group members may be lost; full commitment to implement the decision is absent; full benefit of group interaction is not obtained.	Can be used when enough time is lacking for decision by consensus or when the decision is not so important that consensus needs to be used, and when complete member commitment is not necessary for implementing the decision; closes discussion on issues that are not highly important for the group.
6. Minority control	Does not utilize the resources of many group members; does not establish widespread commitment to implement the decision; unresolved conflict and controversy may damage future group effectiveness; not much benefit from group interaction.	Can be used when everyone cannot meet to decide, when the group is under such time pressure that it must delegate responsibility to a committee, when only a few members have any relevant resources, and when broad member commitment is not needed to implement the decision; useful for simple, routine decisions.

7. Consensus	Takes a great deal of time and psychological energy and a high level of member skill; time pressure must be minimal, and there must be no emergency in progress.	Produces an innovative, creative, and high-quality decision; elicits commitment by all members to implement the decision; uses the resources of all members; the future decision-making ability of the group is enhanced; useful in making serious, important, and complex decisions to which all members are to be committed.

Source: David W. Johnson and Frank P. Johnson, *Joining Together* (1982), pp. 108–109.

===

Suggestions for Arriving at a Consensus

Since in a consensus, one cannot observe a standardized parliamentary procedure, there are some helpful guidelines that would help the chairman in guiding toward a decision:

(1) Clearly define the purposes of the meeting and the problems to be considered.

(2) Call for suggestions (not motions) for a solution of a problem. Continue discussion of all suggestions until each is fully understood by every member.

(3) In general, require that all opposition to any suggestion take the form of proposing an alternative suggestion. One such alternative, of course, may be to refrain from taking any action.

(4) Gauge the nearness of consensus occasionally by taking a preferential straw vote, in which no member commits himself to a final decision. From the results, select the most popular suggestions for continued discussion.

(5) Ask all those who oppose the most popular suggestions to state the reasons for their objections, along with proposals for modifying the popular suggestions to meet their objections.

(6) Continue the discussion in the direction of modifying the most popular suggestions to make them acceptable to nearly all.

(7) Gradually reduce the number of suggestions through the occasional straw vote.

(8) Continue the modification and straw voting until one suggested course of action is acceptable to virtually all members.

(9) Adopt for the present only those courses of action upon which these is almost unanimous agreement.

(10) When there is an irreconcilable conflict between two methods of action, work toward choice of one on a provisional, experimental basis.[292]

"In the characteristic business meeting of Quakers all over the world, the decisions are made without voting and without adherence to ordinary parliamentary rules of order. The hope is that the clerk will be a highly sensitive person who can find the 'sense of the meeting' without a show of hands. He is supposed to try to search for essential unanimity and to judge by 'weight,' rather than by mere numbers. When there is a clear division, the usual practice is to postpone a decision for at least a month or to settle into a time of worship and prayer. Frequently, the effect of such waiting verges on the miraculous. It does not always succeed, but it succeeds so often that there is no serious doubt concerning the wisdom of the method. One beneficent effect is the avoidance of 51–49 decisions which almost always leave a residue of bitterness. The Quaker method of reaching decisions is slow and outwardly inefficient, but the results are often healing. That it has not always been faithfully followed is evidenced by the few unhappy divisions which Quakers have experienced during more than three centuries." (D. Elton Trueblood, *The People Called Quakers*

---

292 Caesar B. Moody, *Preparation for Cooperative Decision Making*, The Association for Student Teaching Bulletin No. 12 (1960).

==

Decision-Making Method[293]   Handout 4

Process	Rationale Communicated
Define the problem in terms of needs	Your needs are important to me; you are important to me. I am important enough to have my needs expressed and heard. We really can understand one another.
Brainstorm	I value your creative thinking and mine and believe that together we can be even more creative in dealing with our common problem.
Select mutual solutions and check for possible consequences	I want you to have your needs satisfied, and I won't accept either one of us denying our uniqueness.
Plan who will do what, where, and by when.	You and I are willing to make joint decisions and coordinated plans to assist each other in getting our needs met.
Implement the plan	You and I have the power to change our behaviors in ways that can enhance our lives and improve our relationship. Our commitment to each other is expressed in action as well as in words.
Evaluate the process	You and I want to continually improve the way we solve problems that arise between us. In honesty and caring, we will discuss our feelings about this interaction.
Evaluate the solution	We are not locked into any solution, policy, or program. If our decision is not as good for us as we had hoped, we have the power to remake it better.

---

293 See Robert Bolton, *People Skills* (Englewood Cliffs, NJ: 1979), pp. 248, 249 footnote 19. Cf. also p. 294 footnote 19.

Exercise
Decision-Making Aid: 294 Step 3 Alternative # _____

7	Positive Anticipations+	Negative Anticipations−
1. Tangible gains + and losses − for *self*		
2. Tangible gains + and losses − for *others*		
3. Self-approval + or self-disapproval −		
4. Social approval + or disapproval −		

---

294 This is adopted from the balance sheet grid of Daniel D. Wheeler and Irving L. Janis, *A Practical Guide for Making Decisions* (New York: Free Press, 1977), p. 407. (Participants are encouraged to use this aid for each option.)

How to Help Others Handle Conflict

A. Session 1: Intervention Process (120 minutes)
    Focus, Facilitator's Goals, Pastors' Terminal Objectives
    Some Intervention Strategies: Adjudication, Arbitration, and Mediation
    Conflict Intervention Evaluation
    Handout 1: Conciliation Procedure Christian Conciliation Service
    Negotiation Process
    Mediation Process
    What to Do When Intervention Fails
    Exercise 1: Characteristics of Third Party
    Break
B. Session 2: Intervention: Personnel (75 minutes)
        Qualifications of the Third Party
        Exercise 2: Paul and Onesimus
        Communication Styles of Successful Third Parties
        Basic Assumptions of Third Parties
        Role Attributes of Third Parties
        Exercise 3: Role Play
        Evaluation of Role Play
        Break
Session 3: Seminar Closing Exercises (45 minutes)
Closing Exercises
        Review of Seminar Goals and Participants' Expectations
        Review of Seminar Modules—Transparencies
        Seminar Feedback
        Vote of Thanks—Facilitator

—

How to Help Others Handle Conflict

Focus

Third-party intervention is often needed to efficiently handle conflicts, equalize perceptions, and initiate rational responses to conflict.

Facilitator's Goals

The goals of this learning module include the following:
1. To provide information useful to pastors that can aid successful third-party intervention and negotiation
2. To increase confidence in using resource persons or aids in conflict management
3. To demonstrate some advantages of referral in conflict management
4. To encourage pastors to perceive other individuals as potential resources for learning
5. To update pastors with the contents and intent of the conciliation procedure of the General Conference of Seventh-day Adventists

Pastors' Terminal Objectives

Upon the completion of this learning module, pastors will be able to
1. recognize when third-party help is needed;
2. identify some intervention strategies for managing conflicts and some of their uses and limitations;
3. identify some qualities, attributes, and characteristic advantages of third-party intervention and interveners; and
4. intentionally enter conflict situations with less apprehension and fear.

INTRODUCTION

Ability to intervene, negotiate, and mediate successfully in conflict situations is increased as one becomes aware of the nature and dynamics of conflict. The likelihood of consistently and permanently resolving differences are quickly enhanced by being able to put the conflict in perspective. The third-party arbitrator or mediator should be amoral in his evaluation of the conflict situation. Since pastors are called upon to serve as neutral third parties to help resolve conflicts, pastors should develop skills in third-party intervention. The mediation process, with its negotiation ingredient, can provide pastors with increased credibility in conflict management as they demonstrate efficiency in this process.

Intervention Process

When Is Third-Party Intervention Necessary?
These are indicators that suggest intervention may be appropriate:
1. The person spends more time with you than usual, asking for advice and sharing feelings.
2. Private information is shared.
3. Your acquaintance indicates that a decision is impending and that the decision is crucial.
4. The person makes you understand that life is not smooth, distress is present, or that things seem out of control.
5. Friends may make dramatic, noticeable changes.

Intervention Strategies
Intervention strategies include adjudication, arbitration, and mediation. They often involve use of excellent communication skills, control of the

process, and a transformation of the conflict elements. The more formal the strategy the less degree of influence the parties have on the outcome.

Adjudication is a process in which parties go before a judge or jury, and the judgment can be put into operation without mutual consent.

Advantages:
1. It gives access to a resolution process to all evidence.
2. It provides rules for fairness such as the admission of evidence.
3. Professionals speak on behalf of the parties.
4. Serves as a backup for other processes of conflict.

Disadvantages:
1. It has been overutilized and is overburdened and misused.
2. Conflict parties no longer make their own decisions although they must live with the consequences.
3. Adjudication guarantees win/lose perceptions which can lead to escalation tactics.

Arbitration—this becomes operational when the parties mutually empower a third party to decide the outcome of their conflict. They assume the need of a neutral third person. When the parties contractually agree to arbitration, the results of the arbitrated judgment are enforceable in court—binding arbitration.

Advantages:
1. Both parties enter arbitration tactics voluntarily.
2. It prevents passive, aggressive, or impasse tactics.
3. Generally, the arbitrator has expertise in the area.
4. It is readily available when communication breakdown exists.
5. Has wide repertoire of content areas.

Disadvantages:
1. It tends to resolve conflicts solely on a content basis.
2. It reinforces the assumption that people cannot handle their differences.
3. It reinforces win-lose mentality.

Despite these disadvantages, arbitration binds parties procedurally for purposes of resolution and often enhances the chances for productive conflict management.

Mediation is a process in which an intervener helps parties to change their positions, so they can reach an agreement. The intervener serves as listener/moderator and facilitates the development and acceptance of an agreement between the parties. Mediation is relationship-oriented and seeks to resolve disputes and reduce conflict as well as provide a forum for decision-making.

A mediator is not empowered to settle the conflict but serves to clarify the positions of both parties and to suggest compromises. Mediation involves introduction, story-telling, problem-solving, and agreement.

Advantages:

1. It relies on the parties' active negotiation and involvement and promotes a mutual stake in the resolution. (The parties created the conflict, and they work for its management.)
2. The solutions often have a higher probability of being integrative and contain elements of creativity.
3. Mediation is a flexible process that is equally adaptable to many types of conflict.
4. Provides a model for future conflict resolution.

Disadvantages:

1. Not all parties will agree to work through the conflict with the enemy.
2. Mediation may not be appropriate where there are either too much involvement or too little (autistic) involvement with the other.
3. The dispute may not be worth the effort of mediation, and an adjudicated or arbitrated judgment would be the better option.

In church settings, the pastor should seek mediation as her/his forum of intervention or conciliation—the hybrid between mediation and arbitration where the third-party changes roles as he or she deems necessary.

Conflict Intervention Evaluation

A successful conflict intervention must do the following:

1. Help persons develop their own personal, psychological power base
2. Develop a relational base of acceptance and trust
3. Establish constructive communication
4. Filter the assumptions, rumors, and changes

6. Establish a covenant

———

317

Handout 1: Conciliation Procedure and Christian Conciliation Service

Negotiation Process

Negotiation processes follow an almost ritual pattern, and any attempt to bypass or to cut short these rituals often destroys the negotiation process. Negotiation follows five phases: (1) exploration, (2) bidding, (3) bargaining, (4) setting, and (5) ratifying.

Phase 1—exploration—is a period of knowing one another's expectations and requirements. It is used to gain an understanding of the issues that need to be settled in the bargaining phase.

In phase 2—bidding—one or both parties put forward their own bids or offers on each of the issues in the deal.

In phase 3—bargaining—each party is negotiating toward the best advantage.

As the bargaining process matures, the setting phase begins as each party recognizes agreement is at hand.

Phase 5—ratifying—is generally concluded either formally, contractually, or by some gesture of goodwill, like the handshake.

Styles in Negotiating
1. Fights
2. Compromise
3. Collaboration

Strategic Considerations
1. Repeatability—goodwill or lasting relationship may be needed.
2. Strength of the other party—only party or other potential
3. Strength of our party—do we dominate the situation?
4. Importance of the deal—cost, consequences of error.
5. Time scale—urgent, timely, future.
6. Negotiating resources—limited or available.

After any negotiation, critique your strategies, your conduct of the negotiation, your team, and the other party. Negotiation should always be toward agreement and not impasse—aim high. Every act of conflict management is an act in the process of negotiation. If persons are willing to negotiate differences in a give-and-take attitude, conflicts will be managed more creatively.

Mediation Process

1. Introduction—creating trust and structure
2. Fact-finding and isolation of issues
3. Creation of options and alternatives
4. Negotiation and decision-making
5. Clarification and writing a plan
6. Legal review and processing
7. Implementation, review, and revision

Remember the Format!

1. Preliminary interviewing
2. Structuring the context for the confrontation
3. Intervening in the ongoing process
4. Assisting follow-up activities

What to Do When Intervention Fails

Even when one's best efforts seem to fail in conflict management, the pastor can still try to do the following:

1. Make clear decisions (of the process)
2. Increase tolerance for difference
3. Reduce aggression
4. Reduce passive behavior
5. Reduce covert, manipulative behavior

Exercise 1: Characteristics of Third Party

Break

Intervention: Personnel

Intervention strategies suggest that personnel are aware of the potential of the assistance available through third-party intervention. Pastors should not be reluctant to involve credible and confidential third parties to help them with conflict management. Reluctance to use third-party resources (government agencies, denominational sources, electronic instructional aids) may indicate diminishing self-esteem.

Qualifications of Third Party
1. Does not take substantive conflict personally
2. Has a high tolerance for ambiguity, ambivalence, and frustration
3. Confident in conflict management and referring
4. Is not an advocate for any solution
5. Credible to both (all) sides
6. Trusted person (and can handle emotional imbalances)
7. Calm and deliberate
8. Listens well and respects the rights and personhood of the other person

All effective third parties—whether superior, peer, or subordinate—should demonstrate at least three major sources of strength:
1. Analytical ability to understand the conflict process
2. Communicative skills
3. Tactical choices

Exercise 2: Paul and Onesimus
Communication Styles of Successful Third Parties
1. Empathetic understanding of the interpersonal process
2. Congruence, openness, and genuineness
3. Regard and respect for the participants
4. Active leadership and intrusiveness

5. Hopefulness
6. Understanding problems from incomplete information
7. Safety—provides opportunity to risk options

Basic Assumptions of Third Parties
1. Conflict is inevitable and resolvable
2. Conformity is not required
3. Few situations are hopeless
4. One part affects another
5. Each side probably has a piece of the truth
6. There is some similarity between parties
7. Present problems are the ones to be solved
8. The process is of great importance
9. There are no right answers

Role Attributes of Third Parties
1. High professional expertise regarding social processes
2. Low power over fate of principals
3. High control over confrontation setting and processes
4. Moderate knowledge about the principals, issues, and background factors
5. Neutrality or balance with respect to substantive outcome, personal relationships, and conflict resolution methodology

Break
Session 3: Closing Exercises (45 minutes)
Review of Seminar Goals
Review of Participants' Expectations of Opening Session
Review of Seminar Modules Using Transparencies (T 1–8)
Rediagnosis of Seminar
Vote of Thanks
Resource Material

Scott, Bill. *The Skills of Negotiating.* New York: John Wiley & Sons, 1981.

Folberg, Jay, and Alison Taylor. *Mediation: A Comprehensive Guide to Resolving Conflict without Litigation.* San Francisco, CA: Jossey-Bass, 1984.

Hocker, Joyce L., and Wm. W. Wilmot. *Interpersonal Conflict*. 2nd ed. Dubuque, IA: Wm. C. Brown, 1985.

Leas, Speed. *A Layperson's Guide to Conflict Management*. Washington, DC: The Alban Institute, 1979.

Exercise 1: Characteristics of a Third Party

Option A: Ordained Pastors
    Situation:
    You are engaged in a conflict with another ordained pastor, and it is becoming very disruptive of a formerly happy relationship. What are the characteristics of the person you would trust to help bring about the reconciliation you both desire to experience? You are given three names of mediators; what would determine your choice? What characteristics would discourage your choice?

Option B: Intern Ministers
    Situation:
    You are engaged in a conflict with your senior pastor, and it is disruptive of your relationship with him and is stressful to you. Would you prefer the president, the ministerial secretary, or another pastor to mediate with you? Why? Why would you choose neither but someone else?

Process:
    Step 1 — Each person works privately on the exercise.
    Step 2 — Get everyone together in a large group and, with use of chalkboard, flip board, etc., list the characteristics. Check for agreement on the list of positive and negative characteristics. Check for correlation between two groups.
    Step 3 — Summarize findings to introduce session 2 (after the break).

Exercise 2: Paul and Onesimus
    Step 1 — Read silently Philemon 1.
    Step 2 — Group Discussion
    A. Did Paul possess the qualities of a third-party mediator? How?
    B. Was there reconciliation, restoration, and restitution? Either? Was there the framework for conciliation?

C. What proposal did Paul make to suggest that maybe Onesimus would be financially incapable of restitution?
D. Identify some good uses of communication skills in Paul's letter to Philemon _____

Exercise 3: Role Play (Mediation)

Goal: To try practical application of theory

Participants: Pastor—Mediator

Person A—Choir Leader

Person B—Youth Leader

Situation:

The music department wishes to have a musical concert, and the young people's society also wants to have an outing on the same day—Easter Sunday. Uncertainty about the concert and the outing is growing, and feelings are becoming tense between the choir leader and the youth leader. The choir is made up of several young persons. The pastor is attempting to mediate the situation before the regular board meeting, scheduled six days later, at which the subject will be discussed. The three persons must role play this situation for about ten to fifteen minutes.

Process: Audience should try to identify numbers 1–4 below:
1. Identify the communication processes.
2. I-you messages.
3. Look for characteristics of mediation and negotiation processes.
4. Try to identify the sentence(s) that identify movement from one stage to another (introduction, storytelling, problem-solving, and agreement).
5. Discuss numbers 1–4 above.
6. What could be done to avoid a situation like this occurring again?
7. What was the basic source of conflict?
8. At the point of mediation at what stage of the conflict cycle is the conflict?

PS: The role play will be videotaped to aid review.

===

Rediagnosis Sheet

Module/Seminar

Directions: Please take a few minutes to give your opinion on the various elements of the seminar listed below. Be specific. What was helpful, not helpful, exciting, stimulating?

Handouts:

Lectures:

Exercises:

Time (seminar length, session length):

How have the concepts in this module affected your attitudes to conflicts? Be specific.

What suggestions do you have for future (conflict) seminars? (You may write on the reverse side.)

CONCILIATION PROCEDURE

In Autumn Council 1976 and 1977, the General Conference included in Policy a Conciliation Procedure. It is a procedure to be undertaken after the Church Manual procedures (personal and pastoral conciliatory efforts) have not resolved an issue. The purpose of Conciliation Procedure is to safeguard the unity of the Church by a timely and appropriate procedure to resolve differences, and as an alternative to litigation.

The Panel.

After due deliberation, the Conference Committee would select seven individuals to constitute a Conciliation Panel. They would be individuals of compassion and wisdom, solid in the truth. The procedure suggests at least one member from a minority group, at least one woman, and at least three individuals who are not employed by the denomination. Consideration should be given to retired ministers to fill some of the positions.

While the panel would consist of seven individuals, only three would be involved in any one issue.

The members of the panel would serve without remuneration, and only reasonable and necessary expenses (e.g., travel, where necessary) would be reimbursed.

The panel would be appointed for the term of the Conference Committee which appointed it.

The Scope of the Procedure.

Section 1(a)2 of the Procedure specifies six areas outside the scope of the Conciliation Procedure:

(e) An individual dispute with a branch of civil government.
(f) An individual dispute with a law enforcement agency.
(g) Problems of marital differences.
(h) Theological differences.
(i) Church election problems.
(j) Debt collections.

That leaves a large scope for purview by the Panel. The following are some examples of areas of conflict where the Panel might conciliate:

(a) Contract disputes between members or members and the Church (including contracts of business association, employment, property, etc.)

(b) Issues over areas of responsibility, authority and the delegation of authority.

(c) Disputes in the nature of tort—e.g., libel, slander, injuries.

(d) Non-marital family disputes.

(e) Financial disputes other than debt collection matters.

(f) Matters of conduct that have potential for church discipline.

(g) Any issue of a potentially litigious nature between members or members and the Church.

(h) Any conflict between the Church Administration and (for example) a local Church, a school board, or a subsidiary organization, that cannot be resolved in the normal course of administrative attempts to resolve the issue.

Numerous examples might be cited, but as well other categories may become evident as the work of the Panel progresses. The scope of the work of the Panel is open for dealing with internal church conflict, limited only by the procedure itself to those six areas designated.

Availability.

At present, conciliation procedure is used only when called upon to deal with specific issues, the panel appointed at the time to deal with the single issue or case. However, the appointment of a Panel to form part of the regular conflict resolution process within the Church, would open to all, members, pastors and administration alike, a forum for the early and expeditious resolution of problems. The availability of the Panel would best be well-known to everyone within the Church, so that problems could be brought at the earliest possible time after the preliminary steps to resolve them had been taken. As the work of the Panel became known, hopefully it would gain in credibility as a viable new source of internal conflict resolution. Increased credibility will result in greater use, and thus the positive purposes of the Policy will be realized.

[Annual Council 1976] *(as amended Annual Council 1977)*
CONCILIATION PROCEDURES

VOTED. To adopt the following conciliation procedures statement for use in North America. Adaptations may be considered by overseas divisions:

Safeguarding Unity of the Church

Christians should make every effort to avoid tendencies that would divide them and bring dishonor to their cause. "It is the purpose of God that His children shall blend in unity. Do they not expect to live together in the same heaven? . . . Those who refuse to work in harmony greatly dishonor God." (8T 240.) The church should discourage every action that would threaten harmony among its members and must encourage unity.

Settling of Differences Among Members—Reconciliation of differences among church members should, in most cases, be possible without recourse to civil litigation. "Contentions, strife, and lawsuits between brethren are a disgrace to the cause of truth. Those who take such a course expose the church to the ridicule of her enemies and cause the powers of darkness to triumph. They are piercing the wounds of Christ afresh and putting Him to an open shame. By ignoring the authority of the church, they show contempt for God, who gave to the church its authority" (5T 242, 243). Personal revenge is not becoming to a child of God. If he is abused, he is to take it patiently; if defrauded of that which is his just due, he is not to appeal to unbelievers in courts of justice. "Christians should not appeal to civil tribunals to settle differences that may arise among church members. Such differences should be settled among themselves, or by the church, in harmony with Christ's instruction" (AA 305, 306).

Much civil litigation is carried on in a spirit of contention that results from and reveals human selfishness. It is this kind of adversary proceedings, prompted by greed or impatience that must be discouraged by a church that seeks to exhibit the spirit of Christ. Christian unselfishness will lead followers of Christ to "suffer . . . (themselves) to be defrauded" (1 Cor 6:7) rather than to "go to law before the unjust, and not before the saints." (1 Cor 6:1).

All steps outlined in the *Church Manual* (pp. 222–229) should first have been followed before other remedial actions are attempted. If personal and pastoral conciliatory efforts have not resolved the differences, the procedures that follow should be undertaken.

Conciliation Guidelines

The establishment of Conciliation Panels may serve to care for unsettled grievances held by members against fellow members or church organizations/institutions. This applies to all institutions excepting those which have established internal procedures. The following guidelines are offered to assist church members to reconcile these differences within the church without recourse to legal proceedings:

1. Local Conference Conciliation Panel

    a. Purpose

1) The local conference Conciliation Panel is structured to provide a procedure within the church to promptly reconcile personal differences and misunderstandings that may arise between individual Christians, an individual and a local church, or an individual and a local conference. The Conciliation Panel is not a quasi-judicial system but is a definitive effort by the church to fulfill its responsibilities of spiritual leadership by providing members timely and objective counseling intended to strengthen the bonds of Christian love and to channel the energies of the membership to the primary spiritual mission of the church.

2) Matters involving an individual's dispute with any branch of civil government or law enforcement agency shall be outside the responsibility of the church's conciliation procedure. The Conciliation Panel is not intended to deal with such problems as those arising from marital differences between husbands and wives, specific theological questions, church elections, or debt collection.

    b. The Pastor

1) The counseling responsibility of the pastor is the initial step in the conciliation process. Where members from more than one church are involved, the conciliation effort should be a joint endeavor by pastoral representatives from each church.

2) In cases where a pastor is a primary party to a misunderstanding involving a member, another pastor, or the conference, the matter should be addressed directly to the conference Conciliation Panel through the conference secretary.

    c. Appointment

1) The conference Conciliation Panel shall be appointed by the Conference Executive Committee and panel members shall serve for a term concurrent with the term of the conference committee.
2) A total of seven panelists shall all be members in good standing in the Seventh-day Adventist Church and shall include at least one-member representative of a minority ethnic group, at least one woman, and at least three individuals who are not denominationally employed.
3) Although no conference officers will be panelists, consideration should be given to capitalizing on the experience of retired ministers.
4) Only three panelists will hear any one issue, appointments will be made on a rotating basis, and the first listed name among any three sitting panelists will automatically serve as chairman. Where the issue involves young people, a young person should be invited to sit with the panelists. In selecting the panelists, latitude is given that the rotation procedure must not be rigidly followed if the nature of the case indicates that a modification would be desirable.
5) All discussions in any of the conciliation proceedings at every level must be regarded as strictly confidential. Topics and personalities should not be discussed outside of the panel meetings. Failure to observe this ethic will erode confidence in the conciliations and render their exacting task still more difficult.

d. Preliminary Procedure

1) The conference secretary shall be responsible for scheduling all panel hearings and assembling and maintaining all pertinent data. The request for a meeting with the Conciliation Panel shall be delivered in writing to the conference secretary and shall include a brief memorandum of the facts, the names and addresses of the interested parties, and the specific question needing resolution.
2) The conference secretary shall obtain oral assurance from the pastor that a conciliation effort by the panel would be timely and appropriate. Thereafter the conference secretary shall recommend a time and place for a conciliation hearing within 30 working days after receipt of the initial written request. The consent of all other interested parties is a condition precedent for such a hearing and all parties shall provide the conference secretary with all written

materials or data that will clarify the issues, at least seven working days prior to the bearing date.

3) Copies of all written materials delivered by the interested parties to the conference secretary will be delivered to the individual panel members prior to the conciliation hearing and concurrently the union conference secretary shall be advised of the issues pending.

e. Hearing Procedure

1) The conciliation hearing shall be limited to the three panelists, the two primary interested parties, with the conference secretary sitting as an observer.

2) Procedure shall be informal with no formal written transcript or electronic record made or kept of any oral discussion and no third parties present to represent either individual.

3) The discussions shall be opened and closed with prayer with each individual party being given an opportunity to participate. Both parties shall give brief opening and closing statements with the individual requesting the hearing giving his statement first. The balance of the time shall be used by the panel members taking turns in directing questions to everyone.

4) Third party witnesses shall not be present but subject to the discretion of the panel chairman, the hearing can be adjourned so that third party witnesses can be questioned privately by the panelists and then reconvened at a subsequent occasion for further discussion with the interested parties.

f. Panel Recommendations

1) 1) Within seven working days after the conclusion of the hearing the chairman of the panel shall provide the conference secretary with a brief written statement summarizing the reconciliation recommendations of the panel. Immediately thereafter, the conference secretary shall arrange a meeting with both interested parties and their pastor or pastors at which time the recommendation of the panel shall be orally presented for discussion and a definite oral response from the parties shall be sought determining whether the recommendation is mutually acceptable. Acceptance must be the result of moral commitment and not legal compulsion since the spiritual conciliation process is not legally binding arbitration.

2) 2) If a church member feels that the proceedings were unfair or the panel's recommendations are unreasonable, it is possible for him to appeal to the union conference Conciliation Panel.

3) 3) When complete, duplicate files of all written material shall be sent to the union conference secretary by the local conference secretary. All files of cases involving administrative affairs of a denominational organization shall be retained under guidelines provided by the General Conference. All other files shall be destroyed 24 months after closing.

2. Institutional Conciliation Panel

   a. Purpose—Each denominational institution except those that have a board approved conciliation plan shall appoint a Conciliation Panel to reconcile differences that may arise as between an employee and the institution or a church member that has a contractual relationship with the institution.

   b. Personnel Director—Any dispute or misunderstanding which cannot be resolved within a department shall initially be brought to the attention of the personnel director, or the management representative carrying comparable responsibility, for discussion and serious efforts to equitably reconcile differences and misunderstandings.

   c. Administrative Committee

1) Issues that cannot be resolved through the conciliation efforts of the personnel director shall be brought to the attention of the administrator who will direct it to an administrative committee appointed specifically to be responsive to employee grievances. Concurrently, the administrator shall also advise the board chairman of the pending issue.

2) The individual employee or other church member concerned with a grievance or misunderstanding with the institution shall deliver a memo to the chief administrative officer summarizing the facts and the issues and requesting a conciliation hearing. Such a hearing shall be scheduled within 30 working days after the receipt of such written request and a brief statement summarizing the recommendation of the committee shall be delivered to the parties within seven working days after the hearing.

3) Procedure for the discussion by the Administrative Committee shall reflect the philosophy of spiritual conciliation within

the context of the unique needs of the institution. Unresolved issues may be appealed by either party to the board-appointed Conciliation Panel. However, all matters relating to professional standards and practices shall be outside the scope of responsibility of the Conciliation Panel and shall be dealt with exclusively within the discretion of the administration of the institution.

    d. Conciliation Panel

1) The Board of Directors shall appoint a Conciliation Panel of seven members who shall serve a term concurrent with the term of the board and shall review appeals from recommendations of the Administrative Committee.

2) The members of the Conciliation Panel shall include at least one-member representative of a minority ethnic group, at least one woman, and at least three laymen, and shall not include administrative personnel from the institution. At least four of the panelists shall be members of the board and all panelists shall be members in good standing of the Seventh-day Adventist Church.

3) A single issue shall be heard by any three members of the panel on a rotating basis with the first listed name among any three sitting panelists automatically serving as chairman.

4) The hearing procedure shall be comparable to that utilized by the local conference Conciliation Panel with duplicate files of completed hearings automatically forwarded to the union conference secretary. The copies filed at the union conference shall be retained under guidelines provided by the General Conference.

3. Union Conference Conciliation Panel

    a. Appeal

1) In the event a party has not accepted the recommendations of either a local conference conciliation panel or an institutional Conciliation Panel, that individual may request a review of procedures by the union conference Conciliation Panel by filing a written request directed to the union conference secretary within 30 working days after the written recommendation of the local Conciliation Panel was written.

2) The union conference Conciliation Panel may also serve as the original panel for seeking resolution to problems that may arise between members of different conferences, or for appeals from

General Conference institutions located within the geographic boundaries of a given union conference.

b. <u>Appointment.</u> The union conference Executive Committee shall elect seven members for its Conciliation Panel for a term concurrent with that of the union conference Executive Committee. Representation shall consist of at least one member from a minority ethnic group, at least one woman, and at least three laymen. Serious consideration should be given to the appointment of retired institutional administrators as well as retired conference officers.

c. <u>Procedures</u>

1) The union conference secretary shall select a mutually convenient time for a conciliation hearing to be held at the conference office in closest proximity to the interested parties and within 30 working days after receipt to the written request for a hearing. Notice of time and place of hearing shall be sent to the interested parties and panel members selected to review the issue.

2) For each matter to be heard, two of the union conference conciliation panelists shall take turns on a rotating basis with the chairman and third panelist to be a General Conference representative designated by the General Conference Secretariat on a case-by-case basis.

3) Hearing procedure shall be comparable to that of the local conference Conciliation Panel hearing with only the interested parties appearing before the three panelists together with the union conference secretary sitting as an observer. However, the issue shall be narrowed to the fairness of procedures and reasonableness of the prior panel's recommendation for conciliation and any other possible alternatives that would be both equitable and satisfactory to the parties.

4) To the extent possible, it is desirable that the panelists' decision shall be made on the day of the appeal hearing and a final effort shall be made to complete the reconciliation of the parties on the occasion with no procedural alternative for further appeal. Immediately afterward, the union conference secretary shall send a brief written statement of the status of the matter to the local conference secretary with copies directed to the interested parties, institutions, and pastors. This final status memo shall be

sent within seven working days after the conciliation meeting of the union conference Conciliation Panel and shall terminate any formal conciliation proceedings by the church.

5) All files shall be retained under guidelines provided by the General Conference.

4. The Time Factor—Time is of crucial importance to the church in dealing decisively, objectively and promptly with an internal issue of dissension before it is aggravated and expanded out of proportion with resultant damage to internal church relationships. There is a heavy responsibility on the shoulders of pastors and institutional officers to act openly, kindly and with spiritual compassion at the first sign of a developing issue. It is also incumbent upon the formal conciliation process to initiate and complete all hearings in a total time not to exceed 90 working days from the first written request for an initial hearing to the final written status report from the union conference secretary after an appeal. It is intended that a serious effort to seek spiritual solutions to confrontations will result in full and complete voluntary reconciliation; however, in cases where this effort may for any reason prove unsuccessful, it is essential that the church have acted in a timely manner so as not to jeopardize any legal rights of the parties.

Christian Conciliation Service
of Sacramento

926 J Street, Suite 716
Sacramento, California 95814
(916) 441-3951

What Is Christian Conciliation Service?

CCS seeks to implement the biblical approaches to dispute resolution indicated in 1 Corinthians 6 and Matthew 18. This ministry is being developed by Christian attorneys and laypersons to assist local churches to resolve differences between Christians without recourse to the courts.

The benefits CCS offer includes the following:

1. It assists, but does not take the place of the local church.
2. It provides training in peacemaking and reconciliation process to local church members.
3. In cases of dispute between two Christians, it provides a reconciliation service upon the consent of the pastors of both parties, typically using a panel of two or three persons following biblical procedures.
4. It relieves the pastor or pastoral staff of much of the time-consuming detail required to handle the cases which it takes.
5. It saves Christians who use its dispute resolution services untold thousands of dollars that would otherwise be spent for attorney fees and court costs.
6. It is a specialized ministry to help churches do better what good churches are already attempting to do to the extent of their resources.

Services Available

Educational Services
- sermons
- lectures
- workshops and seminars

- church awarenessintroduction to biblical principles (3 to 12 hours)
- church leadership orientation workshops (14 hours)
- biblical principles
- communication skills
- awareness of technical problems
- awareness of pitfalls
- biblical problemsolving
- awareness of resources available
- resource materials and support for presentations by pastors or other church leader
- Bible study (7 to 10 weeks)
  "Resolving Our Differences"—teaching outline complete with worksheets and transparencies for overhead projector (for presentation by pastor or other church leader)
- peacemaker training for mediators (14 to 20 hours), for pastors, elders, deacons and other church leaders.
- administrative workshops.

Peacemaking Services
- biblical counseling
- mediation
- arbitration
- referral and coordination
  - referral to Christian counselor or other professionals
  - coordination of panels
  - referrals to trained arbitrators and mediators

Organizational and Administrative Services
- consultation in setting up congregational and area denominational programs
  - awareness promotion
  - administration
  - procedure
  - training
  - leadership

- resources and supplies
    - administrative materials
    - study materials
    - tapes
    - workbooks
    - homework
    - specialized study topics
        - forgiveness
        - reconciliation
        - restitution
        - anger
        - communication
        - etc.

Recommended Reading

- *Tell It to the Church* by Lynn Buzzard and Laury Eck (David C. Cook)
- *Telling Each Other the Truth* by William Backus (Bethany House)
- *Repairing the Breach* by Ronald S. Kraybill (Herald Press)

Transparencies

The Conflict Process (T-1)

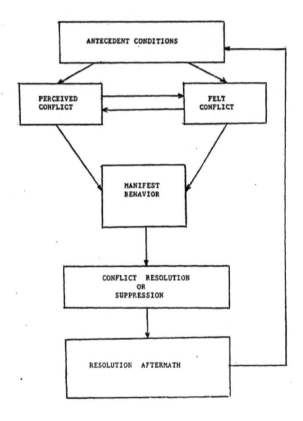

Source: Alan C. Filley, Interpersonal Conflict Resolution (1975), p. 8.

Choice-Action-Resolution (T-2)

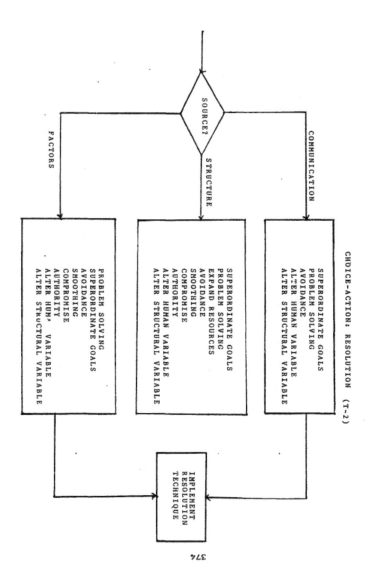

Conflict Management/Resolution Continuum (T-3)

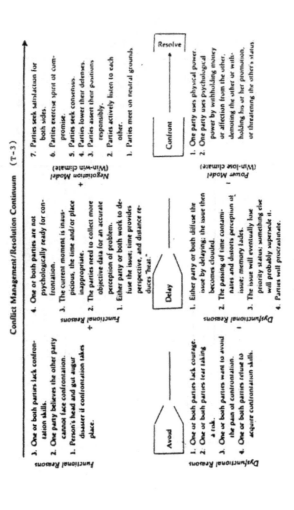

Conflict Management/Resolution Continuum (T-3)

Avoid

Functional Reasons
1. One or both parties lack confrontation skills.
2. One party believes the other party cannot face confrontation.
3. Person's head and gut augur disaster if confrontation takes place.

Dysfunctional Reasons
1. One or both parties lack courage.
2. One or both parties fear taking a risk.
3. One or both parties want to avoid the pain of confrontation.
4. One or both parties refuse to acquire confrontation skills.

Delay

Functional Reasons
1. Either party or both work to defuse the issue; time provides perspective, and distance reduces "heat."
2. The parties need to collect more objective data for an accurate perception of problem.
3. The current moment is inauspicious, the time and/or place inappropriate.
4. One or both parties are not psychologically ready for confrontation.

Dysfunctional Reasons
1. Either party or both diffuse the issue by delaying; the issue then becomes clouded.
2. The passing of time contaminates and distorts perception of issue; memory fades.
3. The issue will eventually lose priority status; something else will probably supersede it.
4. Parties will procrastinate.

Negotiation Model
(Win-win climate) +
1. Parties meet on neutral grounds.
2. Parties actively listen to each other.
3. Parties assert their positions responsibly.
4. Parties lower their defenses.
5. Parties seek consensus.
6. Parties exercise spirit of compromise.
7. Parties seek satisfaction for both sides.

Power Model
(Win-lose climate) −
1. One party uses physical power.
2. One party uses psychological power by withholding money or affection from the other, demoting the other or withholding his or her promotion, or threatening the other's status.

Confront

Resolve

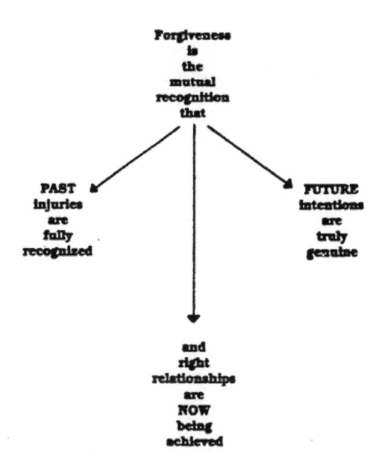

Forgiveness
is
the
mutual
recognition
that

PAST
injuries
are
fully
recognized

FUTURE
intentions
are
truly
genuine

and
right
relationships
are
NOW
being
achieved

(T-4)

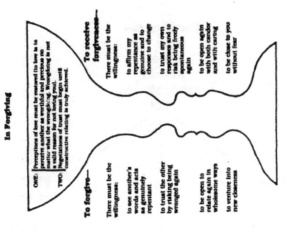

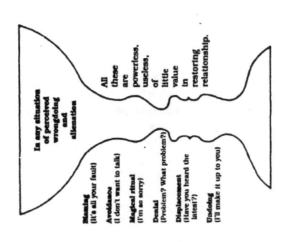

(T-5)

(T-5)

Key Strategies (T-6)

Adjudication

Arbitration

Mediation

Peacemaker

Reconciler

Your Problem Is
Three Problems

OUTCOME PROBLEM

Goal

Target

What we
want
to see
happen

BLOCKAGE PROBLEM

Cause or
hindrance
preventing
outcome

Various causes,
key causes

ACTION PROBLEM

Actions
to take
to remove
blockage
and achieve
outcome

Operational Model

Steps in Decision-Making Model

SELECTED BIBLIOGRAPHY

Books

Abbott, T. K. *Ephesians and Colossians.* International Critical Commentary. Edinburgh: T & T Clark, 1956.

Ahlstrom, Sydney E. *A Religious History of the American People.* New Haven, CT: Yale University Press, 1972.

Apps, Jerold W. *Study Skills for Adults Returning to School.* New York: McGraw-Hill, 1982.

Anderson, Bernard W. *Understanding the Old Testament.* Englewood Cliffs, NJ: Prentice-Hall, 1964.

Arndt, William F., and Wilbur F. Gingrich. *A Greek-English Lexicon of the New Testament and Other Early Christian Literature.* Translation and adaptation of Walter Bauer's *Griechisch-Deutsches Wörterbuch.* Chicago, IL: University of Chicago Press, 1979.

Augsburger, David. *Caring Enough to Confront.* Ventura, CA: Regal Books, 1985.

———. *Caring Enough to Forgive: Caring Enough Not to Forgive.* Ventura, CA: Regal Books, 1981.

Bach, George R., and Peter Wyden. *The Intimate Enemy*. New York: Avon Books, 1969.

Bainton, Roland H. *Christendom*. 2 vols. New York: Harper & Row, 1964.

———. *Christian Attitudes Toward War and Peace*. New York: Abingdon Press, 1960.

———. *Here I Stand*. New York: Mentor Books, 1955.

Barclay, William. *Great Themes of the New Testament*. Edited by Cyril Rodd. Philadelphia, PA: Westminster Press, 1979.

Berkhof, Louis. *Manual of Christian Doctrine*. Grand Rapids, MI: Wm. B. Eerdmans, 1969.

———. *Systematic Theology*. Sussex, England: Banner of Truth Trust, 1969.

Bianchi, Eugene C. *Reconciliation: The Function of the Church*. New York: Sheed & Ward, 1969.

The Bible. The New International Version. New York: International Bible Society, 1983.

Bloomfield, Harold H. *Making Peace with Yourself*. New York: Ballantine Books, 1985.

Bolton, Robert. *People Skills, How to Assert Yourself, Listen to Others and Resolve Conflicts*. Englewood Cliffs, NJ: Prentice-Hall, 1979.

Boulding, Kenneth J. *Conflict and Defense: A General Theory*. New York: Harper & Row, 1962.

Bossart, Donald E. *Creative Conflict in Religious Education and Church Administration*. Birmingham, England: Religious Education Press, 1980.

Brammer, L. M. *The Helping Relationship.* Englewood Cliffs, NJ: Prentice-Hall, 1985.

Brookfield, Stephen D. *Understanding and Facilitating Adult Learning.* San Francisco, CA: Jossey-Bass, 1986.

Bruce, F. F. *The Hard Sayings of Jesus.* Downer's Grove, IL: InterVarsity Press, 1983.

Bruder, Ernest E. *Ministry to Deeply Troubled People.* Philadelphia, PA: Fortress Press, 1964.

Brueggeman, Walter. *Living Toward a Vision: Biblical Reflections on Shalom.* Philadelphia, PA: United Church Press, 1976.

Brundage, D. H., and D. MacKeracher. *Adult Learning Principles and Their Application to Program Learning.* Toronto: Ministry of Education, 1980.

Brunner, Emil. *The Mediator.* Philadelphia, PA: Westminster Press, 1947.

Buzzard, Lynn R., and Juanita Buzzard. *Resolving Our Difficulties.* Elgin, IL: David C. Cook, 1982.

Buzzard, Lynn, and Laurence Eck. *Tell It to the Church.* Wheaton, IL: Tyndale House, 1985.

Cohen, Herb. *You Can Negotiate Anything.* New York: Bantam Books, 1982.

Coleman, James S. *Community Conflict.* New York: Free Press 1957.

Collins, Gary R. *Christian Counseling.* Waco, TX: Word Books, 1980.

Come, Arnold B. *Agents of Reconciliation.* Philadelphia, PA: Westminster Press, 1964.

Cook, Jerry, and Stanley C. Baldwin. *Love, Acceptance and Forgiveness.* Ventura, CA: Regal Books, 1981.

Coser, C. L. *Functions of Social Conflict.* New York: Free Press, 1956.

Cross, K. Patricia. *Adults as Learners.* San Francisco, CA: Jossey-Bass, 1986.

Darkenwald, G. G., and S. B. Merriam. *Adult Education: Foundations of Practice.* New York: Harper & Row, 1982.

Davis, Ron Lee. *A Forgiving God in an Unforgiving World.* Eugene, OR: Harvest House, 1984.

Denny, James. *The Christian Doctrine of Reconciliation.* London: Hodder & Stoughton, 1917.

DesPortes, Elisa. *Congregations in Change.* New York: Seabury Press, 1973.

Deutsch, Morton. *The Resolution of Conflict.* New Haven: Yale University, 1973.

Donnelly, Doris. *Putting Forgiveness into Practice.* Allen, TX: Argus Communications, 1982.

Draves, William A. *How to Teach Adults.* Manhattan, KA: Learning Resources Network, 1984.

Dudley, Roger L. *Passing on the Torch.* Hagerstown, MD: Review & Herald, 1986.

Edwards, Rex. *A New Frontier: Every Believer a Minister.* Mountain View, CA: Pacific Press, 1979.

Egan, Gerard. *The Skilled Helper: A Model for Systematic Helping and Interpersonal Relating.* Monterey, CA: Brooks Cole, 1982.

Eller, Vernard. *War and Peace: From Genesis to Revelation.* 2nd. ed. Scottsdale, PA: Herald Press, 1981.

Ellias John L., and Sharon B. Merriam. *Philosophical Foundations of Adult Education*. New York: Robert E. Krieger, 1980.

Fensterheim, H., and Jean Baer. *Don't Say Yes When You Want to Say No*. New York: David McKay, 1975.

Filley, Alan C. *Interpersonal Conflict Resolution*. Glenview, IL: Scott, Foresman, 1975.

Flynn, Leslie B. *Great Church Fights*. Wheaton, IL: Victor Books, 1976.

Folberg, Jay, and Alison Taylor. *Mediation: A Comprehensive Guide to Resolving Conflicts without Litigation*. San Francisco, CA: Jossey-Bass, 1984.

Gagne, R. M. *The Conditions of Learning*. New York: Holt, Rinehart, & Winston, 1965.

Harkness, Georgia. *The Ministry of Reconciliation*. Nashville, TN: Abingdon Press, 1971.

Hastings, James, ed. *A Dictionary of Christ and the Gospels*. 2 vols. New York: Charles Scribner's Sons, 1808.

———. *The Great Texts of the Bible: 2 Corinthians–Galatians*. Grand Rapids, MI: Wm. B. Eerdmans, 1913.

Hauck, Paul A. *Brief Counseling with RET*. Philadelphia, PA: Westminster Press, 1980.

Herzberg, Frederick. *The Managerial Choice: To Be Efficient and to Be Human*. Homewood, IL: Dow-Jones-Irwin, 1976.

Hocker, Joyce L., and William W. Wilmot. *Interpersonal Conflict*. 2nd ed. Dubuque, IA: Wm. C. Brown, 1985.

Hocking, David L. *Spiritual Gifts: Their Necessity and Use in the Local Church*. Long Beach, CA: Sounds of Grace, 1975.

Huggett, Joyce. *Creative Conflict: How to Confront and Stay Friends.* Downer's Grove, IL: InterVarsity Press, 1984.

Janis, Irving L., and Leon Mann. *Decision Making: A Psychological Analysis of Conflict, Choice and Commitment.* New York: Free Press, 1977.

Johnson, David W., and Frank P. Johnson. *Joining Together.* Englewood Cliffs, NJ: Prentice-Hall, 1982.

Kidd, J. R. *How Adults Learn.* New York: Cambridge Books, 1973.

Kinghorn, Kenneth Cain. *Gifts of the Spirit.* Nashville, TN: Abingdon Press, 1976.

Kinzer, Mark. *The Self Image of a Christian.* Ann Arbor, MI: Servant Books, 1980.

Kittlaus, Paul, and Speed B. Leas. *Church Fights.* Philadelphia, PA: Westminster Press, 1973.

Klimes, Rudolf. *Conflict Management in the Gospels.* Berrien Springs, MI: Andrews University Press, 1977.

Knowles, Malcolm S. *The Adult Learner: A Neglected Species.* 2nd. ed. Houston, TX: Gulf Pub., 1978.

———. *The Modern Practice of Adult Education.* New York: Associated Press, 1970.

Knowles, M. S., and Associates. *Andragogy in Action: Applying Modern Principles of Adult Learning.* San Francisco, CA: Jossey-Bass, 1984.

Knox, A. B. *Adult Development and Learning: A Handbook on Individual Growth and Competence in Adult Years.* San Francisco, CA: Jossey-Bass, 1977.

Knox, A. B., and Associates. *Developing, Administering, and Evaluating Adult Education.* San Francisco, CA: Jossey-Bass, 1980.

Kornhauser, A., R. Dubin, and A. M. Ross. *Industrial Conflict*. New York: McGraw-Hill, 1954.

Kraybill, Ronald S. *Repairing the Breach*. Scottdale, PA: Herald Press, 1981.

Kriesberg, Louis. *The Sociology of Social Conflict*. Englewood Cliffs, NJ: Prentice-Hall, 1973.

Leas, Speed B. *Discover Your Conflict Management Style*. Washington, DC: Alban Institute, 1985.

————. *A Lay Person's Guide to Conflict Management*. Washington, DC: Alban Institute, 1979.

————. *Moving Your Church through Conflict*. Washington, DC: Alban Institute, 1985.

Leas, Speed B., and Paul Kittlaus. *Church Fights*. Philadelphia, PA: Westminster Press, 1973.

Lee, Robert, and Russell Galloway. *The Schizophrenic Church*. Philadelphia, PA: Westminster Press, 1969.

Lewis, G. Douglass. *Resolving Church Conflicts*. San Francisco, CA: Harper & Row, 1981.

Leypoldt, Martha M. *Learning Is Change: Adult Education in the Church*. Valley Forge, PA: Judson Press, 1981.

Likert, Rensis, and Jane Gibson Likert. *New Ways of Managing Conflict*. New York: McGraw-Hill, 1976.

Lindgren, Alvin J., and Norman Shawchuck. *Let My People Go*. Nashville, TN: Abingdon Press, 1980.

McDowell, Josh. *Building Your Self Image*. Wheaton, IL: Tyndale House, 1984.

MacGorman, Jack W. *The Gifts of the Spirit*. Nashville, TN: Broadman Press, 1974.

McSwain, Larry L., and William C. Treadwell Jr. *Conflict Ministry in the Church*. Nashville, TN: Broadman Press, 1981.

Mager, Robert F. *Preparing Instructional Objectives*. Rev. 2nd ed. Belmont, CA: David S. Lake, 1984.

Maloney, H. Newton, Thomas L. Needham, and Samuel Southard. *Clergy Malpractice*. Philadelphia, PA: Westminster Press, 1986.

Maslow, Abraham. *Motivation and Personality*. New York: Harper & Row, 1954.

Miller, H. L. *Teaching and Learning in Education*. New York: Macmillan, 1964.

Miller, John M. *The Contentious Community: Constructive Conflict in the Church*. Philadelphia, PA: Westminster Press, 1978.

Miller, William R., and Kathleen A. Jackson. *A Practical Psychology for Pastors*. Englewood Cliffs, NJ: 1985.

Mork, Wulstan. *The Biblical Meaning of Man*. Milwaukee, WI: Bruce Pub., 1967.

Murphy, Edward F. *Spiritual Gifts and the Great Commission*. South Pasadena, CA: Mandate Press, 1975.

Nierenberg, Gerard I. *The Art of Negotiating*. New York: Hawthorn Books, 1968.

Oglesby, William B., Jr. *Referral in Pastoral Counseling*. Philadelphia, PA: Fortress Press, 1968.

Pelikan, Jaroslav. *The Christian Traditions*. 2 vols. Chicago, IL: University of Chicago Press, 1974.

Pfeiffer, J. William, and John E. Jones. *A Handbook of Structured Experiences for Human Relations Training.* 5 vols. La Jolla, CA: University Associates Press, 1975.

Pneuman, Roy, and Margaret E. Bruehl. *Managing Conflict.* Englewood Cliffs, NJ: Prentice-Hall, 1982.

Rapoport, Anatol. *Fights, Games, and Debates.* Ann Arbor, MI: University of Michigan Press, 1960.

Rice, Richard. *The Reign of God: An Introduction to Christian Theology from a Seventh-day Adventist Perspective.* Berrien Springs, MI: Andrews University Press, 1985.

Robbins, Stephen P. *Essentials of Organizational Behavior.* Englewood Cliffs, NJ: Prentice-Hall, 1984.

———. *Managing Organizational Conflict: A Non-Traditional Approach.* Englewood Cliffs, NJ: Prentice-Hall, 1974.

Robert, Marc. *Managing Conflict from the Inside Out.* Austin, TX: Learning Concepts, 1982.

Rogers, Carl R. *Becoming Partners.* New York: Harper & Row, 1972.

———. *Carl Rogers on Encounter Groups.* New York: Harper & Row, 1970.

———. *Client-Centered Therapy.* Boston, MA: Houghton Mifflin, 1957.

———. *Freedom to Learn.* Columbus, OH: C. E. Merrill, 1964.

———. *In Therapy and in Education.* Boston, MA: Houghton Mifflin, 1961.

———. *On Becoming a Person.* Boston, MA: Houghton Mifflin, 1961.

Rush, Myron. *Management: A Biblical Approach.* Wheaton, IL: Victor Books, 1984.

———

Schaller, Lyle E. *Community Organization: Conflict, and Reconciliation.* New York: Abingdon Press, 1966.

———. *Community Organization: Conflict and Resolution.* Nashville, TN: Abingdon Press, 1966.

Schuller, Robert. *Self-Esteem: The New Reformation.* Waco, TX: Word Books, 1982.

Scott, Bill. *The Skills of Negotiating.* New York: John Wiley & Sons, 1981.

Seamands, David A. *Healing for Damaged Emotions.* Wheaton, IL: Victor Books, 1984.

Seventh-day Adventist Hymnal. Washington, DC: Review & Herald, 1985. No. 578.

Seventh-day Adventist Bible Commentary. Edited by F. D. Nichol. 7 vols. Washington, DC: Review & Herald, 1953–57.

Shawchuck, Norman. *How to Manage Conflict in the Church.* 2 vols. Indianapolis, IN: Spiritual Growth Resources, 1983.

Shelley, Marshall. *Well-Intentioned Dragons.* Carol Stream, IL: Christianity Today, 1985.

Simmel, Georg. *Conflict and the Web of Group Affiliations.* Translated by Reinhard Bendix. Glencoe, IL: Free Press, 1955.

Smedes, Lewis B. *Forgive and Forget: Healing the Hurts We Don't Deserve.* Philadelphia, PA: Harper & Row, 1984.

Smith, Clagett G., ed. *Conflict Resolution: Contributions of the Behavioral Services.* Notre Dame, IN: University of Notre Dame, 1972.

Smith, R. M. *Learning How to Learn: Applied Learning Theory for Adults.* New York: Cambridge Books, 1982.

Stagner, Ross, ed. *The Dimensions of Human Conflict.* Detroit, IL: Wayne State University Press, 1967.

Taylor, Vincent. *Forgiveness and Reconciliation.* London: MacMillan, 1948.

Tedeschi, James T., Barry Schlender, and Thomas V. Bonoma. *Conflict, Power and Games.* Chicago, IL: Aldine Pub., 1973.

Thomas, Kenneth W., and Ralph H. Kilmann. *Thomas-Kilmann Conflict-Mode.* Tuxedo, NY: Xicon, 1974.

Tidwell, Charles A. *Educational Ministry of a Church.* Nashville, TN: Broadman Press, 1982.

Tournier, Paul. *The Meaning of Persons.* New York: Harper & Row, 1957.

Verduin, John R., Harry G. Miller, and Charles E. Greer. *Adults Teaching Adults, Principles and Strategies.* Austin, TX: Learning Concepts, 1977.

Vine, W. E. *An Expository Dictionary of New Testament Words.* Nashville, TN: Thomas Nelson, 1952.

Walker, Williston. *A History of the Christian Church.* New York: Charles Scribner's, 1970.

Wallace, John. *Control in Conflict.* Nashville, TN: Broadman Press, 1982.

Walton, Richard E. *Interpersonal Peacemaking: Confrontations and Third-Party Consultations.* Reading, MA: Addison-Wesley, 1969.

Wheeler, Daniel D., and Irving L. Janis. *A Practical Guide for Making Decisions.* New York: Free Press, 1980.

Ellen G. White. *Adventist Home.* Nashville, TN: Southern Pub., 1952.

———. *Christ's Object Lessons.* Washington, DC: Review & Herald, 1941.

———. *Counsels to Parents, Teachers, and Students*. Mountain View, CA: Pacific Press, 1943.

———. *Counsels to Writers and Editors*. Nashville, TN: Southern Pub., 1946.

———. *Desire of Ages*. Mountain View, CA: Pacific Press, 1940.

———. *Evangelism*. Washington, DC: Review & Herald, 1946.

———. *Gospel Workers*. Washington, DC: Review & Herald, 1915.

———. *Great Controversy*. Mountain View, CA: Pacific Press, 1935.

———. *Mind, Character & Personality*. 2 vols. Nashville, TN: Southern Pub., 1977.

———. *Ministry of Healing*. Mountain View, CA: Pacific Press, 1942.

———. *Patriarchs and Prophets*. Mountain View, CA: Pacific Press, 1945.

———. *Prophets and Kings*. Mountain View, CA: Pacific Press, 1917.

———. *Selected Messages*. 3 vols. Washington, DC: Review & Herald, 1958–80.

———. *Sons and Daughters of God*. Washington, DC: Review & Herald, 1955.

———. *Steps to Christ*. Mountain View, CA: Pacific Press, 1956.

———. *The Story of Redemption*. Washington, DC: Review & Herald, 1947.

———. *Temperance*. Mountain View, CA: Pacific Press, 1949.

———. *Testimonies to the Church*. 9 vols. Mountain View, CA: Pacific Press, 1948.

Worley, R. C. *Change in the Church: A Source of Hope*. Philadelphia, PA: Westminster Press, 1971.

———. *Dry Bones Breathe*. Chicago, IL: Brethren Press, 1978.

———. *A Gathering of Strangers. Understanding the Life of Your Church*. Philadelphia, PA: Westminster Press, 1976.

Yearbook of the Seventh-day Adventist Denomination. Washington, DC: Review & Herald, 1985.

Yost, F. Donald. *123rd Annual Statistical Report*. Washington, DC: Office of Archives and Statistics, 1985.

Young, Robert. *Analytical Concordance of the Bible*. Grand Rapids, MI: Wm. B. Eerdmans, 1964.

Periodicals, Dissertations, and Tapes

Addley, W. P. "Matthew 18 and the Church as the Body of Christ." *Biblical Theology* 26 (June 1976): 12–17.

Bennett, John. "The Missing Dimension." *Christianity and Crisis* 29 (September 1969): 241–242.

Blizzard, Samuel W. "The Minister's Dilemma." *The Christian Century* 73 (April 25, 1956): 508–510.

Breen, David. "Churches in Conflict: A Conflict Management Manual for Church Leaders." DMin project, Western Theological Seminary, Holland, MI, 1983.

Brown, Dale, W. "Who Really Manages Ministry." *The Christian Ministry* 9 (March 1978): 8–12.

Burquest, Donald A. "A Celebration Feast of Forgiveness." *Christianity Today* 26 (January–June 1982): 24–25.

Buzzard, Lynn R., and Lawrence Eck. A cassette tape supplied with *Resolving Our Difference*. Elgin, IL: David C. Cook, 1982.

"Christian Legal Society." Informational Pamphlet. Oak Park, IL: n.d.

Coleman, James S. "Social Cleavage and Religious Conflict." *Journal of Social Issues* 12 (1956): 44–56.

Connors, Kenneth Wray. "Pastoral Partners or Puppets." *The Christian Ministry* 4 (1973): 19–22.

Cosier, Richard, and Thomas L. Ruble. "Research on Conflict-Handling Behavior: An Experimental Approach." *Academy of Management Journal* 24 (December 1981): 816–831.

Cousar, Charles B. "2 Corinthians 5:17–21." *Interpretation* 35 (1981): 180–182.

Dailey, C. A. "The Management of Conflict." *Chicago Theological Seminary Register* 59 (May 1969): 1–7.

Davenport, J., and J. A. Davenport. "A Chronology and Analysis of the Andragogy Debate." *Adult Education Quarterly* 35 (1984): 152–159.

Epstein, N. B., D. S. Bishop, and L. M. Baldwin. "McMaster Model of Family Functioning: A View of the Normal Family." In *Normal Family Processes*, edited by F. Walsh, pp. 115–141. New York: Guilford Press, 1982.

Filley, A. C. "Some Normative Issues in Conflict Management." *California Management Review* 21 (Winter 1978): 61–66.

Fogg, Richard Wendell. "A Repertoire of Creative, Peaceful Approaches." *Journal of Conflict Resolution* 29 (June 1985): 330–358.

Furnish, Victor Paul. "The Ministry of Reconciliation." *Currents in Theology and Mission* 4 (1977): 204–218.

Gibb, J. R. "Learning Theory in Adult Education." In *Handbook of Adult Education in the United States*, edited by M. S. Knowles, pp. 54–64. Washington, DC: Adult Education Association of the USA, 1960.

Good, E. M. "Peace in the Old Testament." *The Interpreter's Dictionary of the Bible*, pp. 704–706. Nashville, TN: Abingdon Press, 1962.

Greenlaw, David E. "An Interpersonal Relationship Workshop Designed for Seventh-day Adventist Congregational Use." DMin project, Andrews University, 1984.

Hall, J., and Williams, M. J. "A Comparison of Decision-Making Performances in Established and Ad Hoc Groups." *Journal of Personality and Social Psychology* 3 (February 1966): 217.

Hill, Barbara J. "An Analysis of Conflict-Resolution Techniques: From Problem-Solving Workshop to Theory." *Journal of Conflict Resolution* 26 (March 1982): 109–138.

Ingo, Herman. "Conflict and Conflict Resolution in the Church." *Concilium* 3 (1972): 107–118.

Jacobsen, Wayne. "Seven Reasons for Staff Conflicts." *Leadership* 4 (Summer 1983): 34–39.

Jarvis, Peter. "The Ministry-Laity Relationship: A Case of Potential Conflict." *Sociological Analysis* 37 (1976): 74–80.

Johnson, Jan Gary. "A Design for Learning and Developing Skills for Handling Interpersonal and Substantive Conflict in the Ardmore, Oklahoma, Seventh-day Adventist Church." DMin project report, Andrews University, 1986.

Joseph, Samuel H. "A Study of the Foundations of Ministry and Laity with Special Reference to the East Caribbean Conference of Seventh-day Adventists." DMin project, Andrews University, 1975.

Kahn-Freund, D. "Intergroup Conflicts and Their Settlement." *British Journal of Sociology* 5 (1954): 196–197.

Kaiser, Odilo, and Rudolf Pesch. "Reconciliation." *Encyclopedia of Biblical Theology*, edited by Johannes B. Bauer, pp. 730–783. New York: Crossroads, 1981.

Kerr, C. "Industrial Conflict and Its Mediation." *American Journal of Sociology* LX (1954): 230.

King, Dennis. "Cheers for Conflict." *Personnel* 58 (January–February 1981): 15–21.

Kreider, Eugene Charles. "Matthew's Contribution to the Eschatological-Ethical Perspective in the Life of the Early Church: A Redaction-Critical Study of Matthew 18." PhD dissertation, Vanderbilt University, 1976.

Kurtz, Arnold. "Leadership in Church Organizations." Class notes—CHMN727, Andrews University, Berrien Springs, MI, 1985.

———. "The Pastor and Institutionalization of Conflict Management in the Church." *Andrews University Seminary Studies* 20 (Autumn 1982): 217–227.

———. "The Pastor as a Manager of Conflict in the Church." *Andrews University Seminary Studies* 20 (Summer 1982): 111–126.

Leas, Speed B. "Strategies for Social Change in the Seventies." In *Creating an Intentional Ministry*, edited by J. E. Biersdorf, pp. 194–215. Nashville, TN: Abingdon Press, 1976.

Lindgren, Alvin. "Church Administration as a Dynamic Process." *Pastoral Psychology* 20 (September 1969): 7–16.

———. "Contemporary Church Administration" (Editorial). *Pastoral Psychology* 20 (September 1969): 5–6.

McGinnis, Thomas C. "Clergymen in Conflict." *Pastoral Psychology* 20 (October 1969): 12–20.

Mack, Raymond W., and Richard C. Synder. "The Analysis of Social Conflict—Toward an Overview and Synthesis." *Journal of Conflict Resolution* 1 (June 1957): 212–248.

McPolin, James. "Peace in Conflict." *The Way* 22 (1982): 262–271.

Manschreck, Clyde L. "Absolutism and Consensus: An Overview of Church History." *Chicago Theological Seminary Register* 59 (May 1969): 40–47.

Martin, R. P. "New Testament Theology: A Proposal—The Theme of Reconciliation." *Expository Times* 91 (1979–1980): 363–364.

Morris, Leon. "Reconciliation." *Christianity Today*, 13 (January 1969): 331–332.

Naden, Roy C. "Pastoral Nurture and Religious Education." Notes of class lectures for CHMN740, Andrews University, Berrien Springs, MI, 1985.

Narramore, S. Bruce. "Parent Leadership Styles and Biblical Anthropology," *Bibliotheca Sacra* 135 (1978): 345–357.

Nebgen, Mary K. "Conflict Management in Schools." *Administrator's Notebook* 26 (1977–78): 7–10.

Nelson, Melvin R. "The Psychology of Spiritual Conflict." *Journal of Psychology and Theology* 4 (Winter 1976): 34–41.

Newbold, Robert T. "Conflict in the Black Church." *Leadership* 1 (Spring 1980): 99–101.

Patton, B. R., and Kim Griffin. "Conflict and Its Resolution." In *Small Group Communication: A Reader*, 3rd ed., edited by R. S. Cathcart and L. A. Samovar, pp. 326–335. Dubuque, IA: Wm. C. Brown, 1979.

Phillips, Eleanor, and Ric Cheston. "Conflict Resolution: What Works?" *California Management Review* 21 (Summer 1979): 76–83.

Pondy, Louis R. "Organizational Conflict: Concepts and Models." *Administrative Science Quarterly* 12 (September 1967): 296–320.

Rapoport A. "Conflict Resolution in the Light of Game Theory and Beyond." In *The Structure of Conflict*, edited by P. W. Swingle, pp. 1–43. New York: Academic Press, 1970.

Rico, Leonard. "Organizational Conflict: A Framework for Reappraisal." *Industrial Management Review* 6 (Fall 1964): 67–80.

Robbins, Stephen P. "'Conflict Management' and 'Conflict Resolution' Are Not Synonymous Terms." *California Management Review* 21 (Winter 1978): 67–75.

Roberts, J. H. "Some Biblical Foundations for a Mission of Reconciliation." *Missionalia* 7 (April 1979): 3–17.

Rogers, Patrick V. "Peace through the Cross." *The Way* 22 (July 1982): 195–203.

Rook, William C. "Understanding Conflict in the Church." *Church Administration*, December 1980, pp. 15–16.

Shawchuck, Norman. A cassette tape supplied with *How to Manage Conflict in the Church: Understanding Church Conflict*. Indianapolis: Spiritual Growth Resources, 1983.

Sorenson, R. C. "The Concept of Conflict in Industrial Sociology." *Forces* 29 (1957): 263.

Stevenson, Ernest Johnson. "Seminars for Professional Improvement: A Pilot Project in Continuing Education for Ministers." DMin project, Andrews University, 1979.

Stimac, Michele. "Strategies for Resolving Conflict: Their Functional and Dysfunctional Sides." *Personnel* 59 (November–December 1982): 54–64.

Swanson, Rolla. "Planning Change and Dealing with Conflict: A Field Theory Model with Eleven Steps to Change." *Chicago Theological Seminary Register* 59 (May 1969): 18–31.

Tannenbaum, Robert, and Warren H. Schmidt. "How to Choose a Leadership Pattern." *Harvard Business Review* 36 (March/April 1958): 95–101.

———. "Management of Differences." *Harvard Business Review* 38 (November/December 1960):107–115.

Thomas, K. W., and W. H. Schmidt. "A Survey of Managerial Interests with Respect to Conflict." *Academy of Management Journal* 19 (June 1976): 315–318.

Thompson, Garth D. "On Pastors as Counselors." *Andrews University Seminary Studies* 22 (Autumn 1984): 341–348.

Thompson, John. "The Doctrine of Reconciliation." *Biblical Theology* 27 (September 1977): 43–52.

Thrall, Margaret E. "Salvation Proclaimed V. 2 Corinthians 5:18–21: Reconciliation with God." *Expository Times* 93 (October 1981): 227–232.

Wansbrough, Henry. "Blessed Are the Peacemakers." *The Way* 22 (January 1982): 10–17.

White, Ellen G. "Be Gentle unto All Men." *The Advent Review and Sabbath Herald* (May 1895): 305–306.

———. "Comments on John 17:20 21," *Seventh-day Adventist Bible Commentary*. Edited by F. D. Nichol. 7 vols. Washington, DC: Review & Herald, 1953–57. 5:1148.

———. "Judge Not." *The Adventist Review and Sabbath Herald* (February 7, 1899): 81–82.

Wilczak, Paul F. "The Pastoral Care of Families: A Ministry of Reconciliation." *Encounter* 39 (Spring 1978): 175–188.

Williams, A. M. "Reconciliation with God." *Expository Times* 31 (1919–20): 280–282.

Zehr, Daniel. "Portrait of a Peacemaker." Mennonite Central Committee Pamphlet, n.d.

VITA

Personal

Winston Anthony Richards was born on May 29, 1943, in Kingston, Jamaica, West Indies. He is the third of a triplet and the seventh of eight children. He was baptized on May 20, 1962. He was married to the former Dorothy Brown on June 2, 1974. They have three beautiful adult daughters—Althea, Karolyn, and Sharon; one son-in-law, Everald; and two grandchildren, Tatyana and Rohan.

Educational

In 1962, Richards graduated from high school and, in 1964, from the Mico Teachers' College. He taught for three years. In 1971, he graduated from West Indies College (Jamaica), now Northern Caribbean University, with a bachelor of theology and an education minor. Richards entered the Andrews University Seventh-day Adventist Theological Seminary, Michigan, that same year (1971) and graduated with a master of divinity on June 2, 1974—the day of his marriage. He completed the doctor of ministry degree in the summer of 1987 at the SDA Seminary at Berrien Springs, Michigan.

Professional

In 1974, Winston Richards was called to the East Caribbean Conference of Seventh-day Adventists to serve as the pastor of the British Virgin Islands. From 1975 to 1978, he was the producer and speaker of a half-hour religious program "Treasure of Truth Broadcast." In 1978, he was transferred to St. John, US Virgin Islands, by then part of the North Caribbean Conference of Seventh-day Adventists. From 1980 to 1984, Richards served as the pastor of six of the churches on Antigua, West Indies, where his interest in conflict management developed. He was ordained on September 2, 1978, in Port-of-Spain, Trinidad. He served on the Union Committee of the Caribbean Union Conference of Seventh-day Adventists from 1982 to 1984 and served as pastor in the USVI from 1988 to 2001 and from 2009 to 2013. Richards also served on the Executive Committee of the North Caribbean Conference of SDA while he was the Stewardship, Trust Services, Communication, Spirit of Prophecy, and Adventist Development Relief Agency (ADRA) director of the conference (2001–2009). He retired in December 2013.